A Question of Identity

A Question of Identity

Iberian Conversos in Historical Perspective

RENÉE LEVINE MELAMMED

OXFORD
UNIVERSITY PRESS

2004

OXFORD
UNIVERSITY PRESS

Oxford   New York
Auckland   Bangkok   Buenos Aires   Cape Town   Chennai
Dar es Salaam   Delhi   Hong Kong   Istanbul   Karachi   Kolkata
Kuala Lumpur   Madrid   Melbourne   Mexico City   Mumbai
Nairobi   São Paulo   Shanghai   Taipei   Tokyo   Toronto

Published by Oxford University Press, Inc.
198 Madison Avenue, New York, New York 10016

www.oup.com

Oxford is a registered trademark of Oxford University Press

Library of Congress Cataloging-in-Publication Data
Melammed, Renée Levine.
A question of identity : Iberian conversos in historical perspective / Renée Levine Melammed
   p. cm
Includes bibliographical references (p.) and index.
ISBN 0-19-517071-7
   1. Marranos—Spain—History.   2. Marranos—Spain—Ethnic identity.   3. Jews—Spain—
Identity.   4. Marranos—Europe—History.   5. Spain—Ethnic relations.   I. Title: Iberian
Conversos in Historical Perspective.   II. Title.
DS135.S7 M43 2004
946'.004924—dc22   2003020145

9 8 7 6 5 4 3 2 1

Printed in the United States of America
on acid-free paper

In memory of my father
Bernard Levine (1916–1987)

In honor of my mother
Saralee Levine

Preface

This book is the product of preparing and teaching courses on the subject of the conversos and studying their movements from locale to locale and from century to century. In no way do I presume to be presenting a comprehensive history of the conversos, but rather to be exposing the reader to a historical perspective. There are many communities that are not included here, such as the conversos of the Ottoman Empire, North Africa, and the New World. In the first two destinations, one witnesses the union of most of the conversos with their Sephardi brethren who left Spain in 1492; thus, it is more difficult to trace the newcomers who were absorbed into established communities. This is not to say that they did not have noteworthy experiences or, for that matter, crises; on the contrary, rabbinic responsa (queries to and replies from legal experts) attest to the legal dilemmas faced by many of the conversos who joined these Jewish communities. Needless to say, the New World also presents a set of problems unique to the colonial experience.

At the same time, I ventured a chronological leap. After dealing with the Western European communities in the sixteenth and seventeenth centuries, I did not follow their progress. Some of them simply disappeared though assimilation, while others became bona fide Sephardi Jews. Most did not continue to deal with the question of identity, which is the concern of this book and the reason why I leaped into the twentieth century. There I chose three groups who faced the dilemma of maintaining and/or forming their identities under completely different conditions. Yet the fact that in the twentieth and twenty-first centuries, descendants of conversos are still grappling with such issues is astonishing to me.

As I researched this topic, I was delighted to see that it still fascinates scholars around the world. Books and articles dealing with the converso experience appear annually.[1] Some scholars have even introduced creative and innovative terms, such as "troubled souls" and "fuzzy Jews."[2] A term that I found quite useful is "cultural commuter," adapted from the world of anthropology.[3] The notion of gliding between cultures, feeling at home in two, moving comfortably back and forth between them, or even being marginal to more than one group, is one that will aptly fit some of the conversos under discussion.

The group identity that developed has its distinct Iberian stamp, and the "men of the Nation" maintained long-lasting ties to their homeland generations after leaving the peninsula. While they had no Jewish memory to speak of, for their Jewish ancestors were long gone, there is a Jewish aspect to their ethnic identity that differentiates them from the Iberian nonconversos. I have attempted to characterize these differences and to seek what it is that made these conversos different and motivated them to choose the paths they chose.

I am grateful to the institutions in which I was fortunate enough to teach courses about converso history, in particular the Schechter Institute of Jewish Studies in Jerusalem, and to my students for making me clarify complicated and often muddled issues. Their enthusiasm always ensured me that the topic was as interesting as I thought it was. I was also encouraged to sharpen my perspective during the July 2000 workshop at Columbia University and the July 2001 conference at the Netherlands Institute for Advanced Study organized by Wayne te Brake and funded by the Ford Foundation. This international group of early modern historians discussed the notion of "religious accommodation," and I analyzed the converso experience in this context; the collegiality and feedback offered was quite helpful to me.

I must offer a special thanks to Claude B. Stuczynski of Bar Ilan University for reading the chapters that dealt with Portugal and with Belmonte and for the advice, recommendations, and continuous support he has provided. His impressive breadth of knowledge has been most beneficial to me, and I have learned a great deal from him and from the endless readings he has suggested.

The group of women that convenes at the National Library of the Hebrew University helped just by being there, usually for lunch and coffee breaks. Esther Chazon, Dena Ordan, Yvonne Friedman, and Betsy Halpern-Amaru provided camaraderie that I greatly appreciated, especially on days when I faced endless hours of printed words. My long-distance friends and colleagues provided endless support, mostly via electronic mail. Lastly, knowing that I have the love of my family, Uri, Shira, and Benjamin Melammed, is a source of strength, as is the love and pride of my mother, Saralee Levine.

A heartfelt thank you to my editor, Cynthia Read, for her continuous and enthusiastic support and to Theo Calderara for his help and patience. Ultimately, I can only hope that I have somehow succeeded in offering insight into the dilemma of living as a converso, and of the changes that made life such a challenge for the descendants of the Iberian conversos. If the reader gains a historical perspective concerning the question of their identity, I will have completed my mission.

Jerusalem, 2003

Contents

A Question of Identity

Introduction

The experience of the Iberian Jews was unique, and continued to be so even after there were no longer bona fide Jewish communities in either Spain or Portugal. Perhaps this is an integral part of the uniqueness of the Iberian Jewish experience. Yosef Hayim Yerushalmi discusses the uniqueness of Spanish Jewry in terms of three features. The first was the fact that the relationship with the host country was so long lasting and intimate. The second was the existence of unusually favorable conditions that led to the rise of numerous powerful courtiers. The third was that the power and stature of Spanish Jewry loomed large beyond realistic proportions and led to a mythical quality concerning its existence.[1] The Jewish community predated the arrival of the Muslims on the peninsula in 711; the conquerors were aware that the Jews were the local residents in Visigothic Spain and, as natives, knew the lay of the land. In addition, they were perceived to be loyal and stable. The developments that transpired while Spanish Jews lived under Islamic rule had no parallel in any other locale; the contact between the dhimmis, a minority group, and the host society was similarly impressive during this period in terms of its lasting effects.[2]

The reconquest of Spain was to alter much more than the rulers and the ruling religion; ultimately the Jewish community would undergo enormous upheaval because of its contact with medieval Christianity. Life under Christian rule could not duplicate or genuinely imitate that of the Islamic period, essentially because of the very nature of Catholicism with its built-in deprecation of Judaism. There is a major difference between being perceived in Islam as rejectors of the Prophet and being considered to be the killers of Christ in Christianity. Because of this, when the Jews were under Muslim rule, a delicately constructed integration was the order of the day. In other words, despite a potential for volatility and occasional eruptions that did occur during this earlier period, a precarious and viable balance was nonetheless maintained. As we will see, while life under Christian rule contained inherent potential tensions as well, the strains that developed were of a different nature and led to eruptions on a level and at an intensity never experienced by the Jews in Muslim Spain.

At the outset of the reconquest, the conquering leaders encouraged Jewish settlement in the northern Christian areas and frontiers by offering tempting arrangements; there was a subsequent movement to the north as the Jews attempted to cement an alliance with the Crown. Individual Jews were even given ownership of lands as Christian armies advanced and conquered territories.[3] A policy of protecting and fortifying the Jews was advocated; Jewish quarters were left intact or new ones were even constructed as proof of goodwill. Jews were offered tax exemptions in the hope that they would settle in and develop the newly conquered territories. Until the end of the thirteenth century, the frontier of Christian Spain was constantly changing as the conquest proceeded. The reconquest began in about 1060, and although it was not fully completed until the fall of Granada in 1492, it was well established by 1250. The first stage of the reconquest is usually dated from 1060 to 1150, during which time Alfonso VI of Castile conquered Toledo (1086) and Alfonso I of Aragon conquered Tudela (1115), Saragossa (1118), and Barcelona (1149). The second stage, dated from 1150 to 1230, is highlighted by the defeat of the Almohads, North African militant tribes, at the Battle of Las Navas. During the next twenty years, Ferdinand III of Castile conquered most of the Andalusian cities, and James "the Conqueror" of Aragon advanced considerably in the east. As a result, by 1250, the conquest was almost complete, although life in these territories was by no means stable.[4] During this time, the conquerors had to face a large population of Muslim subjects whom they obviously viewed as hostile. Consequently, the Jews stood out because unlike the Muslims, they did not present a threat but rather were potentially loyal to the new reign. At the same time, they were urban dwellers who might have skills to offer or who could provide a number of other economic advantages to the developing Christian kingdoms.

Because the early medieval experience in Spain was so different from that of the other western European countries, its socioeconomic structure was also quite different. No burgher or bourgeoisie class had developed in the eleventh or twelfth centuries; no limitations on occupational choices were made either by guilds[5] or because of competition on the part of a Christian middle class. On the whole, the Castilian reconquerors tended to be warriors or farmers, meaning that the rulers either had to find or encourage others to fill in the socioeconomic vacuum. The Jews were perceived to be loyal and experienced as well as economically solvent. In order to build a stable economy, a middle class was desperately needed, and the presence of the Jews provided the ideal solution. In a sense one can say that as the reconquest proceeded, the Jews again made themselves essential to the service of the throne.

Consequently, a strong belief developed on the part of the Iberian Jews that the king was their reliable ally. Choosing to depend upon the state rather than upon the local government stemmed from the desire to obtain a uniform status for the community and to enable it to maintain inner unity. An alliance with local officials was regarded as less stable, less promising, and thus less desirable. In addition, only the Crown could provide for internal communal autonomy. Royal charters were given to each Jewish community that assumed this responsibility; the end result reflected the uniform nature of the Jewish legal system. The fact that the Crown hoped to unify royal law augured well for the Jews. In fact, there had been a plethora of legal systems coexisting in Spain, operating simultaneously and never really accepting one another. The *fueros*, or ancient customary laws, were guarded jealously by the localities. As a result, there was a mixture of Roman, Visigothic, Church, Muslim, and customary laws on the books in the early Middle Ages. King Alfonso the Wise masterminded a comprehensive legal code in the mid-thirteenth century, *Las Siete Partidas*, which became effective by the fourteenth century, and, of course, included laws concerning the Jews. At any rate, this "royal alliance" was essentially a good arrangement for both parties involved. The Jews appreciated being associated with the king, and preferred to bypass the local bureacracy that often viewed them as undesirable competition. The direct line to the Crown was not only a matter of status; the community could generally count on the king for protection and appeal to him when need be.

As for the king's considerations, first and foremost the Jews were a loyal and stable element worthy of cultivating. Their reputation as an industrious group harboring limited political aspirations also carried weight. These mainly urban subjects provided an excellent source of revenue. In short, this community provided loyalty together with direct payment of taxes, a combination not to be belittled. This arrangement was, on the whole, desirable for and suitable to both parties involved. The Crown was guaranteed the loyalty and revenues of the Jews who, as a result, enjoyed a feeling of security and protection.

Needless to say, this arrangement also had its inherent flaws. As long as the Crown was powerful and in control, the Jews were relatively safe. Since the presence of a weak king would leave them vulnerable, it was in their best interests to strive to maintain a strong central authority. However, if popular resentment of the king developed, the Jews would be viewed as guilty by association and would suffer accordingly. At the same time, there was no guarantee that the king might not decide to dispense with the Jews at any given moment or for any given reason; expediency was surely foremost in his mind, and when the situation demanded, he could arbitrarily change the rules when his own self-interest was involved. Needless to say, the king and the municipalities or other groups naturally experienced a conflict of interests concerning control of the Jews. There was often pressure upon the Crown from various interest groups such as the nobility or the church in this matter, which created competition over who would be in charge of certain communities.[6] If and when the king chose not to favor the Jews, the supposedly protected Jews would then be at the mercy of Spanish society, namely, of those very groups or corporate bodies they had bypassed (and probably offended) by forming a direct alliance with the Crown; included here one might find the municipalities, the Church, or the urban dwellers.[7]

Ultimately, the Jews had no choice but to adapt to the ever changing reality of life in the Iberian Peninsula. On the whole, the community flourished as the Christian rulers strengthened their hold on the conquered lands, especially in the early years. No doubt there were signs that might have been interpreted as problematic or as heralding tensions, but they were not so noticeable or extreme that they would have sounded an alarm. It is only via hindsight that the cracks in the seemingly peaceful life under Christian rule can be discerned as having been more serious than met the eye at the time.

Examples of such signs include the level of contact between the religions, ranging from tolerance and cooperation to debates, polemics, and proselytizing. Needless to say, tolerance was not one of the salient features of medieval Christianity. The modus vivendi that existed for the Jews living under Islamic rule can be attributed to the political reality of the isolated Umayyad kingdom, to the usefulness of the Jews, and to an inherent characteristic in Islam of religious tolerance for monotheistic peoples.

The Catholic Church, on the other hand, did not display a similar innate tolerance. On the contrary, the historical memory of its believers associated Jews and Judaism with various crimes and negative attributes; this association was frequently renewed or revived by preachers and churchmen of various stations. Even the best of conditions harbored a passive residue of this memory, which would never entirely dissipate from the scene. In addition, the fact that popes were involved in combating heresies during the thirteenth century did anything but contribute to an aura of tolerance.[8]

One tactic used by the Church was the debate, which was not necessarily a sign of intolerance but rather a tool of multiple purposes that could range from an honest intellectual exercise to a veiled attempt to humiliate and demoralize the opponent in the hope of absolutely defeating him. Yet when religious beliefs and truths were involved, even the most innocent of debates could be potentially volatile. While there seemed to have been genuine interaction on a cultural level between the Jewish and Muslim cultures in the earlier period, the nature of contact with the Christians was different; the Jews were now essentially performing cultural services for Spanish Christian society.

By the thirteenth century, there was a clear change in the tone of Jewish-Christian debates as well as of their potential consequences. An example from neighboring France illustrates this point. The Disputation of Paris was a verbal spar between an apostate, Michaelis Donin, and Rabbi Yehiel. The apostate was an ideal candidate to attack Judaism both because of his zealousness for his new religion and because he knew his former religion and all its faults from within. In this instance, at the close of the debate, the Talmud, whose contents were considered for the first time by the Church in a public forum, was declared heretical because of the errors and blasphemy contained within. One of the factors responsible for this change was the involvement of the mendicant proselytizing orders that were becoming more and more militant. The brilliant idea developed by Raymond de Peñaforte to train the monks in the languages of the texts of the opposition, namely, in Hebrew and Arabic, was potentially devastating. Each of the three religions reveres the language in which its holy scriptures are written, but when one has to rely on translations in a debate, for example, one can easily be defeated because of inaccuracies in translation or due to lack of precise comprehension. Yet when the debater has knowledge of the original language and text, he can quote and often stun his opponent by using his mastery wisely. There are inherent weaknesses in all scriptures, and firsthand knowledge provides powerful ammunition against one's opponent. Quotes taken out of context or that are used to pervert the original sense of the words can be debilitating and devastating in a public forum.[9]

Spain was probably the site of the richest polemic literature and public debates, some of which came after 1391 and will be discussed later in chronological context. The presence of Dominican and Franciscan monks who saw themselves as warriors of the faith most certainly had ramifications for Spanish Christian society. Those who chose to express themselves in writing left powerful polemical works against Judaism, and those who ranted and raved against the Jews in their sermons had more temporal but nevertheless potent influence upon the masses.[10]

The power of the demagogue should not be underestimated. In 1378, the archdeacon of Ecija (near Seville), Ferrant Martínez, began haranguing the Jews in his fiery sermons, moving from parish to parish. Martínez was a canon of Seville and a deputy of the archbishop in legal affairs; as archdeacon, he had "pastoral and administrative oversight of a large section of the wealthy archdiocese of Seville," a very major position in the hierarchy of the Church.[11] His message was more or less consistent: Destroy the synagogues and separate the Jews' residence from the Christians; in addition, he intimated that there would be no punishment by the Crown for those who translated these suggestions into action. The man was relentless, spreading his poison and letting it seep in slowly. He was also patient, realizing that the fruit of his labor would not be borne for a number of years, and in his case, the process took from 1378 to 1391.

During the fourteenth century, there had been other signs of unrest such as anti-Jewish pogroms in the wake of the plague in 1348, economic hardships, and a civil war in Castile between King Pedro (1350–1369) and his half brother, Henry, from 1366 to 1369. Yet the year 1391 was to be the watershed year, both for the Jews of Spain as well as for anti-Semites like Martínez. "As the fourteenth century drew to a close, the Jewish communities in Castile and the Crown of Aragon were impoverished, embattled, and vulnerable to further attacks. Society as a whole had not fared well under the blows of economic decline, depopulation, and civil war; but the Jews also had to face the exacerbation of anti-Jewish feelings—that strange mixture of religious bigotry, greed, envy, and unspoken fears—which always flourish in times of economic and social crisis. It is within this framework that the events of 1391 must be understood."[12] The riots that occurred during that fateful year would change more than just the religion of those who succumbed to forced conversion. The history of the Jews in Spain was changed forever, and the repercussions of this event would affect Spanish history for years to come.

Attempting to explain how and why these riots transpired at this particular time is an almost impossible task. Consequently, the rationales range from socioeconomic to political to religious. In attempting to understand this society, some scholars stress the fact that the aristocrats and other ruling groups were generally more tolerant than the lower classes, while they note that economic interests of oligarchies in towns often determined the economic and social structure of a given community. Thus, social unrest in cities and tensions between the nobility and the bourgeosie at times led to popular violence. When placed alongside one another, the available explanations seem to cover most of the viable options.[13] While there is no doubt that the anti-Semitic vitriolic sermons prepared the groundwork for the pogroms, why did they begin precisely in June 1391? If there was significant economic resentment toward the Jews, why did it not manifest itself previously on a discernable but less drastic level? If there was so much anger on the part of the lower classes toward the predominantly Jewish middle class and a deep disrespect for the king's interest, what happened in 1391 that triggered such a violent reaction? According to Baer, the *gente menuda*, or little people, were responsible; they were well aware that the king protected the Jews, but essentially were not concerned with respecting the monarchy.[14] At the same time, the urban patriarchate resisted the centralization process that was taking place, and its resentment of the royal taxation did not make it sympathetic to the Jews.

Beinart is certain that Henry spread anti-Jewish propaganda in his feverish efforts to fight his sibling, King Pedro the Cruel, and gain control of Castile.

The Jews had remained faithful to Pedro, and Henry exploited this fact, treating them brutally. The anti-Semitic attacks he instigated in the 1360s were verbal, physical, and financial, including serious extortion and destruction of communities.[15] Yom Tov Assis writes that "in the second half of the 14th century, the anti-Jewish trend in the Crown of Aragon increased, though it did not reach the proportions of anti-Jewish propaganda in Castile. At that time the Jewish problem was not in the forefront of the public debate, perhaps because in the 14th century the Jews no longer held political and economic positions and were less involved in public life. . . . [W]ithout the incitement and inspiration which emanated from Castile, this hatred alone would not have provoked the 1391 catastrophe."[16] Others have perceived the developments of 1391 as a triumph of Church over synagogue, in essence a crusade occurring on home soil, for, needless to say, the crusader mentality gave a new edge and a militancy to faith that had not been present previously.

What actually did transpire? While there is no need to go into meticulous detail regarding each community that was involved, it is worthwhile to try to present a general sense of the situation. Not all the Jewish communities were affected, and of those that were, no two communities had identical experiences. Nevertheless, looting was prevalent during the course of most attacks, and destruction of life and property was par for the course. On June 4, Seville was the first community to be assailed, and the riots spread quickly and indiscriminately. No one group or leader was responsible in any instance. For example, while the clerics in some locales joined in or even led the rabble-rousers, in others they actually protected the Jews. The same held true for the nobility and municipal officials, although in Cuenca the latter group joined in the fray. While the final results were similar, the participants and their roles were not at all predictable.

Because there was no master plan, there was no uniform way in which the Jews were treated. At times, they were simply coerced to convert; at others, there were brief attempts to cajole or persuade them. Some groups were more bloodthirsty than others. Again, because nothing had been coordinated, the riots and rioters spread from place to place without warning and in no systematic direction, akin to the progress of a brush fire. As mentioned, in June, Seville's community was the first to suffer, followed by large portions of Andalusia and Castile, including the cities of Cordova, Cuenca, Madrid, and Toledo. The communities of Segovia and Burgos were attacked as the riots moved north.

By July, the news had reached Aragon, and on the ninth of that month, Catalonia's Jewish community was destroyed. In Burgos, some Jews took refuge in Christian homes, while others requested government protection. Occasionally the Jews were savvy enough to hire mercenaries to protect them. There were cases in which local rabble-rousers began the rioting, and others, such as in Valencia, in which outsiders, in this case from Castile, appeared and provoked the locals to action. The king, Henry III, although aged twelve, rebuked the rioters, but it was unclear who had really been involved and who should be punished. Baer intimates that there were aristocratic families, even those of knights, who were at times responsible.[17] Certain elements of the population, if they were in the vicinity, consistently participated in the riots; thus, idle sailors in ports such as Valencia were attracted by the call to action as well as by the prospect of plunder and booty.

Also in July, Majorca faced its own set of trials and tribulations, including an unsuccessful attempt to provide protection for the Jews in a fortress. In August, the city fathers of Barcelona were encouraged to protect their Jews, but Castilians from Valencia and Seville arrived and their ranks were fortified by local peasants. In Gerona, the royal and municipal officials provided resistance and evacuated the Jews to a castle; surprisingly, most were saved. While some managed to find refuge or protection in Tarragona (Catalonia) and in the northeastern corner of Perpignan, it was not always a secure option, as in Lerida or in Tortosa, where those hiding in the fortress were removed one by one and forced to convert. In Saragossa, the presence of King Juan I apparently tipped the scales in favor of the Jews, where they indeed were saved.[18] However, the majority of the Jews whose communities were attacked faced the difficult and fateful choice of dying as martyrs or of converting to Catholicism.[19]

The result of all this upheaval was chaotic. There had been no plan and there still was no plan. The Catholic Church, which officially discouraged and actually opposed forced baptism, faced an embarrassing situation: the overnight creation of tens of thousands of forced converts, far too many to forgive and to allow to revert to Judaism. The Church would have to blatantly ignore its own teachings and consider those forced to convert as legitimate Catholics and to regard their baptism as authentic and binding. One scholar intimates that the only reason these baptisms were considered valid was because the level of theological erudition in Spain was substandard.[20]

The Jewish community, that is, those members who survived as Jews, was in a state of shock. Some had successfully hidden or found protection, whether offered voluntarily or in return for payment. Some fled to Tunisia, Algeria, Morocco,[21] or Portugal, while others were fortunate enough to have been in locales where mobs did not attack. The brunt of the shock only worsened as the nature of the situation was assessed. The loss of lives and property, both personal and communal, including destroyed Jewish quarters and synagogues, was more than enough for any survivor to bear. Yet the trauma did not end here. The Jews who remained loyal to their beliefs discovered that former rabbis and community leaders were also among those who had converted under duress, a discovery that had to have been extremely distressing and demoralizing, making the rebuilding process even harder than imagined. Finally, family members, whether of the immediate or extended family, often discovered that they were no longer of the same religion; the bewilderment and pain that accompanied this discovery cannot possibly be described, although the moving letter written by Rabbi Hasdai Crescas to the Jewish community of Avignon in 1391 provides insight into this trauma. Rabbi Crescas had remained protected in the court of Saragossa while his son was killed by the mobs in Barcelona.[22]

Lastly, there was the plight of the converts themselves. Perhaps some of them were psychologically ready to convert—most likely not because of any moral deterioration that occurred, as claimed by Baer, because they had studied philosophy[23]—but possibly because they were duly impressed by the rise of Christianity in their native land or perhaps as a side effect of the open nature of Spanish society. The golden age of Spanish Jewry had come to an end, and the splendor of the conquering religion on the rise physically represented by its towering cathedrals might have proven attractive or convincing. In the long run, was the reconquest not tantamount to proof of divine favor? Yet there is little doubt that this type of reckoning was not the case for the majority of those who had converted. It is natural to choose life over death, whether or not the act of martyrdom is glorified in the Jewish and Christian traditions. Why should the victims not have believed that this was a matter of temporary insanity and that when things calmed down normalcy would return? Earlier Jewish communities had previously experienced forced conversions in Visigothic Spain as well as in Ashkenazic lands that were later rescinded. How were the individuals under duress to know that the numbers of converts would be so overwhelming as to preclude this option? Is it possible that "history made Spanish Jewry vulnerable to conversion"?[24]

Obviously, it is easier to imagine the mindset of the convert by choice, for in this case, the convert has been convinced of the truth of the other religion. Perhaps some of the Jews were so "Spanish" that they could imagine life as a Catholic without great difficulty. Others might well have been certain that the king, particularly in Aragon where he ostensibly had real power, would amend the situation and protect his Jews in the long run. Did the mythic power of the Royal Alliance and the belief in the king's protection play a role here? Did Spanish Jewry suffer perchance from delusions of grandeur? While it had no real strength, there was a myth of power and glory embedded in this community's historic consciousness. Clearly, no one had a great deal of time during which this decision could be mulled over, and a spontaneously made decision would not necessarily be identical to one made gradually as the result of a calm process of deliberation.

Be that as it may, the result described above was the reality to be faced. The converts, or *conversos* as they would be called, were traumatized as well. Precisely because the Church had neither planned anything of the sort nor had anticipated any such events, the conversos could discern no clear sense of direction. Meanwhile, they were still living in the same abodes and neighborhoods as before. Had the entire community converted, this would not have presented as insurmountable a problem. However, because the conversions were not universal, Jews and conversos were essentially living side by side. The Jews were attending synagogue as before and the conversos were expected to attend mass on Sundays and to abandon their previous lifestyle. This was far from an ideal situation if the Church was hoping to turn the ignorant neophytes into a serious group of believers, particularly in light of the fact that they had all become Catholics virtually overnight.

At this point, it would be absurd to imagine that there was anything akin to a converso identity. Essentially there was a group of former Jews ranging from members of the lower and the artisan classes to the bourgeoisie, to former rabbis and the upper class; for whatever reason, each had decided to convert under duress. Everyone knew who had made that choice, and there was no easy way to alter one's fate. The subsequent behavior and choices made by the conversos would also be made on an individual basis. Some, no doubt, decided to accept their fait accompli and resolved to live as Christians, or at least they were determined to make an attempt to do so. Some might even have rejoiced at having new opportunities and doors opened that previously had been closed to them as Jews. As a Christian, the convert could go to the university, run for municipal office, or join the clergy if he so desired. Some were so anxious to be accepted that they even engaged in anti-Jewish polemics and activities.[25]

On the other hand, many of the conversos were coping with the sinking reality of the irreversibility of the situation and were weighing their options. The truly miserable could attempt to flee the country, and the responsa literature attests to some who did precisely that. For example, Rabbi Isaac bar Sheshet Perfet, who escaped from Valencia in 1391, wrote that he heard of conversos living in Valencia and Barcelona who were faithful to Judaism and hoped to leave. Following riots in Cordova in 1473 and subsequent repercussions in Seville, conversos began to consider places of refuge in Iberia such as Gibraltar and Portugal as well as those outside the peninsula, such as Flanders and Italy.[26] The less adventurous might have tried to join a different Spanish community where he or she was not known in the hope that his or her secret would not be revealed. This was dangerous, as one would always live in fear of recognition, and while there was as yet no Inquisition to be feared, the authorities, or more precisely, the Church, could not help but be dismayed by such a course of action. The majority of the conversos stayed in their homes and maintained their previous professions and lifestyles. At the same time, those whose loyalty to Judaism was strong often continued to observe to the best of their abilities, attempting not to be too obvious or flamboyant in their activities. Others were apathetic and waited to see which way the wind would blow. Marín Padilla claims that the converso existence was dominated by individual passions and collective miseries that were a reflection of hate, animosity, and envy. In her opinion, the indecisive converso might have suffered from anguish, anxiety, insecurity, spiritual suffering, and dissatisfaction, whereas the Judaizer's life was characterized in general by treachery, rebellious-ness, and despair.[27] This is a dismal picture indeed.

On the other hand, the Jewish community at this time had to devote itself to the best of its abilities to rebuilding and repairing the damage inflicted upon it; it could not and would not openly provide or profess support for the con-versos. This is not to say that if and when approached the Jews did not lend them a helping hand. On the contrary, they provided services as well as support to conversos who contacted them and contracted their services.[28] At the same time, the conversos found that Spanish society had changed significantly as the result of the forced conversions of 1391. Previously there had been three clear-cut religious groups: the Jews, the Catholics, and the Muslims. Now there was a new group whose existence was unprecedented. Although they were technically Catholics, they were a marginal group and would be identified as such. These former Jews and nouveaux Catholics had a common experience that would bind them together and leave a serious imprint on the generations to come. The conversos, regardless of their personal inclinations, were destined not to forget or ignore their Jewish origins. Although bona fide Christians by church law, the society that had converted them would create its own set of rules, both written and unwritten. Essentially, Spanish Catholic society deemed the conversos a separate group; as a result, this group would develop its own identity and deal with the reality of fifteenth-century Spain in its own inimitable way.

I

The Aftermath and a New Reality

No one was prepared to deal with the results of the forced conversions. While the Jewish community tried to heal and renew itself, the Spanish Catholics faced an equally shocking situation. Because there had not been serious forethought or direction, it appeared that there was no plan for the aftermath either. Ferrant Martínez had succeeded beyond his wildest dreams, but he had not prepared anyone for the mayhem that might follow such irresponsible actions. Decisions had to be made by those who had not been involved with the riots yet were facing the reality of the morning after.

By the same token, the newly converted had no plan either and presumably were charting their way in unknown territory on an individual basis. Some relied on intuition and pragmatism, some reacted with guilt at having abandoned the faith, and some were resigned to accept their unexpected fate. As we will see, there was not necessarily one sole path that was taken by any given converso; the decision that seemed correct today might not appear to be so tomorrow. Yirmiyahu Yovel discusses the trend of assimilation as opposed to preservation of Jewish identity:

> Although opposite in theory, these two trends were often compatible in reality and sometimes existed in the same family, even in the same person. This produced some of the complex—and more interesting—forms of duality which marked the lives of almost all the Conversos. Not only the wavering or ambivalent converts, but even those who had made a single-minded choice in favor of one option only (Catholicism or secret Judaism) often betrayed the rival option in their actual lives, in

the way they reasoned and behaved, or in the very ardent choice they made against it.[1]

On the other hand, the society at large had to determine what to do with such a group. Whereas discrimination against Jews was acceptable practice, these converts were now considered fully qualified Christians in the eyes of the Church; the Jew had been easily identifiable as an "other," but theoretically the converso was to be welcomed as a peer. At first, assimilation seemed to be a viable and acceptable path for the convert. According to Haliczer, even Vicente Ferrer, who strongly promoted the conversion of Aragonese Jews, advocated the acceptance of conversos by their fellow Christians.[2] Problems arose, however, with various strata of the population. Urban dwellers, for example, attempting to establish themselves as members of the middle class, were threatened by the converso presence precisely because this group was technically entitled to equality. Netanyahu claims that in certain important communities such as Seville and Valencia, the conversos formed a majority, which would clearly present a threat to their Christian neighbors.[3] At the same time, what was to become of traditional popular anti-Semitism? Christians nurtured on the image of Jews as demons or as the killers of Christ would find it difficult to alter that image when they contemplated the nature of the converso. How could the same person have become trustworthy overnight? Ironically, once the conversos could ostensibly take advantage of more opportunities, the threat seemed closer to home and even more disconcerting than before. In modern terms, the conversos had moved from their "unambiguous mode of otherness" into mainstream Christian Spain, defying a religious demarcation and creating a new reality.[4]

If truth be told, there was no reason to believe that those who succumbed to the forced conversions of 1391 were in the least bit sincere. While there were also various converts by choice, there is no doubt about the fact that they were relatively few in number and far less threatening to Spanish Catholics. For example, in 1391, after the forced conversions, the rabbi of Burgos, Solomon ha-Levi, converted, changed his name to Pablo de Santa Maria, and later served as bishop of Burgos (1415–1435). His student Joshua ha-Lorki, with whom he had engaged in polemics, also converted, albeit some twenty years later, and would later be known as Hieronymo de Sancta Fide.[5] These individuals had first acquired a religious education and had been convinced of the truth of Christianity before opting for baptism. Alcalá lists five reasons why a Jew might convert to Christianity by choice in the fifteenth century: a sincere theological conviction, socioeconomic difficulties, agnosticism, rabbinic statements concerning forced baptism (e.g., Maimonides' *Letter on Forced Conversion*) or that Christianity is not idolatry, and an inextinguishable Hispanism.[6] Some of the converts also became spokesmen for the Church and were able to take advantage of weaknesses inherent to Judaism that only they, as insiders, knew. As for the majority who did not choose to convert voluntarily, the Church faced a major dilemma whether or not to recognize their involuntary baptism. In the long run, it opted to ignore its own teachings that reject the use of force to gain believers; consequently, it acknowledged the validity of the forced conversions of 1391.[7] Yet it faced a new dilemma: how to properly educate such a large group so as not to make a mockery of the holy rite of Baptism?

Some of the conversos chose to pursue a path that included entering the literary world or even convents such as the Hieronymite monastery; others chose to enter the university and become lawyers, while yet others served in royal and governmental capacities at various levels.[8] At the same time, many did not take advantage of these new opportunities and simply remained in the same professions as before; there was still a need for artisans, merchants, and royally employed tax farmers, and no pressing reason to embark upon a new career. The majority of the conversos continued to reside in the cities along with the Jews, as pointed out by Coronas Tejada. Despite the fact that they assumed Christian names and surnames, they and their descendants lived in the same neighborhoods and cities in the fifteenth and sixteenth centuries.[9]

Before the conversos had a chance to form any sort of community, they were faced with yet another unexpected situation. The aforementioned Dominican preacher, Vicente Ferrer, who had roamed both Aragon and Castile, teamed up with the anti-pope, Benedict XIII, after he came to reside in his native Aragon. Ferrer tried to introduce the Valladolid laws of 1412 of Castile in Aragon.[10] Among these regulations were orders for separating the areas of Jewish residence, the wearing of modest dress, not using the title *Don* before their names, and not engaging in tax farming, government posts, or court posts. In addition, Jewish physicians were not to treat Christians; neither the patients nor merchants, artisans, or agents should interact with them. If they owned land, no Christian was permitted to work it. Lastly, the autonomy of the Jewish community was to be abolished. In actuality, these regulations were not carried out, although attempts were made to establish Jewish quarters and to deny Jews access to tax farming.[11] Together with the newly appointed King Ferdinand I,[12] Ferrer and the pope arranged for eminent rabbis of the Aragonese and Catalonian communities to come to Tortosa in January 1413 to debate representatives of the Catholic Church under the direction of the convert Hieronymus de Santa Fe. Each community was asked to send two to four scholars as representatives. Consequently, Saragossa sent three rabbis, while other communities, such as Daroca, Alcañiz, and Gerona each sent one. Scholars such as Profet Duran were present at the debate.[13] While this significant group of spiritual leaders was away from home (until December 1414), missionaries inspired and led by none other than Ferrer took advantage of the opportunity and began to harangue the Jewish communities.[14] The weakening of these communities was made easier by means of rumors reporting the conversions of their rabbinic leaders, who were not permitted to return to their flocks for over two years. Consequently, the level of disillusionment and confusion among the Jews was at its height, and the missionaries began to report a considerable number of successful missions.

The outcome of these developments was the creation of yet another group of conversos, who ostensibly had converted by choice, but more likely as the result of disillusionment and desperation. It is extremely difficult to assess the number and nature of the converts during this period, although Netanyahu contends that the number of converts in 1391 and during this period were more or less identical, or that the sum total of the waves neared 400,000.[15] Freund and Ruiz place most of them as members of the "intellectual and mercantile elites."[16] These converts, while not choosing Christianity as the result of coercion, ultimately faced a fate similar to that of their predecessors. As a result, it is extremely difficult to differentiate between the converts of 1391 and those of the early fifteenth century in terms of their acceptance by Christian society and their sense of identity or belonging. When the host society chose not to accept the converts as full members of the group, it did not single out the former group as opposed to the latter or vice versa. No special consideration was given to those who had voluntarily converted or to their descendants; ultimately all were viewed as untrustworthy and unfaithful.

Beinart points to writings such as propaganda, satire, and polemical works, as well as debates that took place in the first half of the fifteenth century concerning the conversos. "The entire debate for and against the absorption of the Conversos indicates the extreme confusion which reigned in Spanish Christian society during the second and third generations following the mass conversions, by which time the assimilation of the converts into Christian society should in fact have been proceeding normally."[17]

The most vehement expression of rejection and distrust took place in the 1440s in the city of Toledo, where there were a number of converso tax collectors. After a coup by Pedro Sarmiento, the supreme judge of appeals, and an unsuccessful attempt to raise funds for the war between Aragon and Castile, riots against conversos erupted on January 17, 1449. Beinart characterizes this as "the manifestation of latent animosity which had been waiting for a propitious moment to erupt. It was the reaction of the masses, incited by religious and secular leaders, to the Conversos."[18]

The aftermath of these riots included a trial of fourteen eminent conversos whose sentence was deprivation of office, clearly aimed at preventing conversos from penetrating into Christian society. Such actions were opposed to Church teachings, for all Christians were to be considered as equals. They were the equivalent of heretical doctrine, as proven by Alonso de Cartagena in his *Defensorium unitatis christianae* and as declared by Pope Nicholas V in the bull *Humani generis inimicus* in 1449.[19] Ignoring this precept, Toledo advocated discriminating against the baptized. This decision was not greeted enthusiastically by the king, the pope (who had already objected to discrimination of this sort in 1427), or various members of the clergy or court.[20] The Toledo statutes, although enacted, were, for the time being, a local phenomenon and not yet an indicator of a national preference. Nevertheless, the notion of purity of blood laws crept into the Hispanic consciousness over the next century, with the aim of keeping conversos out of positions whereby they would have jurisdiction over Christians.[21] By 1547, a model for discrimination had been set and even approved by Pope Paul VI and King Philip II. The bodies or organizations that eventually required proof of purity of blood for its members included military as well as religious orders, cathedrals and chapters, public offices (especially municipal ones), aristocratic colleges at the universities, judicial courts, and brotherhoods.[22]

As a result, new classifications were introduced into Spanish society. No longer were there Christians as opposed to Jews or Muslims; now there were "New Christians" and "Old Christians." The New Christians might be fifty years "new" to Christianity, or they might be second or third generation and pious Catholics, but they were nevertheless viewed as New Christians. Anyone whose ancestry could be traced to Jews was a New Christian; thus, only the Old Christian was of pure Catholic ancestry.

Consequently, the converso was denied access to Spanish society on the basis of ethnic discrimination. Even the most sincere convert was denied equal rights and opportunities. Only by forging documents or by paying for forgeries could he perhaps manage to circumvent these limitations. Some of the conversos tried by these means or others to integrate surreptitiously, but the majority knew it was condemned to second-class citizenship. The Church might teach brotherhood and equality, but life had a different lesson in store. A converso who had never experienced a day in his or her life as a Jew, who might know absolutely nothing about his tainted heritage, was still refused entry into Spanish society, and little or nothing could be done to alter that fact. The host society was perpetuating a converso identity, even for those who might well have assimilated. The descendants of Jews would be reminded of their backgrounds constantly; a converso or New Christian consciousness was being nurtured willy-nilly, and the product was someone different from the Old Christian and different from the Jew. If the conversos had not already formed a group of their own, the collective was now being formed for them, whether they approved or not.[23]

This did not mean that the rate of Judaizing rose or that crypto-Judaism was formed as the result of rejection. This did mean, however, that the converso identity was strengthening and that some of these individuals might turn to their Jewish roots, if only in order to see what it was that made them different and to examine the basis of this differentiation. Spanish society in the mid-fifteenth century was still debating how to deal with the converso phenomenon; the topic appeared in pamphlets, satires in both poetry and prose, and in other literary works. A large portion of the latter aimed to prove how harmful the

Jews as well as the conversos were to Spanish society. While some members of the elite advocated educating them, many others contended that it was pointless to make such efforts, as they would be for naught.[24]

Another example of deterioration was the persecution of conversos that began in Cordova and spread to Jaen. As in the case of the riots of 1391, there was no one clear-cut cause for these disturbances. Coronas Tejada cites famines, devaluation of currency, rising prices, and political intrigues that created an opportunity for the masses to attack the oppressors and for the nobility to take municipal offices held by conversos. This pogrom included murder, looting, and flight of conversos, most of whom later returned.[25] The situation seemed to be deteriorating, although the fate of the conversos would not be sealed for another thirty years—until the establishment of the Inquisition. In the city, however, there was anti-converso feeling on the part of the nobles, the fanatical priests, and the masses. Because their conversion was not taken seriously, as claimed by Tejada, they were an easy target, replacing the previously unpopular Jews.[26]

The transition to this final phase was eased and probably accelerated by the activities of Alonso de Espina. This Franciscan friar devoted most of his career to itinerant preaching in Castile, but is best remembered for the book he wrote toward the end of his career, *Fortalitium fidei* (The Fortress of Faith). Because little is known about his life, scholars still debate whether or not he was a converso. Beinart wrote that he "had either converted or was the son of converts," while Netanyahu was convinced that a converso was incapable of writing about his brethren in the terms that de Espina used; in the latter's opinion, the idea that he was a converso was a figment of the imagination of European scholars of the seventeenth century.[27] On the other hand, according to Meyuhas Ginio, it is clear that he amassed experience from his public sermons, in particular from the interaction he had with the public he encountered. By the 1460s he seemed to have successfully incorporated this experience, as is reflected in his writing. His style appealed to ecclesiastics as well as to laymen, and his use of the vernacular (and not only Latin) kept the latter group interested as well as comfortable with the discourse. It is thought that because de Espina came into contact with so many strata of society, his writings accurately reflected their moods and modes of thinking.[28]

Part of his five-volume work dealt at length with the converso problem—especially with the activities and attitudes of the Judaizers, including classifications of their sins—and offers a program for solving this problem. According to MacKay, this work "not only covered a host of real and imagined enemies, such as Jews, Moors, heretics, and demons, but also constituted a 'ready-made manual' for the establishment of an Inquisition."[29] His solution included the creation of separate living quarters for New and Old Christians, the expulsion of the Jews from Spain, and a call to establish an inquisition. While he did not envision the National Inquisition that was to develop in which the Crown would play a central role, his sermons and magnum opus clearly laid the foundation for what was yet to come.[30] The power of his words was apparently perceived by Jews and conversos alike, for he was supposedly assassinated on the initiative of a converso named Diego Arias Dávila.[31] His book was printed a number of times after his death, and is assumed to have had influence on the policies to be instituted in the decades to follow.

There is no doubt that the subsequent marriage of Isabella to Ferdinand in 1469 and their accession to the throne of Castile in 1474 was decisive for the fate of the conversos. The converts were all suspected of being insincere, and the Jewish community was seen to be contaminating the kingdom of Castile by its presence.[32] The newlyweds fought and overcame rebellious forces, and were clearly anxious to deal with the problem of the conversos (as well as the Jews) as they consolidated their reign. Consequently, in 1477, they requested permission from Pope Sixtus to establish a national inquisition. This request was granted the following year, and in 1481 a tribunal was formed in Seville in order to investigate the heresy considered to be rampant among the conversos.

This innovative institution began functioning in Castile, where its headquarters were to be located, and in Aragon in 1484.

> Unlike the medieval inquisitors, the Spanish Inquisition became and remained a uniquely Spanish institution, its theological and juridical legitimacy conferred originally by the popes, but its institutional existence and personnel dependent upon the rulers of Spain, and it functioned as much to protect a distinctive form of Spanish Christian culture as it did to protect Latin Christian orthodoxy generally. The identification of the Inquisition with Spanish culture and Spanish policies in sixteenth- and seventeenth-century Europe colored its image outside of Spain, and the image of the Inquisition that emerged colored all accounts of all inquisitions throughout history.[33]

While a papal bull was still deemed necessary for initiating procedures, the Crown and not the pope selected the inquisitors. In addition, the Spaniards were by and large operationally autonomous from Rome and insisted upon abiding by a number of rules of their own which were often in flagrant opposition to papal dictates. For example, the pope recommended an unlimited grace period at which time penitents could confess and be reconciled to the Church; in Spain, the grace period began only when a court was preparing to begin trials. During this period, which could range from a few weeks to a few months, two books were compiled. The first was a book of testimonies recording information volunteered by witnesses who had been enlightened about Jewish rites and law by special instructors sent by the Church. The second was a book of confessions. Any converso could freely approach the Inquisition and confess his or her sins and be reconciled to the Church. However, should that individual revert to his or her old ways, mercy would not prevail the second time. As a matter of fact, a relapsed confessant was almost always guaranteed a death sentence.

Conversos had to make choices all the time: whether to appear during the grace period or not to appear, and if one did testify, precisely what to confess regarding oneself as well as others.

> Failure to appear for confession during the Period of Grace, and remaining silent about other Conversos who observed mitzvoth, were also construed by the Inquisition as acts of conspiracy against Christianity. Maintaining silence about a matter of such severity must have weighed heavily upon the soul of the Converso who knew of the practice of Jewish deeds. Hence the Inquisition asked—or rather demanded—that the accused unburden his Christian conscience before it decided his fate. This release from the burden which preyed upon the conscience of the Conversos it tried, and which was also the lot of Conversos who appeared before the tribunal during the Period of Grace and revealed whatever they did, was a fundamental element of Inquisition policy.[34]

In addition to setting a grace period as they saw fit, the Spaniards ignored the ban on allowing servants to testify for the prosecution, and many subsequently appeared in the trials of the conversos. The third Spanish innovation was the fact that the names of the prosecution witnesses were withheld from the defendant and the defense, despite the fact that the pope advocated listing their names so that both the prosecution and the defense would have access to this information. This policy made the task of the defense a formidable one.

At any rate, the Crown and the Church were unified in their determination to deal with the religious and social problems created by the converso presence; the uniqueness of the Spanish Inquisition stemmed from the fact that as a state institution, it was a tool of the state that, despite its religious nature, was intended to consolidate the kingdoms of Castile and Aragon. This reflected a serious turnabout for a Spanish monarchy that had previously considered violence and discrimination to be illegal; in the past, the riots of 1391 were condemned and the acts of the Toledans in 1449 were deemed rebellious. The creation of the Inquisition essentially moved persecution into the public domain and legalized an entire bureaucracy commissioned to implement a new set of rules. MacKay claims that mob violence was replaced by law and that the royally sanctioned Inquisition was now able to create a monopoly on persecution.[35] This clear-cut policy is reflected as well in Ferdinand's actions in Aragon, where there had been inquisitorial tribunals in the thirteenth century.[36] Ferdinand made every effort to link it to the Crown rather than to the pope or to a religious order.

The Spanish Inquisition functioned technically until 1820,[37] and was supervised by the Supreme Council or *Suprema*, made up of eight advisors and the inquisitor general; it was finally abolished in 1834. The Council was located in Madrid but had a secretariat in both Castile and Aragon that was in constant contact with the local courts. There were extremely close ties between the Council and the local inquisitors, who wrote reports to the inquisitor general almost daily. Eventually there were a total of twenty-one (permanent) local tribunals, fourteen in Spain itself and seven in Spanish colonies and possessions ranging from the Mediterranean to the New World. The first and formative period, from 1481 to 1530, predominantly dealt with Judaizers (95 percent of those tried), for their involvement in heresy was the precipitating cause for the institution's establishment. The first years were characterized by very intensive activity, at which point the conversos, in particular those who had been reconciled during grace periods, were under surveillance. Haliczer points out that in Valencia, the hopes harbored by the confessing conversos during the grace period were in vain. Although they were indeed reconciled to the Church and had suffered the humiliation of being paraded in public, the majority were not able to continue their lives in tranquility. In this particular city, 85 percent of these confessants were later tried by the Holy Tribunal.[38] This was part of the increased activity taking place at the beginning of the sixteenth century.

Other offenses appear in the records, most not until after 1539, yet they are considered to be equally serious as heresies; these include the observance of Islam by baptized Muslims (or *moriscos*), Protestantism (Lutheranism), illuminism (a pietism observed by *alumbrados*), and Erasmism. There were other aberrations of a less serious nature, most reflecting the influence of the anti-Reformation. These were considered "second degree" offenses; they include heretical propositions, bigamy, blasphemy, homosexuality, bestiality, witchcraft, and superstition. Those accused of these offenses were later prosecuted as well, especially during the period from 1530 to 1630, at which time there was greater inquisitorial activity in Aragon than in Castile. During both periods, about 1,500 heretics were burned at the stake, but whereas between 1481 and 1530, 95 percent of them were Judaizers, during the second period, only 20 percent were convicted of this heresy. Due to the influx of Portuguese Judaizers who emigrated to Spain during its union with Portugal from 1580 to 1640, Judaizing reappeared as a dominant accusation in the third period, from 1630 to 1730, when, once again, 95 percent of the defendants on trial were faced with these charges. By this time, however, the terror and intensity characterizing the end of the fifteenth century had abated, for "only" 250 Judaizers were burned at the stake during the third period.[39]

The establishment of the Inquisition was to affect the lives of every converso, regardless of his or her affinity to Judaism. The converso anxious to assimilate could not be sure if an adversary might attempt to have him arrested on trumped-up charges. Thus, even a non-Judaizing converso's life was permeated with fear, a fear that may also have served as a prophylactic against the temptation to observe. Once the Holy Tribunal branched out in Iberia as well as in its territorial possessions, the freedom of the conversos was more severely limited. At the same time, conversos who had not made a definite decision regarding their religious loyalty or identity (or the "fuzzy" Jews, for that matter), could not but be influenced by developments on the inquisitorial front. Obviously, the Judaizer's position was the most insecure because the observance of Judaism, albeit clandestinely, might nevertheless be witnessed or have been witnessed by someone who could relay that information to the authorities at any given time.

The confusion here was ubiquitous; no one was truly certain what to do or how to proceed. An example of a thoroughly confused converso from Albarracín, an inland community in Valencia not far from Teruel, proves illuminating. Pedro de Ripoll was a tax farmer and a merchant who at times expressed himself like a faithful Catholic and at other times appeared to be a Judaizer. As we will see, this is not an example of a successful crypto-Jew who maintained a façade as a believing Catholic while scrupulously observing Jewish law. Pedro's identity is extremely difficult to fathom, for at times he seemed to intend to be both both Jew and Christian. Witnesses attested to his observance of the Sabbath and holidays, partaking of *matzoh* and kosher meat and consorting with Jews who visited him at his home.

At the same time, he maligned his first wife as a bad Christian on more than one occasion, including during an incident in 1473 when he was beating her. When the Inquisition began to function, he first maligned that institution as well, but then refused to admit Jews to his home, began to eat pork, and quarreled with his second wife regarding observance of dietary laws. Of course, it is possible that his fear of the Inquisition was responsible for his abandonment of Judaizing, despite the fact that his spouse continued to Judaize. Yet his abuse of his first wife a decade beforehand, where he not only called her a bad Christian but denounced her for consorting with Jews, seems to reflect an ambivalence that was tearing him apart. His first marriage was clearly deteriorating, but the fact that he again married a New Christian Judaizer seems to reflect this inner conflict. Pedro was trying to be both Jew and Catholic, and if he had abandoned his Judaism completely, his choice of a second mate made little sense. In order not to be suspected by the Inquisition, an Old Christian wife or, at the very least, a New Christian woman faithful to the Church would have been more logical and less risky. Logic, however, does not seem to have been the order of the day.[40]

It is also clear that there were divisions within communities as well as within families. A conversa Judaizer who had already been reconciled to the Church and yet continued her heretical activities was unhappy with the Catholic piety of her son's fiancée. Rather than keep her comments to herself, she openly criticized and alienated the young lady, who later, in 1491, reported the

Judaizing activities she had seen in this household. She also confessed to observing the Sabbath there, which she probably depicted as having done so reluctantly or under pressure. Her fiancé then confirmed his mother's activities, thereby condemning his own mother.[41] Unfortunately, he was not the only child who implicated his mother in the course of a trial.

The irony was that the Church was judging Christians and not Jews; these New Christians had all been baptized and were not formally aligned with the Jewish world. Yet the fact that they or their forefathers had originally been Jews left even the most sincere converts prey to suspicion and derision. The reality was that some conversos harbored emotional or psychological ties to Judaism, some truly felt inextricably bound to the fate of the Jewish people, and still others secretly observed some of the Jewish laws and rituals. By the same token, some were completely alienated from their religious past, while others were anxious to free themselves of past ties and to assimilate, but, as has been seen, Spanish society was not willing to let them break these ties. Contreras claims that assimilation was the goal of those who converted during the fifteenth century, but that the difficulties of assimilation became clearer following the act of conversion.[42] Between the discriminatory laws and the activities of the tribunals, no convert could pretend to be immune to his or her surroundings. On the contrary, the fifteenth century was laden with developments providing constant reminders of one's past, and even those anxious to deny it would probably eventually confront that past if only in order to discover the nature of this powerful ancestral religion.

A draper from Valencia had learned about Judaism sometime between 1570 and 1580 when he had observed it as a teenager in his parents' home. He had abandoned these practices as an adult, never seeming to have learned any rationale for their observance. When he was an adult in his fifties, he was forced to face an interrogation. This converso, who considered himself to be a faithful Christian, recalled some of the Judaizing experiences of his youth, but the inquisitors felt he was not telling all. This court meted out particularly harsh punishment at this time because he had not confessed to fasting on Yom Kippur and had not named those with whom he had observed. The assimilation process that had been well underway was thwarted here, as the defendant was burned at the stake in 1518.[43] A second example from this city concerns an artisan who had been initiated into Judaism while serving as an apprentice; his masters were obviously Judaizers. This system not only allowed for Judaizing lessons but also helped develop business ties and endogamous marriages. Yet in this case, according to Haliczer, he had been attending church and was serious about his Catholicism. Unfortunately, he was unable to cope with his arrest, which delivered "a shattering blow to his precarious new identity." As a result, he killed himself while on trial in 1520.[44]

Equally ironic was the fact that an individual whom the rabbis might not judge to be halakhically Jewish might be viewed as a Judaizer by the inquisitorial court. Again, these were Christians on trial, and while those who were forced to convert were treated with far more leniency by the rabbis, halakhic problems arose when attempting to assess the status of a second, third, or even fourth generation converso. An additional factor to be considered was the Jewishness of the parentage, that is to say, whether there had been an Old Christian grandmother or great grandmother in the picture, or whether the family had managed to arrange endogamous marriages among the New Christians.

Questions of this nature usually arose when the converso left the mainland and attempted to join a Jewish community, not while he or she was still in Iberia. This is logical due to the fact that between 1391 and 1492, a New Christian would not turn to a rabbi for a legal decision, as the rabbi could not prescribe or proscribe anything to a baptized Christian. Off the record, however, rabbis might converse, console, and instruct New Christians. For seven months during the course of 1471, a rabbi named Fernando de Trujillo provided guidance to a group of conversos who fled Ciudad Real and arrived in Palma near Cordova. Unfortunately, this very rabbi later decided to convert and then, as a good Christian should, he proceeded to inform the court of all the activities he had witnessed while serving as a rabbi.[45]

As one can surmise, the establishment of the Inquisition undoubedly played a role in the formation of the identity of many a converso; the very rumor of its pending appearance was enough to motivate some conversos to flee their homes. According to Andrés Bernáldez, when the first court was set up in Seville, a substantial number of conversos fled. Bernáldez mentioned their destinations as Portugal, Granada, and even Rome.[46] Those who fled their homes once the Inquisition was established were creating a converso diaspora already in the 1480s.[47] The fact that at many of the early trials the defendants were tried in absentia and burned in effigy attests to the terrifying effect the establishment of the Inquisition had on certain conversos, most probably Judaizers. For example, over two hundred conversos from Ciudad Real and more than a hundred in Barcelona and Lerida and elsewhere were tried and condemned in their absence.[48]

A famous, complicated, and heartbreaking case is that of Juan de la Sierra. Juan had been a loyal Catholic who was reconciled to the Church after a grace period confession in 1483; as a matter of fact, he was so loyal that he volunteered to bring back his mother, Leonor González, from Portugal where she had fled in order to observe Judaism. Consequently, she was condemned to death at her trial; later in his life, her son, responsible for her demise, decided to revert to his ancestral ways. He fled to Santarem, Portugal, in or before 1511, only to be tried in absentia in 1515.[49] Others were not as fortunate as Juan; for example, a note was found regarding a converso couple that had fled Castile and attempted to exit Spain via Valencia but was caught.[50] Likewise, reports from Jaén confirm this general impression that conversos were fleeing, for there are royal documents that refer to the property of conversos who were sentenced and had their property confiscated in their absence. One individual is referred to as he who fled and reconverted, and later as one who crossed the frontier.[51]

Some of the conversos who had been reconciled to the Church during the grace periods in the 1480s were fearful for their future; if the court was to decide either that their confessions had been incomplete or that they had relapsed, a merciless trial would ensue. Consequently, among the reconciled, there were also those who fled, both to destinations inside and outside of the peninsula.[52] The converso historian and royal secretary Fernando de Pulgar wrote that some fled to Portugal[53] and to the "land of the Muslims" and later added that some chose France and Italy and other destinations as well.[54] Those who chose Portugal will reappear in the discussion of the Portuguese situation; however, it will prove more difficult to locate those who fled to France and Italy.

There is no doubt that those who were tried by the Holy Tribunal clearly had soul-searching experiences; while sitting in the prison chambers, there was more than enough time to contemplate one's past as well as one's future. An actual Judaizer might choose to die for his or her faith, to seek reconciliation with the Church and disavow any connection with Judaism, or to attempt to dissimulate. A converso falsely accused of Judaizing might ardently seek to defend his or her loyalty to the Church, might feign having observed even if he or she had not done so in order to end the travail,[55] or might become interested in the religion he or she was wrongly accused of observing. It was difficult to remain apathetic when faced with the prospect of a trial and the array of prospective punishments if found guilty. It was equally difficult to ignore the activities of the Inquisition even if one was not personally affected; there was perpetual uncertainty about whether one's turn might be in the offing, regardless of one's fidelity to Catholicism and to the Church. In addition, there were priests who took it upon themselves to incite the masses against the conversos; one Dominican monk insisted that these conversos were more Jewish than the converts of 1391.[56]

In addition, one must take into account the use of the *sanbenito*, or penitential garb. At the public and very ostentatious auto-da-fé, all of the accused appeared in the sanbenito and the headgear intended to accentuate their disgrace. Even after the sentences had been publicly carried out, the community was not to be permitted to forget the identity of those very individuals. To begin with, the direct descendants of the guilty had numerous limitations, ranging from inability to attain public office, bear arms, serve in various professions, and what clothes they might wear. But this did not suffice as a means of perpetuating the infamy and heresy. Thus, the sanbenitos of those punished were put on display in the churches; all who attended church would be reminded constantly who was guilty of apostasy.[57] Even the converso who was the most faithful of Catholics could not help but incorporate a sense of awareness of his or her heritage, whether it be filled with guilt and shame or pride. This phenomenon must have played a part in forming the converso identity.

The information known to us about the activities of the Inquisition are available mainly through the proceedings of the trials conducted by the Holy Tribunal. However, there has been a great deal of controversy concerning the reliability of the documents as sources. Jean-Pierre Dedieu points out that they are a "magnificent source from which specialists in various disciplines can glean valuable information,"[58] but also points to some difficulties that arise when using them:

> The Holy Office was an ideological tribunal; and even though the legend that it fabricated accusations has long since been laid to rest, it is nonetheless true that the material which it offers may well have been heavily biased. I think that the problem is real and that a good share of our information has been re-thought and re-shaped according to the preoccupations and mental "filters" of the judges. . . . But with certain precautions, when we are in possession of the best classes of documents, the Holy Office papers are an extremely reliable source, and they are far richer than most.[59]

After assessing the reliability of the sources, Dedieu discusses certain limitations that could be expected, such as geographical, chronological, and thematic. Dedieu correctly notes that a great deal of this material had been lost due to moves and revolutions. In conclusion, he refers to the massiveness of this source material and the fact that many parts of the trials "were recorded with exceptional scrupulousness and detail, thus furnishing an unusually rich complex of beliefs, customs, and interpersonal situations for us to study."[60] Edwards comes to a similar conclusion when discussing the pros and cons of using inquisitorial material; he also notes that "scholars have increasingly come to regard inquisitorial records as worthwhile historical sources, as often as not for what they can say about personal and social beliefs and practices, hopes and fears, social conflicts and economic difficulties."[61]

Any discussion of the validity and use of inquisitorial documents would not be complete without referring to Yerushalmi's apt assessment:

> The basic credibility of the inquisitorial documents is the more easily established, and to do so it is not necessary to enter into the controversy on the original aims of the Spanish Inquisition itself. We can easily concede that its purposes were not exclusively religious but were mixed with certain political and pragmatic considerations. Still, one fact is germane: the archival records of the Inquisition were kept in the very strictest secrecy for the use of inquisitors

alone, and remained so until the abolition of the Holy Office in the nineteenth century. To regard these documents as a means of spreading the fiction of crypto-Judaism for propaganda purposes presents a strange dilemma. It would mean that, in recording the details of Judaizing practices into the dossiers of the accused, the inquisitors were purposely transcribing a tissue of lies for the perusal of other inquisitors who were engaged in the same conspiracy. But this is manifestly absurd. Certainly we must approach these documents critically, bearing in mind the possibility of false denunciations, motives of confiscation, confessions extracted under torture, and similar factors. This is merely an invitation to the exercise of scholarly caution. It cannot possibly justify an a priori rejection of masses of inquisitorial documents spanning some three centuries and ranging from Spain and Portugal to Goa in the east and Chile in the west.[62]

The juxtaposition of the attitudes of the Church and the rabbinate always seems to loom large when evaluating the conversos. In many ways, the position of the Church was the more clear-cut of the two. A baptized Catholic who believed that another religion or its laws or rites would lead to salvation was most certain to be deemed as a heretic who must be prosecuted in order to save his or her soul. For the rabbis, the problem of dealing with a Jew who had converted to another religion was far more complex. To begin with, there were numerous factors involved, such as whether the conversion was by choice or the result of coercion,[63] and whether the individual under consideration was a convert or a descendant of a convert. In addition, it was important to determine whether or not there had been an opportunity to flee, whether the convert had publicly abrogated the Sabbath, and if there were other factors involved such as lack of funds or justified fear that might have prevented either departure or secret observance of Judaism.

At the same time, it is worthwhile to consider the level of expertise in Jewish law possessed by the conversos, in particular the most active Judaizers. Only those who had experienced Jewish life as bona fide Jews would qualify as knowledgeable; included here would be the generation of forced converts of 1391, the voluntary converts of the first half of the fifteenth century, and the converts of 1492 who chose not to leave with the exiles or left and later returned to Spain. The descendants of those who converted between 1391 and 1492 had not experienced Judaism personally, and thus the knowledge they acquired was secondhand and often distilled.

Essentially the Inquisition was concerned with the Judaizing activities of these baptized Christians and with the intent behind the deed, whereas the rabbis were dealing with individual problems that arose once a converso left the Iberian Peninsula. As is evident, these sources do not overlap but rather present two different groups or, at best, the same individuals but at different stages of life and in different locales.

Of the rabbinic material available, the most frequently consulted and most abundant consists of responsa, or questions put to the court and answered by the scholar consulted in that particular matter. There is an enormous quantity of responsa material concerning the conversos,[64] and the severity or leniency of a particular decision is often related to the time and place of the question along with the personal experience and personality of the decision-making rabbi.[65]

One can discern the problem involved in interpreting the repercussions of these rabbinic decisions, for the personal opinion of the rabbinic scholar is not always obvious. For example, if a woman left her husband in order to rejoin a Jewish community, she is not allowed to remarry until he grants her a writ of divorce. If the rabbi rules that she is indeed a Jewess, he is essentially condemning her to the status of *agunah*, a bound woman, who can never remarry. On the other hand, if he declares her to be a non-Jew, she can more easily resume a normal family life after undergoing a token conversion; such a pronouncement on the part of a rabbi does not necessarily mean that he truly perceived her to be a non-Jew, but rather that he was seeking a compassionate means to enable her reentry into the community.

Interestingly, most of the cases in the responsa either relate to property and financial issues or to personal and marital status. This division is pointed out in the responsa by Rabbi Samuel de Medina (Rashdam) of Salonika (1506–1589), himself a descendant of exiles from Spain. He needed to make this distinction when determining whether a daughter who was clearly a Jewess living in the Ottoman Empire should inherit after her father's death if there was a brother living in Portugal as a non-Jew. The rabbis always raised the possibility that the converso might repent, but in this case, since he had been born a Catholic and ample time had passed, the assumption was that the chance of his conversion was nil. When dealing with personal and marital matters, there was a possibility of being considered to be what we will term "partially Jewish." This term, however, did not apply to financial matters.[66]

Many of the problems concerned those who had not chosen to leave, such as a wife who needed to receive a writ of divorce from a husband yet on the peninsula, or a son who had remained behind whose father could not decide if he should be included in his will or not, and so on. There were also issues that dealt with local or non-Jewish law that was at odds with Jewish law; often they dealt with marriage contracts and inheritance. For example, Portuguese inheritance laws automatically entitled the widow to half of her husband's property, while Jewish law only grants the wife her *ketubah* (marriage contract) and the dowry she originally brought with her. This problem is clearly reflected in the battle for Dona Gracia Nasi's inheritance in the sixteenth century. A number of rabbis ruled on this issue, and despite the fact that some of them clearly rejected Portuguese law, they did not succeed in overturning the status of her inheritance.[67] When the issue dealt with an emigrant joining a Jewish community, there were also specific questions asked concerning the ancestry or parentage of the individual and how to best carry out a transition to the Jewish world.

Of course, there were issues far more complex than these. For example, there were problems of mixed marriages between Old and New Christians; if the mother happened to have been an Old Christian, this posed a considerable problem when determining Jewishness. The rabbis also had to decide how they would view the status of couples that were not married halakhically (which was the majority), and how significant this was. Could the conversos' testimony and their charity be accepted? Did they need to do penance once they joined the community? How should the rabbis view uncircumcised men? Should ritual immersion be demanded for all those who openly entered the fold? Was it feasible to recognize the priestly status of those who claimed to belong to that category? The transition from converso to Jew was fraught with difficulties, both expected and unexpected; in the chapters to follow, these difficulties will be discussed and analyzed.

2

The Expulsion and
Its Consequences

According to Yosef Hayim Yerushalmi, Shlomo Ibn Verga maintained that "on the scale of catastrophe exile is a lesser evil than forced conversion, but it is terrifying enough."[1] In a discussion of the significance and primacy of the Spanish expulsion in Jewish memory, this contemporary historian points to three significant factors: Spanish Jewry had reveled in a glory that was unprecedented; accounts of other exiled Jewries are rare; and the size of the expelled population was also unprecedented. He adds yet another factor to be taken into account: "the traditionally high, even inflated degree of self-awareness on the part of Spanish Jews of their special identity and destiny as 'the exile of Jerusalem that is in Spain.' "[2] This was the most traumatic of the European expulsions, and both the Jews and the conversos would have to seek a way to accept this fact and deal with the changes and challenges it presented.

Explanations vary for why the decision was made to expel the Jews of Spain. The classic rationale is that the Crown sought to create a country that was solely Catholic. In my opinion, this claim can be easily dismissed once one realizes that there was still a significant Muslim population in Spain at the end of the fifteenth century. Roth is convinced that the king and queen were not really religious fanatics and that most historians incorrectly assess their motives for the expulsion. In his opinion, there was no plan for a unified Catholic country. The crown had been too preoccupied to have developed such a plan because it was attending to noblemen who were not cooperating with Ferdinand, issues with the Portuguese, the war in Granada, and other time-consuming problems.[3]

A more realistic position is presented by Gerber, who refers to a unification process that had indeed been part of royal policy. Economic jealousy does not seem applicable here; except for a few individuals, the Jewish community was no longer particularly wealthy. Anti-Semitism was not especially strong at this time, and the nobility was not unusually hostile to the Jews. In fact, the conversos might have been perceived to have been more threatening than were the Jews.[4] Beinart, nonetheless, prefers to advocate religious motivation as pivotal, adopting a position akin to that of Baer: "There can be no possible doubt that the cause of the Expulsion was religious in nature, and that no economic considerations concerning the seizure of Jewish property entered into it."[5] This at least was the claim of the Crown in the decree itself; the Jews were a bad influence on the conversos, and as long as they remained in the kingdom, they would corrupt the conversos and encourage Judaizing.[6]

This claim does not seem to be so far-fetched. Encarnación Marin Padilla engaged in extensive research regarding relations between Jews and conversos during the second half of the fifteenth century in Aragon. She claims that the contact between conversos and Jews continued until 1492 and that there were extensive relations and broad friendships involved as well as complex family ties. There are even claims that the Jewish community survived in part because of its "powerful and often superior converso neighbours."[7] At any rate, Marín Padilla emphasizes the fact that these ties were intensified by family events such as births, hadas, circumcisions, weddings, illnesses, deaths, and holidays, Sabbaths, festivals, and fast days. In addition, there were extensive economic ties as reflected by joint contracts, journeys to fairs, and hospitality offered.[8] One interesting case is that of Simón de Santa Clara of the Buenavida family in Calatayud who, in 1391, was forced by his parents to convert as a teenager. In 1478, this centenarian still remembered prayers in Hebrew and listened to Sabbath services.[9] Examples also exist of conversos who attended Jewish circumcisions, especially of relatives,[10] and of others who sought to have their sons circumcised.[11] In 1478, one defendant recounted how he was born Christian but decided that the law of Moses was superior. At this point he proceeded to visit a Jew who arranged for his circumcision; Jaco then procured a Jewish wedding contract, made arrangements for ritual immersion for his wife, and the two left Seville and lived in Saragossa as Jews for some twenty years.[12] Other examples exist of conversos lending money to Jews for expenses such as dowries, as well as Jews and conversos attending each others' weddings.[13]

It is somewhat surprising to encounter the claim by Haliczer that it is unusual to find instances of contact and support between the two communities in Valencia. Nonetheless, he relates that in 1488 a Jew from Sagunto, just north of the city of Valencia, "was fined and exiled for having invited conversos to his home for kosher meals, reading the Old Testament to them in Hebrew, and teaching Hebrew to converso children."[14] In a similar vein, Marín Padilla found a converso who had married an Old Christian but who maintained a

Jewish mistress in the Jewish quarter with whom he had children, who were, needless to say, Jewish.[15]

In retrospect, the expulsion is perceived to be the next logical step following the establishment of the Inquisition. The problem of heresy was well on its way to being solved, but with the Jews present, how could this institution achieve its goal of extirpation? If one considers the economic aspect, there was sure to be a financial drain following the exit of the Jewish community. As pointed out earlier, during the reconquest, the Jews were essential for the creation of an economically sound structure for the developing country. They constituted the middle class, and while the native Christians were slowly moving upward, the Jews were the more established of the two groups. The irony is that because of the forced conversions of 1391 (and the damage done to the Jewish communities), there were now Christians, albeit New Christians, who remained active in traditionally Jewish roles.[16] Thus, the conversos formed the majority of the urban middle class.

One cannot help but wonder if, at the time of the expulsion, the Crown considered the possibility that a side benefit would be the addition of new converts to the Christian middle and upper classes, especially since it was pressuring the wealthy court Jews to convert. For example, in the community of Soria in Castile, the conversos of 1492 continued functioning in commerce, tax farming, and lending as before, as noted in a study of this community.[17] Another example was the converso community in Toledo, which, according to Linda Martz, was by no means a simple matter of numbers: "The upper and middle echelons of the Toledo converso society were intelligent, educated, talented and dedicated to achievement. Their skills and perseverance made them far more important in the economy, politics, society, and culture of Toledo and Castile than their numbers would indicate."[18]

It is interesting to note that after establishing the first inquisitorial court in Seville in 1481, the Inquisition itself and not the Crown initiated the expulsion in 1483 of the Jews of Andalusia, including those in the city of Seville. Consequently, Henry Kamen writes that "the general expulsion was no more than an extension of the regional expulsions that the Inquisition had been carrying out, with Ferdinand's support, since 1481."[19] Some scholars have even raised the possibility that there were conversos who were interested in ridding Spain of the Jews, possibly linked to the fact that there were Jews who were hostile to the conversos. For example, Haliczer cites Rabbi Samuel de Cuellar of Castile as having sought revenge on the conversos who were, in his opinion, forcing the Jews out of the country. As a result, this religious leader made a rather drastic suggestion, namely, to inform on them to the Inquisition.[20] Perhaps the ratio of Jews to conversos in any given community is another factor that should be taken into consideration, for some communities, such as Valencia, were destroyed in 1391 while others, such as Murviedro, were barely affected at this time.

While such a possibility forces one to reconsider the relationship between the Jewish and converso communities,[21] one nonetheless encounters numerous examples of cooperation and support that the Jewish community offered to the interested Judaizer. Jews and conversos often lived so close to each other that conversos could hear the praying and chanting in the synagogue. "The picture that emerges from testimony in the late fifteenth century is one of daily interactions between Jews and *conversos*, centered on family and religious events."[22] Evidence can be found of cordial and intimate ties between the two groups, whether financial, social, or religious.[23] There was a report made in 1396 to King Juan I of Aragon informing him that nothing had changed since 1391 because the conversos were living with the Jews and dressing like them, so the Old Christians could not differentiate between them.[24] Gitlitz claims that

> in most Iberian cities prior to the Expulsion the entire population of Jews and *conversos* formed a single extended family, laced together through generations of marriage within their small communities. ... No matter what the beliefs of individual family members, families continued to celebrate important occasions together, at least until the Inquisition made this dangerous. ... Prior to the Expulsion, weddings in the *judería* were usually attended by friends and relatives on both sides of the religious line. *Converso* relatives sent gifts of clothing or jewels to the Jewish bride and groom, while the couple's parents sent gifts of kosher food to their *converso* family. *Conversa* women came to the *judería* to help adorn the house and the bride. They witnessed the ceremony, and ate and drank and danced and sang with their Jewish friends and relatives.[25]

Marín Padilla provides evidence of sick conversos approaching Jews for cures, many of which belonged to the realm of superstition and magic. There were conversas who turned to Jewish doctors and female healers for fertility treatment, and others who went to Jewish astrologers.[26] In addition, there were conversos who visited ailing Jews and Jews who visited ailing conversos; some of them would also offer help when needed. The fact that the conversos were treated by so many Jewish doctors is not coincidental; likewise, the women employed Jewish midwives.[27] For example, in Calatayud in Aragón, a converso named Pedro Sánchez gave or sent gifts to a Jewish surgeon named Yehuda Lupiel as well as to another Jewish doctor; the gifts of friendship and gratitude for treatment included fruit and melons.[28] Another telling account reveals more than medical treatment: Juan Díez went with a Jewish physician to visit his ailing son, who was, no less, a vicar. In the son's home, they sent for a Jewish woman who prepared and cooked a pair of chickens that the doctor had received. The men then sat down together to a tasty meal; the Jewish doctor clearly trusted these conversos and their knowledge of dietary laws to the point that he felt comfortable eating at their table![29]

Marín Padilla also found numerous examples of conversos who were involved in funerals, burials, and mourning of Jews. This is not at all surprising because there were still extensive familial relationships between Jews and conversos. Therefore, when a Jewish relative passed away, it seemed natural for the converso to help, whether in the preparation of shrouds, attending funerals, sitting shiva, or paying shiva calls.[30] One incident was double edged: In 1476 the conversa María López was seen at the home of Moshe Qatorce after he died. There she was seen to be crying and lamenting along with the widow Soli and her children. However, it appears that the real reason she had come to this home was in order to claim the money owed her and her husband. When she arrived, she was not aware that he was on his deathbed, and thought his sons were attempting deception when they tried to dissuade her from entering the father's room. They eventually let her see him from afar, at which point this apparently unflappable woman insisted that the sons honor their father's debt anyway.[31] These were certainly complex relations that nonetheless reflect the natural intertwining of human lives.

When a relative did not have the means, his or her kinsmen would help with funeral expenses; the fact that one or the other was a converso or a Jew did not seem to deter the donor, at least not prior to the establishment of the Inquisition. In about 1470, one Pedro Navarro, a converso clog maker (or seller), covered all the costs of his Jewish mother's funeral including the shroud and coffin. While she was still alive, he had sent his mother money and frequently provided her with help. After the funeral, his conversa wife, dressed in mourning garb, came to see the two sisters-in-law, bringing them some sort of handkerchief for drying their tears.[32]

By contrast, when a converso died, what transpired clearly reflected his or her stance vis-à-vis Judaism. For example, Pablo de Daroca thought he was dying in 1472 and thus sent for Rabbi Salomon Axequo. The converso convinced the rabbi that his illness was terminal and asked if he could borrow a prayer book of confessions which contained the confession that is recited on Yom Kippur. The rabbi complied and the patient recited this prayer in his presence, convinced that he would die while adhering to the law of Moses. It appears that Pablo did not die at this time, but he kept the prayer book nonetheless.[33] The rabbi had respected his "last wishes," as would any conscientious man of God.

On the other hand, when conversos initiated Jewish rites themselves, according to Marín Padilla, one of three reasons could explain such actions: The conversos had personal experience from which to draw; they had attended a Jewish funeral or shiva of an acquaintance or relative and thus learned from observations; they were counseled by Jewish friends or relatives.[34] For instance,

Luis de Santángel, a converso, had left instructions that when he died he should be cared for in the Jewish way and wrapped in a shroud for which linen should be purchased, just as had been done for his grandfather and other Jewish relatives.[35]

A more general account of Judaizing that included direct contact with Jews can be found in the 1490 accusation presented to an Aragonese converso who was none other than the king's steward. This fellow, Luis Sánchez, had a Jewish cook in his home and had been seen reading from a Hebrew book and eating kosher meat. He was described as a great Talmudist who also taught Talmud to others, swore Jewish oaths, and prayed Jewish prayers. When he traveled, he was accused of lodging with Jews and eating their food and wine; while in Tudela, his business dealings were with Jews at whose table he ate. It turns out that when important guests would come to his house, his aforementioned cook would prepare food with the help of another Jewess who lived nearby. On the Sabbath, he supposedly sent someone to light a fire for the Jews, namely, the *goy shel shabbat*, a non-Jew who can perform tasks forbidden the Jew on the Sabbath. What is interesting here is that the converso, ostensibly a converted baptized Catholic, chose not to perform this task but rather sent someone else. We can only presume that he sent an Old Christian in his employ. In addition, he was friendly with the physician Todroz and attended his brother's wedding in the Jewish quarter. The list of his transgressions is long and impressive, but what stands out most is the amount of contact, codependence, and coexistence with Jews in his own and in other communities.[36]

Beinart, in his study of Ciudad Real, a Jewish community that was converted in its entirety in 1391, examines Jewish-converso relations after there were no longer Jews in town. He discovered a grace period confession from 1483 by Juan González in which González relates how a Jew from Cáceres had come to the town to buy fabric in 1462. While there, the Jewish draper, who was apparently a ritual circumciser as well, performed this act on ten young men in Ciudad Real.[37] Neither the defendant nor members of his family were included in this group, but he knew of the event and precisely who had been circumcised from among the converso males.

Baer presents a fascinating account regarding events in Huesca, which had been a well-established Jewish community in northern Aragon. Apparently, Castilian conversos who had fled their homes were attracted to Huesca. Among them was a wealthy man named Juan de Ciudad who, together with his son, approached Rabbis Abraham Bivach and Moses Arrundi in 1465, asking to be circumcised.

His request was honored, not in secret and quietly, but with considerable solemnity. On the eve of the day of the circumcision, Rabbi Bivach called a meeting of the local notables at the home of his friend Rabbi Abraham Almosnino, a broker by vocation, and grandfather of Moses Almosnino, the well-known rabbi of Salonica. The next morning, after services in the synagogue,

Rabbi Bivach asked to have a meeting of the community council convened, and the meeting was held that same evening in the community house. There Rabbi Bivach explained that a great man by the name of Juan de Ciudad had come to Huesca to embrace the Jewish religion, after which he would journey to Jerusalem; those present were duty bound to help him carry out his intention. Rabbi Bivach then swore the members of the council to secrecy, forbidding them to mention the matter even to their own families. The circumcision was then performed in the home of the Bivach brothers in the presence of twenty or thirty men—rabbis, learned physicians, prominent merchants, artisans and visiting students—who were studying Torah under the scholars of Huesca.[38]

The remainder of the account is interesting as well, as it not only alludes to the rabbi's comments but also describes de Ciudad's peregrinations. He had left Castile bound for Valencia, but having become destitute, toured the country in order to collect money and eventually arrived in Huesca. The converso was subjected to penitential treatment, and his son was later circumcised less bombastically; later the two set forth for the Holy Land. Baer not only names another converso who underwent the same ceremony, but claims that other converts joined the Jewish community of Huesca during this period.[39]

Brianda Besant of Teruel not only was an active Judaizer, but in addition to praying in Hebrew she attended the synagogue on the Sabbath on three different occasions. Haliczer reports that on "High Holy Days when it was too dangerous to go to the synagogue, she and several other devout conversos would go to a house near the Jewish quarter from where they could hear the Jews pray and sing."[40] In this community there were conversos who gave charity to Jews in need, supported the synagogues with donations of money and oil, bought *matzoh*, kosher wine, and meat, and even dared to bring a Jewish slaughterer to their homes. It was reported that the aforementioned Brianda actually paid for a seat in the synagogue for the High Holy Days, although if it were too dangerous for her to attend, one wonders why she bought a seat.[41]

A conversa named Teresa López from Castillo de Garcimuñoz provided information in the confession she offered in 1491 when she was reconciled to the Church: "One day some women and I went to Castillo to a Jewish wedding of a friend of ours" and ate in a Jewish home. In addition, once, when she was ill and had an infant whom she was nursing, in order not to infect the child, she found a Jewess to feed him,[42] an act frowned upon by the Catholic Church. A neighbor of hers, Diego de Madrid, was reported to have been visiting the home of Rabbi Yehuda de la Moneda, a physician, and conversing with him and other conversos for an extended period of time, perhaps in the context of a medical consultation; the witness claimed that this group of conversos was remiss in attending mass.[43]

A deceased woman named Blanca Fernández, who was accused of Judaizing, has two interesting items in her file. First, the aforementioned Rabbi Yehuda's wife attested to this conversa's participation in Jewish ritual and prayer. Secondly, the son of this Jewish couple, himself a surgeon, claimed that before her passing in 1475, Blanca sent wheat to the community in Huete, where this surgeon and his parents now lived, in order to ensure prayers for her soul.⁴⁴ The contact between the Jews and conversos obviously did not cease at the time of death, but continued beyond with prayers for the dead.

A different episode highlights the fact that while conversos might have gone to Jews for help or guidance, there was no guarantee that those Jews could be completely trusted. As mentioned in the previous chapter, between 1474 and 1477, a group of more than twenty conversos fled Ciudad Real, following anticonverso riots that transpired in 1474, and settled in Palma.⁴⁵ The local rabbi, Fernando de Trujillo, with whom they had contact, provided testimony that was incredibly detailed and precise. In 1484, he testified that while in Palma, a certain conversa named María Díaz fastidiously observed the Sabbath and the three pilgrimage festivals. He included details concerning the Passover seder, the kosher utensils used, and how they were prepared for that holiday. He mentioned Sukkot, Shavuot, Hanukah, Rosh Hashana, and Yom Kippur. This conversa had a Hebrew name, as did her daughter; the rabbi even recalled being present at the latter's naming ceremony. The meat she ate was slaughtered by Jews, and María would forego meat rather than accept that which was slaughtered by Christian hands. In the seven months during which they had been in contact, she never engaged in any act of the Christian faith. The rabbi also declared that her knowledge of Judaism was as good as his own!⁴⁶ Another witness in this trial, a conversa named Catalina de Zamora, elaborated upon her supervision of the immersion of a young woman prior to her wedding. She mentioned the fact that this Rabbi Trujillo then appeared with a glass of wine, said some words, and gave the bride and groom wine to drink. At this point, one of the participating women's husbands came on the scene and began to object vehemently, beating his wife and insisting that they were Christians and not Jews.⁴⁷

Another rabbi provided information in 1485 regarding a converso from Teruel. The two had business dealings, and the rabbi knew that this Manuel and his wife had Jewish "opinions" and that they had both fasted on Yom Kippur. In the same trial, another Jew testified that Manuel continued in his father's ways without specifying what they were, and yet another Jew described him as having the will and intention of a Jew, although again, he gave no specific details other than Yom Kippur.⁴⁸

The aforementioned rabbi related how another converso and his sons had observed Yom Kippur, slaughtering hens which they ate at the meal prior to the fast and sometimes fasting with the Jews.⁴⁹ Apparently, the Judaizers in Teruel were somewhat frustrated because they could not attend synagogue during Yom Kippur, but it seems that many of them would get together on that day in a house that either was adjacent to the synagogue or situated as close to it as possible.⁵⁰ Sometimes they could hear the prayers from the synagogue.[51] At other times, they procured books, occasionally with a Jew to guide them,[52] or even convinced a rabbi to come to conduct private prayers for them.[53]

In his study of Valencian conversos, Haliczer concludes that most of the Jews were not actively seeking contact with the conversos: "Far from seeking to attract conversos back to their old religion by active proselytizing as implied in the degree of expulsion, the Jews were content to let the conversos come to them for services, products, and occasional instruction while maintaining an attitude of coolness and reserve toward even those who seemed most devout."[54]

Thus, there are images of Jews helping conversos and conversos furious with their brethren for observing; alongside these images are others attesting to mounting tension between the Jews and the conversos.[55] On the other hand, Meyerson claims that most of the tensions between Jews and conversos in Murviedro were legal disputes, although he found an order in 1415 by King Ferdinand protect the local Jews from the conversos, who were suspected of malicious intent.[56] Therefore, it is not surprising to occasionally discover Jews who testified against conversos in inquisitorial trials. "In Toledo the rabbis were ordered to declare a ban on all Jews who did not come before the Inquisition to give evidence on Conversos who observed Jewish precepts. (A similar order had been issued to the Jews of Aragon by Ferdinand on 10 December 1484.)"[57] The aforementioned Fernando de Trujillo, who had been a rabbi, did not testify as a Jew but, ironically, as a former Jew. The crypto-Jew never knew who might serve as an informant for the Tribunal, and in this case, it was none other than a former leader.

As for Fernando de Trujillo, of whose origins we know nothing bar the fact that he was apparently from Trujillo, he was, as has been noted, the rabbi of the converso refugees in Palma. He served the Inquisition as an apostate, a first-generation convert, and revealed to that institution the innermost secrets of the way of life led by many conversos who had reverted to Judaism. So great were the repercussions of his deeds that the very rumor of his arrival in Ciudad Real about the time when the Inquisition began operating there was enough to provoke the flight of many conversos from the town.[58]

Carrete Parrondo claims that the Jews were "spurred on not by religious zealotry, as would be expected, but by social intrigues."[59] In his opinion, there had been a "total disintegration of Jewish and *converso* society" in the 1480s.[60] This could have been perceived as a chance for the believer to take revenge on the apostate.

By the same token, if there were Jews who were providing information for the prosecution, there were conversos who were beginning to advocate the expulsion of the Jews. Haliczer claims that the "entire notion of physically removing Jews from the society of Christian Spaniards was not invented in 1484 by royal bureaucrats but emerged from among a small group of prominent, highly educated converted Jews during the 1460's and 1470's."[61] In addition, court intrigue involving some malintentioned conversos may have played a part in the edict's evolution. Nevertheless, it is clear that this small group of intellectuals and courtiers could not have directly orchestrated the expulsion,[62] for there were other factors that came into play, including popular hatred of tax farmers and the sentiments aroused by the La Guardia trial with its blood libel overtones and the implication of collusion between Jews and conversos.[63]

Clearly, the ties between the two communities and their fates were incredibly complicated. Some conversos left or planned to leave Spain even before the pressure of the Inquisition began; some fled right after the pogroms. The claims made against Jacob Façan of Murviedro in 1393 were that he and his family convinced his son David, a forced convert of 1391, to return to Judaism; consequently, the son was sent by ship to North Africa.[64] There are references in trials to defendants who, like María Díaz, hoped to reach Constantinople and a Jewish community during the fifteenth century.[65] Actually, evidence exists regarding similar departures on the part of conversos. The fall of Constantinople fed messianic hopes, as did the phenomenon of falling comets in 1453. Beinart refers to a movement in the direction of Turkey at the time, but "neither in the records of the Inquisition nor in other sources is there any indication of the route they followed."[66] Leonor Alvarez confessed to eating matzoh with her cousin, Isabel de Lobon, and her daughter Leonor, who, according to Beinart, left for Istanbul sometime after 1453.[67]

Interestingly, a significant number of exiles, with the majority hailing from Aragon, chose the kingdom of Navarre as their destination. There is a debate over whether Navarre was to be mainly a way station for the Aragonese Jews or a final stop.[68] Gampel is convinced that many considered it to be their new home; in his opinion, the fact that "the Jews from the other Spanish kingdoms not only remained a distinct group but eventually formed their own community within Navarre was an unprecedented development in medieval Navarrese history and indeed in all medieval Iberian history."[69] The irony here, of course, is that in March 1498, the Jews of Navarre faced their own expulsion decree; few succeeded in escaping for, unlike in 1492, there were no routes of flight available to the residents of this landlocked kingdom. The majority of the community had no choice but to convert.[70] Thus, those who arrived in 1492 experienced both exile and conversion.

If we return for a moment to the opening comments by Ibn Verga, that "on the scale of catastrophe exile is a lesser evil than forced conversion," we again need to take the other option into consideration. While in 1391 the only choices presented to the Jews under attack were to convert or to die, in 1492 the choice was not identical. In the second case, Jews could opt to leave their homes, or they could remain by converting to Catholicism, an act that would now be voluntary. This choice also qualified as catastrophic, presumably on a lower scale than either exile or forced conversion, but a catastrophe nonetheless.

At this time, the aforementioned Spanish historian Andrés Bernaldez documented scenes in which the vulnerability of the émigrés as they abandoned their homes became all too apparent.[71] Numerous priests and demagogues roamed the countryside, trying to woo the heavy hearted and despondent exiles to stay, if only they would agree to baptism.[72] Some of them chose this path, whether for reasons of expediency, or because they had been worn down due to a reluctance to part with their homes, property and lifestyles, or because they lacked the means to travel elsewhere. Choosing to convert in 1492 could also be viewed as a sign of accepting the inevitable. Culturally assimilated Jews had witnessed the influence wielded by the New Christians and thus might have been more open to this option at that particular time.

Many factors contributed to Jewish willingness to convert. The long war against Granada had been expensive, and throughout the 1480s Jews converting to Christianity were freed from these onerous taxes at the same time that restrictions hitherto placed upon their participation in trade and commerce were lifted. One must consider the importance of continuity in personal contacts in commerce. All aspects of international trade—from the accumulation of capital through shipping of goods halfway around the world, from their point of manufacture to the marketing of goods when roads were poor and highwaymen dangerous—were precarious at best and depended upon strong personal ties with other businessmen. Converts were better able to maintain their value to, and relationships with, foreign merchants elsewhere, whereas those leaving Spain for Arab port cities often found themselves at a disadvantage. Last, but too easily ignored, 1492 provided Jews with a wonderful opportunity to join with victorious Spain in the fulfillment of an age-old national religious and cultural project. With Spain at last fully Christian, there was no end to the possibilities open to this society and to those Spanish Jews accepting Christianity. The completion of the *reconquista* initiated an age of great hope and optimism. Indeed, Spain dominated much of European life for the next century and a half.[73]

Some made this decision once the edict of expulsion was announced, or between that fateful March 31 and the time of final departure on July 31. Included here were prominent individuals such as Rabbi Abraham de Córdoba, who converted in May, Abraham Senior, the most outstanding court Jew in Spain, and Senior's son-in-law, Meir Melamed, who were baptized in June.[74]

The peripatetic proselytizing preachers awaited their prey as they slowly parted with their possessions, their lives, their homeland, and their history; they would be able to point to a considerable degree of success as the numbers of converts to Catholicism in 1492 would increase substantially. In retrospect, perhaps the conversos of 1492 should be referred to as the "New" New Christians, and their brethren who had converted between 1391 and 1491 as the "Old" New Christians.[75] These latest recruits did not "see the light" and then convert; neither they nor their forefathers in 1391 chose to abandon their religion because they had been convinced of the truth of the Church and its teachings. According to Gitlitz, for large numbers of half-assimilated Jews, Jews from divided families, and Jews financially entangled or skeptical about the duration of these hard times, the choice was much harder. For these Jews, the acceptance of baptism might seem a rather trivial price to pay for security, even the very problematic security of an Inquisition-dominated environment. Some converted with the intent to continue to Judaize behind closed doors, to liquidate their property at a convenient pace that would ensure a maximum price, and eventually to emigrate at their leisure. Others converted with the intention of waiting out the storm, confident that before long they might begin to practice Judaism again openly. Some converted because the pull of their Catholic loved ones, their possessions, their hometowns, or the opportunity for social mobility as Christians was stronger than the weak attraction of their Judaism. Others were caught up in the enthusiasm of the missionaries who went door-to-door in the Jewish districts inviting conversion. Some were attracted by the financial incentives that were occasionally offered to new converts. Still others converted because they interpreted the expulsion as final evidence that Christianity had truly replaced Judaism as God's favored religion. Some followed the example of their political and spiritual leaders, for the most noteworthy conversions were deliberately made highly visible.[76]

Like the first group created in 1391, this final group was also conversant with Jewish law and custom. Both groups were made up of full-fledged Jews who had made the choice to convert but who brought with them familiarity and knowledge of their previous religion. This fact stands out in clear contrast to the other conversos in Spain, the majority of whom were descendants of conversos or descendants of descendants and so on.

Oddly enough, it was due to the existence of this intermediary group, comprised of those born into Christianity who never experienced a day as a bona fide Jew, that the promoters of the Inquisition as well as of the expulsion justified their actions. While there is no doubt that some of them indeed were Judaizers, it is nevertheless ironic that they were the first to be suspected as heretics by the Holy Tribunal; their existence was the very rationale for ridding the land of the pernicious Jewish influence. Yet in reality they were extremely different from the converts who began and ended this hundred-year cycle of conversion and exile.

Be that as it may, this third group of converts was fated to appear on the scene, and the Crown realized that it was dealing with yet another type of Jewish converso. Here were Jews who were not able to face leaving their homes or their fortunes, as well as those who had a change of heart after attempting to abandon their homes.[77] Some only managed part of the trek, and others got as far as the border, at which point their will broke. Others opted to move to the kingdom of Navarre and joined Castilian and Aragonese conversos who had fled after the Inquisition was established or in 1492 because Navarre had no inquisition (until 1513).[78] Others went to Portugal and then relented. If and when this happened, what did this signify? What policy was being advocated from above? Could they turn back and recoup their losses? Would the Crown allow them to repossess their homes and property that they had often sold at a pittance? How would Old Christian society accept these last-minute or after-the-fact converts?

The basic policy of King Ferdinand and Queen Isabella was to permit the return of the exiles, provided they had converted or agreed to convert once they returned. The expulsion was ostensibly enacted for religious reasons, and once the religious obstacle was removed, there did not seem to be a justification in opposing the presence of individuals who made a considerable financial contribution to the state's finances. The Crown had historically protected the Jews, reinstating them to their positions after riots and helping them reclaim property in the past;[79] it had also employed them until the final moments. A grant by the king and the queen published in Barcelona and dated November 10, 1492, provides security to those Jews who return in order to convert to Catholicism or who already converted. The Crown specified the sites of exit available to the exiles, such as Badajoz and Ciudad Rodrigo, both on the Portuguese border, and Portugal. The returnees had the right to recover property sold or left behind.[80]

Individuals who returned approached the Crown in order to attain royal support in their struggles to regain property and goods. For example, Francisco de Aguila of Atienza received royal support in December 1492;[81] and in March 1493, those who took possession of the houses and property of Fernán Gómez de la Cueva of Cuéllar were ordered to return them to him.[82] Don Çague Abuacar, a physician, along with his associates were to receive their property back within three months of their return, providing they converted either in Portugal or at a station on their return route. Abuacar was allowed to bring only Hebrew and Arabic books that were for scientific purposes with him; no Talmud, Bible, or legal texts could be included under the rubric of professional literature.[83]

In the community of Torrelaguna, north of Madrid, there had been some two hundred Jews before the expulsion. Enrique Cantera Montenegro surmised that while the majority of the Jews chose exile to conversion in 1492, about half of them returned by 1497 because they had suffered severely while in exile.[84] For example, Rabbi Levy returned from Portugal with his family to reclaim his vineyards, as did Rabbi Abraham Çalama and his wife Inés Díaz; the latter reclaimed her houses, vineyards, and lands.[85] Others received their property back, but only after successfully clearing their names; they had been victims of false accusations claiming they had departed in 1492 with gold or silver, both of which had been forbidden.[86] One Jew had been enslaved in Portugal, but his son had converted and returned to claim his father's property, which had been given to a monastery in Alcalá de Henares made up of *beatas*, or laywomen who lived in piety and seclusion, usually wearing religious habits.[87] Each returnee had complications that needed to be dealt with in order to facilitate the return.

Vicen Bienveniste, a wealthy Jew from Soria, left his home in 1492, having deposited monies with none other than Fernán Núñez Coronel, the former Meir Melamed, who served the Crown with his father-in-law. Bienveniste arrived in Portugal, as attested to by a Jewish tailor who worked for him, but he changed his mind and returned to Spain to convert, as did his tailor. The convert Nicolao Beltrán then reclaimed his wealth and property, achieving the honor of *hidalgo* by April 1493 and adapting to life as a Castilian nobleman who was able to purchase lands and lordships.[88]

Another document proves fascinating as it reveals the intricacies of these forever changing lives. Prior to 1492, a marriage contract had taken place between Diego Sánchez and Moses Hen; the conditions included a considerable dowry of 30,000 maravedis for the bride. The groom, Hen, agreed that if he should die before he and his wife had children, not only would Sánchez's daughter be returned her dowry, but he promised to leave an additional 15,000 maravedis for her from his estate. By Jewish law, a widow does not inherit her husband's estate unless it is specified in a contract or in his will; he could name her as guardian of his estate and/or of his children,[89] and if he chose to doubly secure this specification, he might leave a Latin will as well.[90] As fate would have it, after the couple left Spain for Portugal in 1492, the groom died. His brother, however, in clear violation of the aforementioned agreement, appropriated the funds and property, claiming that they had belonged to his deceased sibling. The father of the bride and his daughter then returned to Spain and both converted. Subsequently, the brother-in-law of the bride also converted, thereby allowing the father to appeal to the Christian courts for justice. The Crown ruled in favor of Sánchez, granting him 45,000 maravedis plus costs and damages.[91]

In this case, the conversion only serves to emphasize the stronger position of the widow in Christian society than in Jewish society. Here the agreement was made regarding both the dowry and a portion of the groom's property. The brother-in-law chose to ignore this arrangement, which might have been a condition in the *ketubah*, or wedding contract, between the groom and the bride's father, and might have been specified in the husband's will. The law in Portugal stipulated that the widow receive half of her husband's property, yet Sánchez did not choose to take the groom's brother to court in Portugal. He waited until he was on his home soil, had attained the status of a Christian, and would not have to rely on the Jewish rule stating that "the law of the land is the law" since he was no longer a Jew! Once the third party had converted, all involved parties would be completely subject to the law of the land with no recourse to rabbis. As mentioned in the previous chapter, Dona Gracia Mendes later dealt with similar issues, although her case reflects the opposite side of the coin, for she was married as a New Christian in Portugal under civil law, and thus eligible for half her husband's property upon his demise according to their marriage contract, Portuguese custom, and his will. When this wealthy conversa eventually reached Constantinople, she asked the rabbinic authorities to assess her situation and determine if more than this half was rightfully hers.[92]

While the king and queen seemed untroubled by the presence of "nouveaux" Catholics on their territory, the Old Christians were not necessarily as enthusiastic. This is none too surprising, considering the events of the previous century on Spanish soil, as well as considering human nature. For example, those who had purchased Jewish property at a pittance would be none too thrilled to learn that the returning Jew had the right to buy back his possessions on the same terms as the original sale. While these changes were occurring, the Inquisition was working full speed ahead in order to extirpate the Judaizing heresy, and the general population was none too convinced that any of these very New Christians were serious Catholics.

If the social and ethnic situation was not problematic enough, additional converts were now coming on the scene whose motivations were as suspicious as ever. Beinart contends that "the act of conversion did not obscure or destroy the foundations of anti-Jewish hatred. For generations the Conversos were not allowed to forget their origins, even if there were some who wished to do so, stopping at nothing in their attempts to obliterate the memory of their past and their Jewish origin."[93] Thus, it should come as no surprise to learn that in October 1493, the Crown issued a decree in Barcelona stating that New Christians were to be treated properly. The locales that were singled out were Cuenca, Osmo,[94] and Siguenza, but the message was intended for all of Spain. The New Christians were not to be denigrated, humiliated, or intimidated, but rather treated properly; examples of such mistreatment include the calling of names—for example, "Jews" and/or "turncoats" (tornadizos)—and intimidation to the point that some New Christians were afraid to leave the confines of their own houses.[95] The execution of this decree would obviously be very difficult to monitor.

Leniency on the part of the Crown regarding ongoing conversions would continue for seven years following the edict of expulsion. Jews could change their minds and return to the land from which they had been evicted as long as they agreed to be baptized and renounced their ancestral faith. In July 1493, the Crown called for Jews who had sought refuge in Portugal or Navarre to convert so that they could return to Aragon and Castile.[96] But seven years was as long as the king and queen were willing to be flexible; the proof is in a final decree from Granada dated September 5, 1499. After this date, Jews were no longer to be allowed on Spanish soil, and unless a particular Jew had already declared his or her intention of converting, the penalty was death.[97] This stipulation had been articulated very clearly in the edict of expulsion; July 31, 1492, was ostensibly the last day when it would be safe for a Jew to be in Spain. Obviously this clause was not truly in effect for another seven years, during which time the option of changing one's mind was still viable, as long as it meant a return to Spain in order to convert to Christianity.

Ironically, while the plan to physically remove the Jews from Spain succeeded by means of the expulsion, Judaism was not as easy to remove. Clearly, the expulsion and the alternatives facing the Jews created a situation in which the number of conversos in Spanish society was now far greater than before. Moreover, as Kamen explains, "Ferdinand and Isabella had hoped that the expulsion would shut off the sources of Judaism, but their solution created new problems, provoked social discord and continued to be criticized by Spaniards both then and thereafter."[98]

The Crown had probably not considered the ramifications of such a large conversion in the midst of an already fragmented society. Its aim was to expel the Jews, and by 1499 it could claim victory on that front. The Edict of Expulsion declared that the Jewish presence negatively influenced the New Christian population. Indeed, there were no longer any representatives of the Jewish community, there were no longer any leaders or functionaries or institutions, and there was no Jewish literature available. Ostensibly, there was no official Jewish presence. However, in truth, despite the expulsion, the Jewish presence was still a reality, albeit modified.

The presence of so many new converts,[99] most of whom were not convinced of the truth of Catholicism, kept the Jewish presence hovering in some places more noticeably than in others, and obviously for different lengths of time. When reading Inquisition documents from this period, one cannot help but notice that there are numerous cases of conversos who dated their conversion to 1492 or thereafter alongside trials that began after 1492 containing information pertaining to both periods. Sometimes trials were delayed because the inquisitors had to wait until they had two witness testimonies before beginning the investigation. Some conversos chose to confess during a grace period and were reconciled to the church, only to relapse into heresy once again after 1492. Whether a converso had begun to Judaize before or after the expulsion, the final assessment was the same: Each had been unfaithful to the church and had either admitted to this or had been accused of apostasy or, if reconciled, had undergone both experiences. Again, the expulsion, while succeeding in ridding Spain of many faithful Jews, increased the size of the problematic group of conversos already plaguing Spanish society.

For example, a tailor named Luis Fernández left Spain for Portugal in 1492. However, after his conversion in Evora, Portugal, probably in 1497, he returned to Spain, choosing to live in Ciudad Real where he proceeded to Judaize. His trial, which took place in 1503–1504, revealed that he observed the Sabbath and Passover, kashered his meat, and prayed Hebrew prayers. For some reason, the court did not treat him as harshly as it might have done twenty years earlier, only confiscating his property and making sure he abjured Judaism publicly at an auto-da-fé.[100]

The Inquisition dealt far more harshly with the followers of the messianic movement that took place in Extremadura around 1500. While this was clearly a local phenomenon and thus limited in scope, it reflects the depth of the ties some conversos maintained to their roots. There were a few bearers of these tidings, the most successful being a young girl named Inés of Herrera. All of the prophetic figures promised redemption for the downtrodden conversos.[101]

The appeal of this movement was clear: Judaize and be transported to the promised land. The followers included men and women and, in particular, young girls such as the prophetess Inés herself. Once the Inquisition discovered the existence of such subversive activity, it knew it must do its utmost to destroy the movement. Consequently, numerous persons were arrested including the twelve-year-old Inés and her relatives and followers. Interestingly, among the believers were seasoned conversos, or preexpulsion New Christians, many of whom had reconciled themselves to the Church during a grace period in the 1480s. Two decades later they were tempted to revert to their heretical ways, at the risk of their lives.

In addition, there were nouveaux converts, mostly post-1492, including young girls, some of whom were toddlers when their families converted and thus had little to no Jewish memory from which to draw. The Inquisition, which helped to create a converso identity as much as it aimed to eradicate the Jewish portion of it, could not ignore this phenomenon.[102] The trauma of the expulsion and the conversions between 1492 and 1497 certainly played a role in the psychological readiness of these conversos to follow a messianic calling. Here was an alternative to the unbearable for the Judaizing converso in Spain, where observance of Judaism was banned after 1492 and where the crypto-Jew dared to practice his or her faith only at great risk. Granted, this messianic movement created a temptation based on prophecy and imagination, but it must have been real to these conversos. This, too, was part and parcel of the postexpulsion converso identity.

After 1492, the expulsion continued to play a role in the converso's life. Mayor Meléndez had been a Jewess named Reyna who converted in 1493 while in her thirties; she belonged to the group of post-1492 converts, many of whom had returned from Portugal. Although she was accused of Judaizing in 1520, the prosecution did not prove its case. Almost thirty years after her conversion, this conversa from Guadalajara still was not entitled to a quiet life, and although she was absolved, suspicion most likely accompanied her for the rest of her days.[103]

Isabel García was about fifty years old when her trial began, also in 1520. Until 1493, she had lived as a Jewess named Clara, but then she converted in Badajoz. This resident of Hita, while accused of numerous Judaizing activities, succeeding in casting doubt on the reliability of the witnesses for the prosecution; in addition, she withstood torture without breaking. During her trial, Isabel referred to the activities in which she had engaged as a good Catholic, which included taking Communion and going on pilgrimages. Isabel was also successful in her own defense, although she is another example of the disruption in the life of a conversa who claimed to be a sincere convert.[104]

A third trial that began in 1520 also had an expulsion conversa as the defendant. Bellida recounted how she was baptized in Lisbon in 1496. Most likely, she was an exile who relented after living in Portugal for four years and then returned to Hita. By the time she was tried, she was already eighty years old. The defendant, now known as Beatriz, was accused of many Judaizing activities, which she denied one by one, although she did not manage to disprove the claims of the prosecution or to invalidate the testimony of the defense witnesses. She insisted that she had been a faithful Catholic, and although the *consulta-da-fé* or consultation suggested torture, it was not implemented, probably because of her advanced age. The court was not sure how to assess this conversa's status; eventually she was absolved, as were the other two women. In this case, however, she was subject to a number of penances, and instructions were presented to her along with a fine.[105]

This conversa was being harassed by the Holy Tribunal, in this case, twenty-four years after her conversion. The Jews had been expelled from Spain, but Judaism was still present both in expected and unexpected places such as Herrera. From the Church's perspective, whether in 1492, 1500, or 1520, extirpating heresy among the conversos was still top priority. In truth, despite the absence of the Jewish community and the fact that it could no longer be blamed for having influenced and corrupted the conversos, no one was certain whether or not the Jewishness or the Judaism of the conversos had been extinguished or not. Despite the fact that the Holy Tribunal sought to prevent it, there were signs that a new postexpulsion converso identity was in formation.

3

The Portuguese Experience

The history of the Jews of Portugal is not well known, nor is it well documented in any language other than Portuguese. A flurry of interest in this community began in the last decade of the twentieth century, and hopefully we will soon be privy to a parallel flurry of publications that will be more accessible to the non-Portuguese reading public. In the meantime, I will attempt here to assess the nature of the converso community in Portugal in light of its history as well as to assess the characteristics of the group or individual identity that developed in this particular community.

The fifteenth-century Portuguese Jewish community was small, especially in comparison to that of Spain. There were probably no more than 30,000 Jews in Portugal in 1491, or about 3 percent of the population, although some estimates go as high as 75,000.[1] While sharing the Iberian Peninsula, the two regions did not have identical experiences; the western community was spared the trauma of the riots and mass conversions of 1391 and was not subjected to ongoing conversionist propaganda as was Spanish Jewry.[2] There are references to an attack in 1449 on the Jews of Lisbon; Salomon wrote that "even that limited eruption was devoid of religious motivation and solely inspired by lust for loot."[3] Apparently, there were many familial ties between the two communities, as illustrated by the fact that prior to 1492 Spanish Jews often visited relatives there, or, in more dire situations, they fled to Portugal for sanctuary, sometimes after having succumbed to conversion.[4]

Those in the latter group apparently were perceived by the Portuguese as being problematic as early as the 1390s. While many of them had Christian names, there was a sense that they had strong ties to Judaism and to the Jews. Once the Spanish Inquisition was established in 1478, more conversos arrived in Portugal; the general assumption was that they had fled precisely because they were Judaizers or "false Christians." This situation was potentially explosive, especially as popular resentment toward the Spanish conversos began to develop. For example, in 1483 and 1484 there were epidemics of the plague; the conversos were accused of being the source of this woe. The city of Lisbon expelled conversos from Castile in August 1484, and similar situations developed in other cities such as Evora and Porto.[5] Those who were given permission to leave had to choose Christian destinations, for the Crown did not want to appear to be encouraging Judaizers or Judaizing. Eventually inquisitors were brought in to deal with some of these suspected heretics after the king received the pope's permission to begin prosecuting Judaizers, most likely in 1487. As a result, there were trials of conversos in Lisbon and Santarém with convictions that included death sentences.[6]

Maria José Pimienta Ferro Tavares writes, "The mistrust surrounding the Castilian marranos finally fell upon the Portuguese Jews themselves, mainly on those in the large cities, where there existed religiously based social instability. The frequency of plague epidemics was perceived as a punishment for human sins, and one of these was the heresy of the marranos and society's acceptance of these heretics in its midst."[7] In other words, although Portuguese society had not experienced upheavals akin to those in Spain, distrust of the Spanish converso led to general distrust of their own native Jews as well.[8]

The situation was destined to change radically following the expulsion of the Jews of Spain. The king of Portugal, John II, was aware that many exiles would turn to Portugal because of its proximity, which was not only geographical but linguistic, cultural, and ethnic. In addition, this neighboring land was a likely option for the émigré because the expense and the danger involved were far less than they were to any other destination. As a result, a delegation arrived to negotiate the entrance of the Spanish exiles. According to Yerushalmi, "The terms under which the refugees were accepted by John II were hardly generous but, given the emergency, at least tolerable."[9] Representing the Jews were Rabbi Isaac Aboab and Don Vidal Benveniste de la Cavalleria who apparently arrived with the exiles. The king decreed that Jews would be permitted to enter the country legally at five points of entry for a period of eight months, paying a fee of eight *cruzados* per capita.[10] Certain artisans would be allowed to settle without fees, more specifically, those involved with weapon making and shipbuilding. Ultimately, a group could remain (after the eight months) that would be comprised of six hundred "houses" or families that had paid one hundred cruzados each.[11] Anyone who had crossed the border surreptitiously and was later caught would be imprisoned and made a slave of the Crown along with those who had entered but could not pay the entrance fees. This group of slaves became an eyesore for the king; thus, on October 19, 1492, he promised numerous rights to those among them who would convert, creating a group of Spanish conversos who were willfully baptized on Portuguese soil.[12]

At the same time, forced conversions of Jews in Portugal were also on the king's agenda. The monarch had already ordered the seizure of two groups: minors from among the exiles and debtors who had entered legally. Samuel Usque referred to 1493 as the year when "my children were sent to the lizards," referring to the island of São Tomé,[13] where "almost all were swallowed up by the huge lizards on the island, and the remainder, who escaped these reptiles, wasted away from hunger and abandonment."[14] Solomon Ibn Verga called them the *Islas Perdidas* or lost islands, and reported that many died en route or upon arrival because of what were apparently crocodiles. He also claimed that over "the course of time, brothers married their sisters,"[15] a dreadful fate to which they were oblivious.

Other reports present a somewhat different picture. The actual number of children taken to the island is uncertain; one of the largest estimates is 2,000, of whom 600 were said to have survived. It appears that malaria was rampant, and the Christians or whites were most susceptible to it, rarely living beyond the age of fifty.[16] The idea of sending newly converted Jewish children to São Tomé was supposed to help solve the problem of the Jews inundating the country while simultaneously contributing to the development of the island. "They would provide labor, an immediate younger generation and possibly some stability in a society that otherwise would consist only of slaves and the dregs of Lisbon."[17] The Portuguese accounts claim that they were not mistreated but rather were placed in the care of couples sent off with them to the island. Many of them would become extremely wealthy and powerful, which accounts for the lingering paranoia about their presence on the island; according to Garfield, the obsession with crypto-Judaism that was probably nonexistent was essentially a political ploy.[18] Needless to say, the episode was to prove traumatic for the Jewish parents as well as for the children; the latter and their descendants would grow up branded as New Christians and Jews, while the majority of them did not have an inkling of what made them different from their neighbors.

In the meantime, the multitude of remaining Spanish Jews, who numbered anywhere from 60,000 to 120,000, fell victim to unexpected changes.[19] The king died, and his successor, Manuel I, had his own ideas and plans. Although he freed those who had been made slaves, the Jewish community as a whole was subject to a new set of orders that appeared in December 1496; by October 1497, an expulsion would be carried out via three ports of embarkation.[20] While this decree appeared to be similar to that of the Spanish precedent, the Portuguese king was not serious about carrying it out. While the Spanish Crown was willing to have a country without Jews, the Portuguese Crown knew that such a move would be against its own interests, for an expulsion would be far too detrimental to its economy. Nonetheless, Manuel had to consider the demands of the Spanish monarchs and of his future bride, Princess Isabella, their eldest daughter, who insisted he rid the country of the Jews before she would set foot in his kingdom.

Thus the path was prepared for the conversion of the Jews in Portugal, both those of Spanish and Portuguese ancestry. Those who had paid their fees or had not paid them were subjected to the same fate. King Manuel simply decided to give the impression that he would allow the Jews to leave his land, instructing them all to depart from Lisbon, but he had essentially decided to keep the majority of them under his tutelage. His officers were instructed to confiscate synagogues and religious objects as well as cemeteries, but the Jews were to remain.[21] As already noted, a method viewed as effective was to baptize the young and either separate them from their parents or hope that they would provide the impetus for the older generation to join the younger. Two baptisms of adolescents during the Easter season were recorded.[22]

In the long run, there was no unified or mass conversion of these Jews, but rather an ongoing process that eventually succeeding in achieving the royal goal. There appear to have been groups baptized en masse, particularly in Lisbon, both before and after May 30, but the traditional image of all of the Jews waiting at the port and being converted in one fell swoop has been shattered. There was a concerted attempt to separate the youth from the adults. Yerushalmi refers to children between the ages of four and fourteen,[23] while Samuel Usque wrote that they "decreed that all the Jewish youth up to the age of twenty-five should be separated from their elders."[24] In the *Chronicle of the Most Happy King Manuel*, Damião de Góis explained that those children who were under the age of fourteen should be "distributed among the villages and places of the kingdom where, at his [the king's] expense, they would be raised and indoctrinated in the Faith of our Savior Jesus Christ."[25] Another chronicler of the king's life was more graphic, for he referred to taking the children and indoctrinating them:

> But the king did not accomplish this without great spiritual afflic-
> tion. It was such a piteous thing to see the children being wrested
> from the breasts of their mothers, and the parents being dragged,
> struck, and whipped as they clutched their little children in their
> arms. A cry was raised and the air trembled with the laments and
> the weeping of the women. There were some among them who, tur-
> bid with indignation, drowned their little children in the wells; some
> of them fell into such madness that they killed themselves.[26]

According to another eyewitness account, that of Ibn Faradj, the king first took away all children thirteen years or younger to be baptized and given their parents' fortunes:

In spite of all this they did not allow the parents to leave the country, even without their money, unless they were baptized. When the
time had passed, and the Jews did not want to change their faith of
their own free will, they were taken in by force in all the king's provinces, and were beaten with sticks and straps, and carried to the
churches. There they sprinkled water on them, and gave them
Christian names, men and women alike.[27]

Interestingly, the king proceeded to declare that he would not investigate the
religious behavior of these converts for twenty years; if a denunciation were
made, it had to be done within twenty days of the heretical act. Even a convicted
heretic would not have his property confiscated, and, if necessary, physicians
could use Hebrew books. In other words, Manuel encouraged conversion by
guaranteeing that conditions in his land would be tolerable for the convert.
The careful Judaizer could manage to survive and the unfortunate one, even
if convicted, would be able to bequeath his possessions to his descendants.
The delinquent Jew would be forgiven his or her crime provided the conversion
took place by May 30. This set of decrees has been nicknamed "the magna
carta of the Portuguese New Christians."[28] Yerushalmi contends that "at the
outset, no Inquisition was envisioned, nor any discrimination in law between
'New' and 'Old' Christians. The king appeared convinced that what had been
initiated by force would eventually be accepted out of faith, and that with the
passage of time the converts, or their progeny, would be assimilated into Portuguese Christian society."[29] Such a liberal approach was due to the fact that
the king was certain that despite the forced nature of the conversions, the
converts or their descendants would eventually assimilate into the Portuguese
Catholic society. There had been no plan for establishing an inquisition or for
discriminating between Old and New Christians.

What essentially had happened? The core of the most faithful Jews of Spain
had suffered the worst of fates. If exile is a lesser evil than forced conversion
on the scale of catastrophes, what can be said about the experiences of this
group of Spanish Jews? They chose what they perceived to be the lesser of two
evils, namely, exile, and suffered the trauma of losing their homes and possessions and their history.[30] The sense of trauma on the part of these Jews of
Spain cannot be compared to any previous exile in the history of Jewry.[31] Yet
there must have been strength in numbers, a strength that would provide faith
and security. This was a group experience, this crossing of borders, this loss
of one's homeland, and while no choice had been made on their part, their
experience had been identical.

Who ever dreamed that this greater evil was yet to befall them? Certainly
not Judah Abravanel, who sent his son Isaac to Portugal in 1492, hoping to
protect him because he had heard that his one-year-old was going to be kid-
napped and converted in an effort to persuade the eminent family of Isaac

Abravanel to remain in Spain. Yet the fact that this family was so eminent or that Judah and his father Isaac had fled Portugal in 1483 did not help the child's situation. Consequently, King John detained the boy and did not permit his Portuguese-born father to procure his release; he was then included in the group of children to be baptized. The poem Judah later wrote in 1503 resembles a lamentation that reflects a father's frustration at making precisely the wrong choice; it is simultaneously an appeal to his son not to abandon his ancestral faith.[32] Presumably this child was being instructed in Judaism, most likely in the home of an aunt who had remained in Portugal. Judah also assumed that if the poem indeed reached his son, he would have a sophisticated knowledge of Hebrew, which would have been quite an accomplishment. Scheindlin contends that "the poem's address to the boy appears not to be a mere rhetorical apostrophe but an actual address meant to be read by the addressee. The urgency of the tone toward the end lends credence to the idea that Judah expected the poem to be delivered and that he had hopes of the boy's imminent release."[33] Thus, while Judah (and his father) had hopes of freeing the boy, he essentially had little control over his own son's destiny.

It is difficult to know what the son actually experienced along with the thousands of others whose fate was linked to his. He clearly did not have any memories from his first year of life in Spain when he was still a Jew; thus, he began his life with a dual identity as soon as he could absorb such notions. While his father assumed he was being methodically instructed in Judaism and functioning as a serious crypto-Jew, the fact is that he was without his parents and grandparents, his primary teachers in the faith. While he was presumably aware of their eminent roles in Iberia as well as in the Sephardi diaspora, he did not know them. He was being nurtured in Portugal, ostensibly by his aunt, and the distance from the rest of his family must have played a significant psychological role in the way he coped with his situation. The irony here is, of course, that his great-great-grandfather had converted in Spain in 1391, possibly even voluntarily prior to the riots; as a result, part of the family, including Isaac's grandfather, relocated to Portugal. Netanyahu claims that

> the conversion of Don Samuel, and his failure to "return," left a
> deep impression on the consciousness of the Abravanels. Not by so
> much as a word does Don Isaac, in his copious works, mention the
> conversion of his grandfather. . . . But behind his complex attitude
> toward the Marranos, behind the harsh chastisement and deep com-
> passion with which he repeatedly treats them in his writings, there
> may lie not only his considered reaction to the grave Marrano prob-
> lem of his time, but also a reflection of his personal attitude towards
> the sad, and perhaps disreputable, experiences of the grandfather
> which he wanted to—but, alas, could not—forget.[34]

Although this contention cannot be proved or disproved, it is a fact that Don Isaac's grandfather, the court Jew and his namesake, had fled Portugal in 1483 because his patron was associated with a rebellion against the king. Ultimately, when Don Isaac and his son Judah left Spain in 1492, little Isaac was already in Portugal for "safekeeping." Unfortunately, nothing was safe for the Iberian Jew after 1391.

When historians of Spanish Jewry chart out the path to the expulsion, the signs they have located en route intimate that the policy of the Crown was comprehensible and perhaps even predictable. However, it is highly unlikely that the Jews in Portugal or their brethren who joined them were even vaguely aware of the fate awaiting them. The exiles, desperate to find a niche in Portugal or to find a way to continue onward to a safe destination, never dreamed that Manuel planned as he did.[35]

The decree of expulsion from Portugal must have seemed like deja vu to the exiles; they had not yet spent five years in their new environs, and the king already decided to imitate the Spanish monarchs. One would assume that the exiles resigned themselves to the fact that Jewish life in the Iberian Peninsula had come to an end. But in this case, the choice of the lesser evil was not theirs to make. The fate awaiting them was not the culmination of unbridled pogroms and demagoguery; the baptismal font was not the site of an act of ultimate faith after having been convinced of the truth of Catholicism. There was no sense of despair that drove them to the Church, and they were not given an alternative as in 1492. While the conversion experience was not new to Spanish Jewry, initiation of forced conversion by the Crown was most certainly an unexpected first-time experience. The Spanish Jews had believed in the Royal Alliance and the protection it had always provided them, right up until the last minute and even for the seven years to follow (for returnees); the Portuguese king attempted to project this image while advocating conversion. Because he was concerned with the problems that would arise when such a large group of neophytes would come upon the scene, and because he knew he needed this particular group, he immediately tried to project himself as the protector of the conversos. No longer was the Crown protecting the Jews; the conversos had replaced the Jews, and while conversion had been involuntary, there must have been an immediate sense of relief to some degree. At least the Inquisition was not around the corner; protection was being offered along with various offers including amnesty. The Portuguese king was informing his New Christian subjects that while he had no choice but to keep them hostage and to convert them, they would receive more reasonable and tolerant treatment than they had in Spain.[36]

Could the king be trusted? What options, if any, were available for the Portuguese conversos, the majority of whom were actually Spanish? The victims of this final Iberian conversion had no choice but to hope the king could be trusted; they were conditioned from their past experience as the "king's Jews," a deep-rooted belief that their alliance with him was sacred.[37] If truth be told, the options were extremely limited: to Judaize or not to Judaize. As long as there was no Inquisition, this was not such a problematic decision, although there had been some inquiries regarding heresy in Portugal. Ironically, because the final result was the conversion of a large group, there must have been, once again, a sense of unity and common fate. This was not a repetition of the conversions of 1391 but rather a fate without incrimination. No one had weakened or had made any choice at all, for that matter. There was no one to judge or to blame. Nonetheless, the fact was that there were no longer Jews on the soil of Iberia; there were only conversos. Those in Spain were a heterogeneous group; the latest to join did so by choice, either in 1492 or during the following decade. Those in Portugal never had an option and represented the stalwart Jews from Spain and their Portuguese brethren who were all subjected to the *force majeure*; they would be more likely to form their own particular identity.

Despite the king's attempt to allow for integration of this group into Portuguese society, no smooth transition was to transpire in either the short or long run. Those who had been uncomfortable with the ever growing Jewish presence would transfer their discomfort to the New Christian group.[38] In all honesty, they had no reason to assume that these converts were sincere or that the situation was destined to change in the near future. At the same time, the king issued decrees in 1499 to prevent them from emigrating; he was anxious to keep these Christians stationary, and forbade buying their property or selling them bills of exchange. At times, he even tried to encourage their assimilation and to open doors to the nobility for them. For example, the decree that was in effect from 1497 to 1507, that New Christians could not marry one another, was intended to open the door to the Old Christian world.[39] At the same time, although they were not sincere converts, they nonetheless were not subject to any legal restrictions; for example, those baptized in 1497 were to enjoy identical inheritance laws to their baptized brethren.

Nevertheless, the distrust and resentment faced by the Spanish converts a century earlier were experienced on a larger scale by their brethren in Portugal. The scapegoat in the form of the Jew had disappeared, and the New Christian who had taken his place was in some ways more threatening precisely because he was not a Jew. The lack of delineation was unnerving; it was most likely only a matter of time until a catalyst would provide the means for an expression of unrest, anger, or frustration.

In May 1504, a group of New Christians in Lisbon were insulted, tempers flared, and the fight erupted into a mob scene, followed by arrests.[40] In the fall of 1505, the city was to suffer a major bout of the plague that would last almost two years. The king himself abandoned his residence and advocated evacuation of the city. It was during this unfortunate time, on April 17, that there were reports of a New Christian Passover Seder which, ironically, was not being held on the correct date but had been delayed in the hope of avoiding detection. At any rate, in April 1506, these reports led to sixteen arrests followed by the release of the prisoners. This triggered understandable anger among the masses because the "infidels" had probably succeeded in purchasing their freedom.[41]

On April 19, the masses and the clergy unexpectedly found themselves with an excuse to incite violence. According to the accounts, at the site of a Dominican convent, a New Christian made an inappropriate and rather cynical remark about a miracle that had supposedly taken place there; the incensed crowd beat and killed him and then killed his brother who later appeared on the scene. The authorities were unsuccessful in their attempt to intervene, and subsequently some Dominican friars encouraged the populace to pursue the path of destruction. According to some reports, approximately six hundred New Christians were slaughtered in Lisbon in one day! Sailors from foreign ships joined in the fray; there are records that wood was purchased to enable the burning of the cadavers. A major effort was made to capture a New Christian royal tax collector, who eventually was located and beaten to death. The crowds and the friars called out for the death of the "Jews."[42] In other words, nine years after the mass conversions, a term that should already have been defunct in this society, namely, "Jew" (rather than "New Christian") was freely and successfully used to incite the masses.

The riots continued for three days, and perhaps as many as two thousand New Christians of all ages were murdered.[43] King Manuel himself played an odd role, remaining outside of the city ostensibly because of the plague, but apparently responding rather slowly to the developments. He likewise allowed his officials to remain outside the city (which had occurred due to fear) for as many as eight days after the incidents. On May 22, the king decided to punish the city, arresting and sentencing the two Dominican leaders to death, confiscating property of those who participated and of those who did not oppose them, and generally asserting his power over the city. The New Christians, in the meantime, requested the right to leave the country, and after a year of negotiations, in 1507, their wish was granted along with the right to leave and return and to sell their property. Rivkin has his own interpretation concerning the repercussions of this decree. He perceives "a release of New Christian energies" enabling new opportunities because of their ability to move freely in the Christian world. They did not exit en masse, but rather took this "as a sign of the monarch's trust in the permanence and sincerity of their Christian affiliation" and were determined not to betray this trust. In Rivkin's eyes, they never considered "a change of religious identity" until the Inquisition was established (in 1536) and exerted its power by 1542.[44] In later years, the right of New Christians to emigrate would be granted and denied. Yet in 1507, the king began an active policy to integrate those who remained, and in 1512, promised not to initiate any investigations in the religious realm for sixteen years.[45]

Ironically, as early as 1515, the king began to examine the possibility of setting up an inquisition in Portugal. In response, the conversos immediately sent emissaries to Rome to offer pleas as well as bribes. If one considers why these conversos were not yet arranging to leave Portugal, there are various possibilities. Some of them might have feared creating a division within their families as the result of such a decision; others might not have had ample funds to emigrate; yet others may have had problems liquidating their property. The historical proclivity of the previously Jewish community to rely on the king might also have provided them with a false sense of security. On the other hand, the historian Herculano claimed that their attempts to buy off the Church served to anger the masses; it did not require a great deal to spark anti-Jewish sentiment.[46] They and the Portuguese clergy, with its share of fanatics, resented the Vatican's corruption and were duly agitated by the New Christian successes there.

In addition, the appearance on the scene of David Reubeni, a Jew and "a messianic adventurer,"[47] both in Rome (1524) and in Portugal (1525) must be taken into consideration. While Reubeni had assured the king of Portugal that he would not be proselytizing among the conversos, his very presence created a high level of excitement in the community, for he had a letter of introduction from the pope.[48] In his accounts, he referred to the conversos he met as Jews, and his presence in a Jew-free country clearly provided his brethren with a sense of pride and identification. His visit inspired a Lisbon converso with mystical inclinations named Diogo Pires to circumcise himself (against Reubeni's advice) and then flee the country; he eventually appeared in Salonika where he exhibited impressive prophetic talents. Diogo met the pope, who unexpectedly saved him from the stake by supposedly substituting someone else for him.[49] In 1532, after joining forces with Reubeni, the two visited Emperor Charles V, who was less generous with this dubious duo than the pope had been. Reubeni was sent to a Spanish prison in Badajoz and died there in 1518, whereas the Portuguese converso, now named Solomon Molkho, was burned as a heretic in Mantua despite his so-called letter of protection.

In the meantime, the conversos exerted tremendous efforts to thwart the inevitable, namely, the establishment of the Portuguese Inquisition. Yerushalmi writes, "Though essentially mere pawns between the interests of Lisbon and Rome, they refused to regard themselves as such. . . . That they did not finally achieve their goal does not mean that they were not vouchsafed repeated partial successes along the way. Indeed, it was these minor triumphs that may have deluded them into overestimating their own strength."[50] The fact that they organized themselves on the basis of religious and ethnic identity speaks for itself. They managed to collect large sums of money and organize representatives, most likely New Christians living outside the peninsula, to help them execute their ideas. "It was a remarkable accomplishment," continues Yerushalmi, "and it reminds us once more that the Portuguese New Christians were not merely a conglomeration of baptized Jews, but a metamorphosed Jewish community that somehow retained vestiges of its collective character and vitality."[51] Quite possibly, the fact that they were Christians now gave them a sense of strength, for it was the pope himself whom they were trying to influence. In addition to bribes, they were arguing that there was no Judaizing heresy to justify the establishment of the Inquisition. One can also perceive a sense of unity for a common cause as well as the maneuvering of a network of strategically located agents who came forth at the appropriate times.[52]

There are those who believe that the Inquisition was established in part to cripple the wealthy conversos, or that the trials represented a class struggle since the New Christians were members of the urban middle class; yet others feel it was "a struggle of interests that cut across class lines."[53] In truth, it is hard to prove that there were no economic motives involved, although during the negotiations, King John II displayed a willingness to confiscate property within the bounds of the power of the Inquisition. Salomon emphasizes the role of the state as compared to the church and insists that it was the moving force behind the conversions of 1497 as well as the Inquisition in Portugal.[54] Others consider the process to have been the result of royal and clerical involvement, for negotiations were taking place between Clement VII and the Holy Roman Emperor, Charles V, the brother-in-law of the next king of Portugal.[55] Despite the Herculean efforts made by the Portuguese conversos, those in favor of establishing an Inquisition prevailed, albeit not until 1536 during the rule of Manuel's son and successor, John III, who hoped to make it a national institution as in Spain. While the Inquisition might have been late in arriving, it began with intensity, held its first auto-da-fé in 1540, was operating at full speed by 1547, and is considered to have been more ruthless and fanatic than its Spanish counterpart.[56] Herculano believed "that the Inquisition was established through a naked power struggle between Lisbon and Rome, in which the Portuguese New Christians were cynically exploited by both sides."[57]

There is no doubt that once it was clear that the Inquisition was there to stay, many Portuguese New Christians felt the need to weigh their options. Some harbored personal fears, other worried about economic insecurity or felt unable to leave, and many must have been afraid of government reprisal. The latter was due to the fact that prohibitions against emigration began as early as 1521 and were repeated in 1532 and 1535. The risks of flight had to be weighed as a factor now. Some, like Samuel Usque, left before they witnessed the ferocity of the tribunal. Usque himself was influential in this community after he left because he wrote in a tongue that "the Nation" could easily read, namely, Portuguese. It is significant that his magnum opus appeared on the Portuguese index of forbidden books; the Inquisition was aware that such a historiographic piece might create sympathy on the part of the conversos for their lost religion.[58] Yerushalmi refers to its "capacity to stir the often sluggish currents of collective memory."[59] A figure like this author represents the Portuguese New Christian who received a Christian-Iberian education but yet had a sense of self as "other." It might have taken a major trauma like the establishment and actual activity of the Inquisition to mobilize latent religio-ethnic identification. However, individuals such as Usque and Dona Gracia, despite their mysterious pasts, succeeded in becoming central figures in the Sephardi diaspora and devoted themselves to their fellow members of the Nation.[60]

The degree of Jewishness or religious attachment of these conversos to the ancestral religion is still a matter of debate among scholars. Yerushalmi contends that while some of the converso population assimilated, "crypto-Judaism was still a living phenomenon" that can be assessed by noting the waves of emigrations, for conversos left Portugal whether or not emigration was legal.[61] Others, such as A. J. Saraiva, prefer socioeconomic explanations when assessing the conversos and their minimal ties to Judaism, whereas I. S. Révah is closer to Yerushalmi when reviewing the situation.[62] In their discussions of crypto-Judaism and the identity chosen by the New Christians, the Spanish and Portuguese are not always considered separately, which indeed they must be. Yerushalmi explains,

> Apart from its social consequences, the simultaneous conversion in Portugal of the entire Jewry of the land must have had an equally profound impact on the self-image of the converts. . . . Here conversion was normative for the entire Jewish group. This was now "Jewry"; there was no other. It is that very corporate nature of conversion in Portugal which invested the New Christians with the solidarity of having shared a common destiny from the very outset. To a degree not paralleled by the Spanish New Christians, those of Portugal possessed a genuinely historical group character of which even Portuguese state and society showed an instinctive awareness.[63]

This is what developed in Portuguese New Christian society. Even the least religious member still felt a tie to the others, which led to long lasting affiliations on all levels. The *homens de negócios*, or "men of affairs," was an economic term used to refer to the Portuguese conversos who later referred to themselves as the *homens da nação*, or "men of the nation," a more ethnic identification. The term "Nation" was the coded term understood to mean one of the group, and as we will see later, no more needed to be said if one was a member of "the Nation."[64] Some of them observed the ancestral laws, while others took no interest in observance or in defying the Church. Yet this ethno-religious affiliation would prove to be incredibly powerful, and even more so for the

Iberian conversos after leaving the peninsula. These ties were bound on many levels: marriage, business associations, familial origins, common traumatic experience, and more.

One was a member of the nation whether or not one was a crypto-Jew; those who joined Jewish communities would not turn their backs on those who yet remained in the peninsula. The two major events that created these inextricable ties for the Portuguese community were the conversions of 1497 and the establishment of the Inquisition in 1536. The trust and cooperation offered by one member to another were, on the whole, steadfast. In the long run, the economic structure created by the Portuguese conversos was based on the notion of group solidarity. The amazing degree to which they supported and cooperated with one another precisely because they all belonged to "the Nation" was one of the outstanding characteristics of the Portuguese converso.

If one tries to assess the Judaizing of the members of this group, one way of ascertaining whether or not they identified with Judaism is to determine if and when they left Portugal to join their Jewish brethren. Some fled immediately after the conversions of 1497, but when the ports were legally opened between 1507 and 1521, more of them took advantage of the opportunity, and others continued to do so even afterward. The fact that many still remained does not negate the possibility that they may have been crypto-Jews. Famous individuals such as Solomon Ibn Verga were clearly still in Portugal in 1506, at the time of the Lisbon massacres, and Samuel Usque was also on hand in 1531. Dona Gracia, as we know, chose to leave only in 1536, although her brother-in-law had been in Antwerp for years.[65] In truth, there is little information in this regard until the Inquisition began to function in 1536. At the same time, the level of awareness on the part of the converso could range from a simple sense of belonging to an ethnic group descended from Jews to living as a bona fide crypto-Jew. As we will see, there was no way to measure the degree to which one identified with the group or to predict the path one might take during one's lifetime. There were no set formulae; one powerful experience might trigger a need to discover one's roots or successfully dissuade one from seeking any connection to them. Unfortunately, there is not a great deal of information about Judaizers' lives in Portugal prior to 1536.

At the same time, there are major discrepancies with the numbers of New Christians identifying themselves with Judaism. For example, Salomon claims that although "the overwhelming majority of 'Portuguese New Christians' were either paragons of Catholic piety or completely indifferent to any form of piety, the Inquisitorial propaganda created the 'Portuguese syndrome,' the idea that the 'Portuguese' as a group were pulled irresistibly, as if by atavism, toward the 'Jewish heresy.' "[66] Révah refers to potential Judaism,[67] while Salomon prefers to see the individuals as "potential prisoners of the Inquisition and consequently disgraced members of their society."[68] It is hard to know if those who observed had inherited a legacy of Judaism from their ancestors or had chosen to adopt the religion only after being hounded by the Inquisition.[69] Yet it is significant that so many of those who eventually left their homeland returned to Judaism in one form or another; this phenomenon cannot be ignored.[70]

After the establishment of the Inquisition, the next major significant development in converso history was the unification of Spain and Portugal in 1580; the fates of the two countries would be intertwined for the next sixty years. King Philip II (1556–1597) was not known for his love of conversos, which might have played a factor in their moving to Spain during his rule, although between 1587 and 1601, they were not allowed to leave Portugal. Essentially, because Spain was larger, there were greater opportunities in addition to more ports, fewer possibilities of being discovered if Judaizing, and more options if leaving by a northern route. In 1601, King Philip, in exchange for payment, allowed the Portuguese New Christians freedom of movement, and many subsequently fled. While it is possible that he might have been planning the upcoming expulsion of the Moriscos (1609–1614), there was no guarantee that these conversos would choose Spain as their destination. However, should they choose to come and contribute to the Spanish economy, the king had no objections.[71] In fact, the potential economic prospects in cities such as Seville and Madrid proved attractive, as did the policy of Prime Minister Olivares (1587–1645), who was willing to offer them protection on the assumption that they would bring economic prosperity to Spain. There is even a highly unusual account of a Portuguese converso named Manuel López Pereira, who moved to Holland only to abandon it for a career at the court of Madrid. The rationale for his decisions was unclear, but he became "the most prolific, and one of the most influential, of the foreign advisors on trade whom Olivares gathered around him in the 1620s."[72] In addition, the Portuguese Inquisition was considered more cruel than that of Spain, making the option of a move across the border even more tempting. The pope, Clement VIII, actually intervened during this time, instructing the Portuguese inquisitorial prisons to free 410 prisoners in exchange for payment to the Crown; after the "General Pardon" in 1605, there were even some Portuguese émigrés who returned home from abroad. When the pardon expired in 1606, arrests began once again, and according to some, the Portuguese Inquisition renewed its activities with vigor and fanaticism.[73]

Because of the outstanding economic participation of these conversos both in Portugal and in Spain, and because of the establishment of the Inquisition, more material is available about them after 1536.[74] Some of this information is found in the files themselves, especially relating to religious observance and family reconstructions.[75] At the same time, there is a wealth of material available elsewhere, such as from royal offices,[76] as well as economic documents that cannot be ignored, including loan contracts and other banking records.

One of the most interesting studies on the subject is by an economic historian who attempted to probe the notion of identity by means of a study of the bankers in Lisbon via a reconstruction of families that comprised seven large banking houses.[77] While at first the New Christians dealt solely with others of their ilk, in dealings ranging from business transactions to marriage contracts, Boyajian discovered that mixed marriages sometimes took place between Old and New Christian banking families. The motives involved here were usually economic, such as hoping to enlarge capital resources and to expand international venues. Sometimes families sought new alliances in order to consolidate financial ventures, in light of the "shifting fortunes of Lisbon's Old Christian families, aristocratic and commoner, and the wealth that New Christians acquired from commerce, [which] enabled New Christians to contract advantageous marriages."[78] Since all these families had resided in this urban center for generations, it is not surprising to discover that they came in contact with one another not only at the port but in other places as well. All of those involved were Iberians with a strong claim to Iberian heritage and pride.

Boyajian claims that these intermarriages angered the inquisitors and the church leaders, who subsequently attempted to limit fraternization and widen the racial barriers.[79] Yet by analyzing this complex situation only from an economic angle, one might tend to overlook other factors. For example, there was resentment and discontent concerning the New Christian problem in numerous circles in seventeenth-century Portugal. Polemical works circulated during this period, and writers, poets, chroniclers, travelers, kings, courtiers, statesmen, inquisitors, monks, and sermonizing priests were all involved in these debates. According to Faingold, this problem and the search for a solution to "the problem" represented a serious concern of Portuguese society. There were suggestions to expel the conversos, recommendations to continue the strenuously working Inquisition, to impose taxes, and to more stringently distinguish between Old and New Christians. The latter is surely linked to the fact that members of some of the wealthiest banking families were intermarrying.[80] The data seems to indicate that these wealthy conversos managed to attain honors and to assimilate into the banking society of Lisbon, angering those who strived to maintain a distinction between New and Old Christians. Interestingly, when some of these families chose to leave in the 1600s, they often crossed the border to Seville, Madrid, and Toledo, where they were in competition with the local merchants. Resentment again developed, and as Portuguese, they posed a distinct threat as competitors, and so were perceived as "foreign interlopers, crypto-Jews and enemies of Spain."[81] The fact that they were all but invited to come did not increase their popularity; the temptation to exploit the Inquisition as a means to cripple them financially was far too great. Boyajian claims that those who managed to escape the Inquisition's tentacles succeeded in doing so because of their own reputations and previous connections that were formed in Portugal, namely, with Old Christians and with members of the aristocracy.[82]

As a result, while some Portuguese conversos were felled by the Holy Tribunal, it appears that members of the large banking families managed to escape this fate.[83]

So what influenced the decision by many of these conversos to leave the peninsula and join Jewish communities? Some surely left for purely economic motives, or because it was convenient or beneficial to their families and their financial interests. As we shall see, each locale had its own appeal and attraction, and not all émigrés became Jewish overnight or even at all. But there was often more than just financial motivation. Some obviously were unnerved by close encounters with the Inquisition, for whether or not they had stood trial, the experience was unnerving. Some simply fled or were exiled by the courts. Others were unable to enter certain professions because they were New Christians, and yet others joined family members who had already emigrated to one of the numerous destinations in the Old or New World. Émigrés almost always seek to consort with those from their place of birth, and here the highly developed ethnic sensibility of the conversos together with the search for business ties would naturally and inevitably led them to join their brethren.

Boyajian's conclusion is that there was no continuous Jewish religious tradition in Portugal from the fifteenth to the seventeenth centuries, as demonstrated by the assimilation efforts of Portuguese banking families. The clans disintegrated or became diluted, and those who chose Judaism were ignorant.[84] Of course, Boyajian only deals with a limited number of prominent and wealthy families. We should not assume that their experience or what he perceives to be their experience was the norm for all of Portuguese Jewry, for there are other sources to be examined, such as the correspondence between converso businessmen and their family members on trial and high officials of the Holy Office. These letters reveal a solidarity among the conversos that aided them in resisting the Inquisition, and seem to reflect a different aspect of the converso reality.[85]

As for those who left the peninsula, it is feasible that they sought out Sephardi enclaves because in that environment they could continue their financial and business interests. If those enclaves were in locations where Jewish communities had been established, then it was expected of the newly arrived to join that community. If no Jewish community had been established, then the decision could be made on an individual or a group basis, depending upon the circumstances. In some places, it was still illegal for Jews to settle; sometimes it was safest to pose as a Catholic. In some cases, due to religious or political tensions, the Catholic or the Portuguese was not welcomed but rather viewed suspiciously or with hostility.

The task ahead is to determine how and why these Iberian conversos went where they did, chose to align themselves as they did, and just how large a consideration was the financial motive. Again, no matter what was decided or when it was decided, the Portuguese converso was a member of "the Nation," whether in his homeland, in Spain, or outside the Iberian Peninsula. This sense of identity may have been the sole basis for his decision to leave or to choose a particular destination. The irony is that both the conversos and the nonconversos all perceived this ethnic identity, which was often combined with an economic identity since so many of the émigrés were merchants. This identity provided a common denominator for all the members of the Nation, yet allowed for great variations from individual to individual and from locale to locale. Nevertheless, it was the Portuguese experience that shaped and created this phenomenon.

4

Amsterdam

The western converso diaspora comprised communities whose histories varied considerably, depending mainly upon economic, religious, and political factors. For the sake of comparison, we will examine four destinations chosen by the Iberian émigrés, namely, Amsterdam, France, London, and Italy. Each choice had built-in limitations along with an array of options that would influence the development of the individual converso as well as the group identity. Consequently, no two communities would or could be identical, although all would be connected, as were their constituents.

The choice available to the Sephardim who sought northern ports consisted of Antwerp, Amsterdam, and Hamburg. Antwerp was the most risky alternative because it was still part of the Spanish Empire and subject to inquisitorial intervention, thus truly safe only for the faithful Catholic. Nevertheless, Portuguese conversos took the risk and chose to do business there in the sixteenth century. Many of them used this city as a temporary way station, while others remained there for a considerable amount of time. Among the most eminent residents were Diogo Mendes, who arrived in 1512 and died there in 1543, and his sister-in-law and her family, namely, her daughter, sister, and nephews, who arrived in 1536.

Mainly as the result of jealousy by his competitors, Diogo was arrested on seventeen counts in 1532, imprisoned for a few months, and finally released after paying a 50,000 ducat "fine" as an interest-free loan to Charles V. Ironically, his brother Francisco had thought he had bought protection for himself and his family from Pope Clement in 1531, but he was obviously mistaken. Diogo was tried again postmortem, at which time his sister-in-law, Dona Gracia, offered more loans to appease the emperor. There are different versions of whether Gracia was also arrested and whether a trial began in absentia after she surreptitiously left for the springs in France in 1545. There is no doubt about the fact that her property was confiscated and that her nephew Joao contested the claim, eventually fleeing as well and forfeiting a significant part of the family fortune.[1] Clearly the risk taken by the Judaizer residing in Antwerp was formidable, for not only could he or she be charged with heresy but business competitors might try to inflict economic damage by means of prosecution by the Holy Tribunal. The attempts to damage the Mendes family and their commercial prowess by means of the tribunal accurately reflect the insecurity that plagued the lives and fortunes of these merchants.

At any rate, the New Christian population of Antwerp in 1545 was between 800 and 900.[2] The situation changed, however, when the provinces of the Low Countries engaged in a rebellion against Spain. In 1585, when Antwerp faced a naval blockade by rebels, some eighty New Christian families there fled north. When Antwerp ultimately fell, the Calvinists living there fled and more conversos followed. When the Dutch laid siege to Antwerp in 1595, they effectively damaged its trade and role as the center of Portuguese routes. Kaplan recounts what happened next:

> As a result of the blow dealt to Antwerp's economy, the Portuguese merchants sought alternative port cities which would serve as safe and efficient entreats, and would enable them to pursue their mercantile activity, particularly in Portugal and its colonies. Initially they gave preference to Hamburg which was more highly developed and eminently suitable to meet these requirements. But once Amsterdam began to grow and prosper, particularly after the armistice agreement between Holland and Spain in 1609, it became a main center for Portuguese merchants, and the metropolis of international trading activity or the western Sephardi Diaspora.[3]

A slightly different interpretation of the fate of this converso community is presented by Swetschinski: "In 1598 Antwerp still harboured ninety-three Portuguese commercial firms, as many as there had been in 1572. Thereafter their number does indeed slowly decline, but apparently as a result more of attrition than of emigration."[4]

Those who fled north chose Cologne, Hamburg, or Amsterdam; some even went east to Leghorn. A small group of interrelated Portuguese seem to have resided in Cologne as early as 1566; some remained Christians and other professed Judaism. Unfortunately, there seems to be very limited data available concerning this group.[5] On the other hand, Kellenbenz claims that in 1580 the first settlers arrived in Hamburg and that by 1595 there were seven families, twenty by 1610, and forty by 1612, when they, members of the "Nation," obtained a contract granting them a five-year residency, although no reference was made to their religious rights.[6] Hamburg was apparently unique in the sixteenth century because of its tolerance of non-Lutherans, in particular Catholics. Thus, a converso who kept a low profile could appear to be a Catholic and not feel threatened in this large commercial center and free port. Marion and Ramon Sarraga divide the community's history into four periods: The first began with the establishment of its cemetery in 1611 and ended when the various synagogues joined together in 1652; the second period reflected the heyday of the community, from 1652 to 1715; the third period ended in 1805; and the fourth lasted until 1869 when the cemetery was closed.[7]

As it turned out, Hamburg never grew to be a demographically large community, although its members, along with those of Amsterdam, were incredibly active in economic enterprises. Be that as it may, the extensive activity of this small group seems to be responsible for creating the impression that the numbers involved were larger.[8] In 1640 there were between 700 and 800 Sephardim in Hamburg and about the same number in Amsterdam. In 1660, the former grew to 900 and then declined, while the latter rose to 1,800 and to 3,000 by the mid-eighteenth century. Some scholars claim that the Hamburg community "never recovered its relative importance after the economic shock caused by the departure of the Teixeira clan around 1698,"[9] thereby crediting one family with an extremely pivotal position. A slightly more viable explanation for this decline is that the power of the *Burgerschaft*, which was hostile to the Jews, rose at this time and led to the imposition of a hefty tax on the community. According to Pinkus, "These events and the deteriorating relations between some distinguished families within the community caused several prominent families to leave the city in 1697."[10]

Interestingly enough, whereas one does not expect to find Jewish knowledge in these fledgling converso communities, it appears that in Hamburg

the overwhelming majority of even the earliest epitaphs have a clearly Judaic cultural content. Moreover, this content is not handled awkwardly, as is the case with many epitaphs we have seen in the Sefardic cemeteries of southwestern France. . . . [S]ome of the earliest epitaphs contain quite respectable compositions in Hebrew, and almost all the early Hebrew epitaphs show that the author (not necessarily the engraver) had solid training in Hebrew orthography and epitaphic terminology.[11]

Surely this indicates a clear Jewish identity on the part of the deceased or at least of those who made arrangements for their burial. Nevertheless, as has been noted, the Hamburg community was not destined for notoriety as was its Dutch neighbor.

As it turns out, the community of Amsterdam is the most researched of the diaspora communities created by the conversos, probably because it was economically and culturally the most impressive of them, and because there is ample material available. Bodian writes that "no other converso community rivals Amsterdam for the wealth of its archival material. The records of the Spanish and Portuguese Jewish community of Amsterdam . . . are unequaled in their richness and depth by those of any other European Jewish community."[12]

Although the origins of the Amsterdam Sephardim are shrouded in mystery, there are, nonetheless, numerous myths regarding the beginning of the community.[13] One, most likely traceable to Daniel Levi de Barrios, concerns a Portuguese ship that was captured by the English en route to Amsterdam. A beautiful maiden on board, María Nuñes, dazzled the court of London but refused to remain there, for she was determined to live as a Jewess in Amsterdam. Another story, probably based on a Portuguese account, refers to two ships docked in Emden. While there, the group of conversos on board met an Ashkenazi rabbi, Uri ha-Levi, who advised them to continue to Amsterdam, where he would join them. This rabbi also appears in the last two versions, in which he and his son were arrested by the mayor of Amsterdam, at which point they told him that they were observing Judaism for the glory of the city and that their considerable riches would surely benefit local and international trade. In the final story, the rabbi again organized clandestine prayers; according to this saga, in 1595 the authorities discovered him engaged in Yom Kippur services, precisely at the time of the closing prayers of this fast day.[14] The original suspicion that he and other worshipers were despised papists was soon dispelled, at which time the Jews were asked to pray for the government of Amsterdam. They readily agreed to do so, and the saga ends with them being allowed to openly practice their Judaism from that day on.

Historians of the community also differ over dating the actual founding of the community. One claims that the first merchants to arrive came in the 1580s, emanating mainly from Portugal and Hamburg and that "the earliest known official document concerning one of them, Emanuel Rodrigues Vega, is dated 1595."[15] Another insists that there were none present until 1595.[16] All agree that one Portuguese merchant received the right of residence in 1597, although his religious status was not part of the deal. The first official text was supposedly drawn up in 1598 by the burgomaster and dealt with the citizenship of Portuguese merchants. According to Huussen, they "were to be allowed to acquire citizenship if they so desired; but the authorities assumed that they were Christians."[17] Many of the immigrants to follow came directly from the Iberian Peninsula, in anticipation of taking advantage of the opportunities awaiting them there.

Economic activities were of the essence, and the conversos drawn to Amsterdam were anxious to be part of the boom in trade that the city was experiencing. Common sense dictated that a Protestant country that had recently gained its independence from Catholic Spain would be more hospitable to Jews than to Catholics, especially Iberian Catholics. Oddly enough, there was never a formal granting of freedom of worship to the Jews. Other smaller municipal councils had granted charters to the Portuguese and Spanish Jews, but this was not the case here. In the meantime, the Portuguese established their first congregation, Beit Ya'akov, between 1602 and 1604; a second, Neveh Shalom, in 1608; and yet a third, Ets Haim, in 1618. When a large house was built by the community in 1612, the municipal council prohibited the practice of religion by the Portuguese "Nation," yet once it was put into use as a synagogue, "the Portuguese nation gained *de facto* recognition of their right to practise Judaism publicly; and once *de facto* recognition had been granted, the right of public worship no longer needed to be translated into law."[18]

Essentially, these conversos had never experienced life in a Jewish community and had to create their own without having any past experience from which to draw. Apparently the fact that official recognition was not granted immediately did not fluster them, possibly because they were simply grateful to be living in a land without a Catholic Church or without the shadow of the Inquisition over them. As far as they were concerned, the details of recognition and Judaism itself could be worked out at a more convenient time, or learned from brethren in places such as Venice, Salonika, or even Leghorn; these were the communities that supplied them with knowledge and rabbis in the first half of the sixteenth century. In the meanwhile, they would learn how to organize congregations, burial societies, and a cemetery (1614), schools (1616), a dowry society (1615), charitable organizations (1609, 1625), and the like. If they needed to maintain a low profile regarding their public identity for a little bit longer, this was part of their life experience, and at least in this case, amelioration was en route. No trauma appears to have been involved, for this was a lifestyle to which many had been accustomed, and was certainly an improvement over the past. The fact that they organized these institutions points to the degree of freedom they assumed to be acceptable in Holland.

Even their early attempts to organize themselves were a far cry from the world of crypto-Judaism. These immigrants were learning the basics of Jewish community building, and would eventually create a proud Sephardi community, totally committed to Jewish law and tradition, but ever so aware of their own selves as Portuguese. While it was clear that eventually a Sephardi Jewish community would develop, the fact that a charter had not been provided did not seem to deter these émigrés. If any one factor would influence a converso's decision to come, it would be an economic one; trade routes were of the essence for the merchant and, for example, if a war erupted that closed crucial routes, a Sephardi merchant might change his place of residence in order to improve his commercial prospects.

The Portuguese who came to Amsterdam were a very tightly knit economic group that started with a narrow commercial base that widened during the seventeenth century. Jonathan Israel has analyzed their economic activities by means of periodization: His two main periods of activity are from 1513 to 1648 and from 1648 to 1713. Each stage has been divided into a number of subdivisions, which are usually the result of changes in international relations.[19] Essentially, a picture emerges of a closely knit merchant community; Israel refers to these ties as their secret of success precisely because they were multifaceted. In other words, there was not just a social or cultural connection but a religious and economic one as well. This reflected the nature of the world of the converso émigrés; the majority of them had intermarried in order to retain the family fortunes and to limit their social intermingling. Culturally, they had an Iberian heritage, rich with linguistic and literary Spanish and Portuguese influence, and a unique *mentalité*.[20] Religiously, they had similar life experiences, as they had moved from the Catholic world to the Protestant one as descendants of converted Jews who were beginning to identify themselves as Jews after all these years. Finally, they had ties with their brethren outside of Holland, and this gave them a serious advantage over other merchants.[21] There was rarely a problem of trust or loyalty; information that was reliable could easily be obtained, and cooperation was the rule. Thus, these trading communities could be developed over geographical distances; this feat could not be matched by either the non-Jewish merchant or the Ashkenazi, as emphasized by Israel, who writes that "no other Jewish community has ever exerted so appreciable an economic influence, over several continents, as Dutch Sephardi Jewry in the seventeenth century."[22]

Economically, the members of the Nation establishing themselves in Amsterdam adapted extremely well, both to the Dutch economy and to the international scene. These individuals have been described as "among the most advanced in education, intellectual activity and commercial undertaking of all 17th century Europeans."[23] Socially, they remained a self-contained group, with internal divisions that developed naturally. Religiously, they were seeking a Jewish framework, but essentially had nothing in the past upon which to create foundations. Popkin called them "a group of Iberian intellectuals, trained in the Catholic tradition, seek[ing] to come to terms with their existence as living protagonists of continuing Jewish history."[24] In order to link themselves with the Jewish world, they turned to more established communities, in particular to Venice, for aid and guidance, and essentially to serve as a role model.[25] For example, the Venetian born Saul Levi Morteira (ca. 1596–1660), who arrived in Amsterdam via Paris in 1616 (and married a Portuguese woman), was a leader in helping foster ties between Venice and Amsterdam.[26]

While open to the influence of others, there were certain conditions that enabled these conversos to remain uniquely Portuguese. These included the geographic location of Amsterdam, for it was somewhat set off from other communities, and the fact that they were not joining an already established community but rather creating their own, taking care to maintain ties with other new Jews or New Christians whether in the diaspora or in Iberia. Bodian claims that "the term 'the Nation' evoked an entire world of vivid memories and feelings; in contrast, 'the Jewish people' remained a somewhat cerebral theological concept—one that had its place primarily in the synagogue and in theological discussion."[27] Thus, "the rabbinic leadership was sufficiently wise to accept the powerful, deep-rooted 'Portuguese' allegiances of their congregants (which they sometimes shared), as long as they served ends consistent with Jewish life."[28]

A great deal of attention has been paid to the way in which these individuals struggled to find a modus vivendi and how the *Mahamad*, or governing board of seven, tried to set up rules and regulations. One can immediately discern signs of a Jewish community under construction, such as through the establishment of charitable organizations[29] and the use of the *herem*, or ban, aimed at keeping its members in line by denying part or all of one's membership in the community. In the latter case, the choices for the banned individual were to yield to the demands of the *Mahamad* and settle their differences or to cut one's ties with the community. This community overused the ban at times; eventually the ban became secularized and represented more of a social and communal sanction than a religious one. Activities in the economic sphere remained independent of the community, however; this condition was crucial for the merchants. Both aforementioned institutions, the charitable organizations and the ban, were to be found in other Jewish communities as well.[30] The Hamburg community, for example, also declared a ban on some of its members and eventually decided that four transgressions would be listed as the most serious in their eyes: informing to non-Jews, shaving the beard incorrectly (with a razor), playing certain games of chance, and gambling on either Yom Kippur or the Ninth of Av.[31]

In Amsterdam, the two most renowned cases of conflict with individuals concerned Uriel da Costa[32] and Baruch Spinoza.[33] Two others who were considered heretics were Daniel de Prado and Daniel de Ribeira.[34] While the converso background of these individuals was thought to be responsible for their unacceptable stances, this explanation is not universally accepted. As Swetschinski points out, the "combination of relative social isolation, economic failure, and intellectual self-esteem . . . certainly accounts much better for the alienation of these men from tradition than their ubiquitously cited Marrano background."[35] These individuals were critical of the tradition, of the basis for the leaders' authority, and also questioned the Jewish identity in formation. If one's tradition is not perceived as legitimate, then "collective identity becomes a hollow construct."[36]

There has been a tendency to present these new Jews as engaged in a century long struggle to define their identity; this then allows for a romanticization of their past as they encountered Judaism and the beginnings of modernity.[37] In Swetschinski's opinion, these New Christians integrated into Jewish contemporary life rather smoothly; the fact that modern scholars have difficulty accepting this fact reflects their own agenda.[38] This struggle, however, was not as long or as hard as depicted, nor were all the Portuguese confronting their past and their present having as difficult a time as portrayed. As Yerush-almi points out, the marvel is not that a few intellectuals were unable to adjust to Judaism or to the demands of the Amsterdam orthodox community. On the contrary, it should strike us as simply astounding that the majority of the members of the Nation who came to Amsterdam were indeed able to partici-pate in Jewish life and to adjust to the demands of Judaism.[39] Needless to say, we do not hear about those individuals who, essentially, had made an amaz-ingly smooth transition to life as Jews.

The nature of this transition is of utmost interest. When considering the travails of these conversos, terms such as "return" were used, but is this indeed accurate? Wilke contends that to refer to their "return" to Judaism is essentially to resort to a national allegory.[40] After all, these were not apostates who chose to abandon Christianity in 1391 or 1492, but rather descendants of converts who succumbed to baptism over a century beforehand. The "return" was purely psychological, and perhaps the fact that the Amsterdam Jews created their community themselves exemplifies this point; quite truthfully, they were start-ing from scratch. Memories of Judaism were relegated to the realm of history; none of them could remember being Jewish or could conjure up life as a Jew, and consequently, scholars such as Kaplan have begun to refer to them as "New Jews" rather than as returnees.[41] While some had indeed been crypto-Jews, this too was a far cry from normative Judaism; while they might have had access to certain texts and sources of information,[42] they were not prepared for a normative Jewish experience.

In addition, the choices that they made were often unusual. Some insisted upon visiting and revisiting Spain, Portugal, and their colonies, which the Jewish community referred to as "lands of idolatry."[43] While the rationale for such trips ranged from economic to nostalgic, the fact is that they often created tension in the community, usually because the male travelers were reluctant to be circumcised in Amsterdam. Once circumcised, baptized conversos could no longer travel safely to the "lands of idolatry," in fear that their commitment to Judaizing might be revealed. Needless to say, an uncircumcised male in the synagogue was problematic for the community. As we will see, in other com-munities, such as France and England, where they could not as easily or safely establish themselves openly as Jews, there was a natural proclivity to opt for less than a run of the mill Jewish existence. Although the situation differed in Holland, there are nonetheless numerous examples of behavior on the part of certain individuals that would be considered unusual, concerning decorum in the synagogue and Sabbath conduct and involving activities such as gambling, engaging in stock transactions, and chewing tobacco in the synagogue on the Sabbath. The community leaders made great efforts to sanction certain behav-ior, both in the synagogue and outside, but their sanctions were often in vain.[44]

Although the rabbinic leaders attempted to control the lifestyle of these individuals, the latter did not seem to be suffering from dissonance as the result of their actions. Bodian refers to aims of communal leaders that were "somewhat conflicting (though not contradictory)," leaders affiliated to the rabbinic Jewish world, and "preserving a distinct identity based on quasi-ethnic foundations alien to rabbinic Judaism."[45]

Loyalty to the group was a given, and a commitment to Judaism was a developing part of their consciousness, but exigencies would take precedence when there were conflicting demands between the Jewish world and the reality of the Portuguese "New Jew." Thus, the importance of being a member of the Nation as well as of being Portuguese played a major role in adapting to diaspora life. In the long run, each world influenced the other; the conversos became more Jewish socially, but their Portuguese heritage affected their religious world.[46] The roots to Iberia, whether cultural, linguistic, or psychological, were not to be disparaged; pride in their deep-seated roots was undeniable. The past, although lacking in Jewish content, provided emotional and traumatic connections that constituted part of their very ethnicity.[47] Interestingly enough, the terms "Portuguese of the Hebrew Nation" or "Portuguese of the Nation" apparently developed in Spain in order to differentiate between Spanish and Portuguese conversos, and would be applied there for a few generations. When they left the peninsula, the term was used "with obvious pride and in a way that showed their basic acceptance of Iberian ethnic concepts."[48]

There has been a traditional view that considered the former conversos settling in the western diaspora to have been living a contradiction, but this seems to be the perspective of the outsider looking in. On the whole, the Portuguese émigrés themselves were not overwhelmed by these perceived tensions. Swetschinski explains that

> the distinction made by the Portuguese Jews between a hatred of the
> Inquisition and all it stood for and a general appreciation for the
> secular authorities and Iberian culture in general was not a mask
> covering an irresolvable deeper tension. . . . No doubt, Amsterdam's
> Portuguese Jews, as well as others of the early modern era, often ex-
> perienced within one life-span two distinct and in some respects an-
> tagonistic religious traditions, lived under the authority of two or
> more often hostile governments, and had been forced to make
> themselves at home as best they could in a variety of cultures. Yet,
> more often than not, the tensions engendered by these changes
> were resolved quite smoothly and gave rise to no apparent psycho-
> logical trauma nor to repressed undercurrents of social pathology.[49]

This appears to be a variation of cultural commuting, or of simultaneously living in two cultures but without the commute. These conversos were open to secular culture because that was a part of their past that they could retain.

On the other hand, what could be called their converso past was much harder to define. In all honesty, one has to ask if memories existed from which this group could draw and if they were the bearers of anything that could be called a collective memory. Swetschinski relates to the fact that there are scarcely any autobiographies written by the members of this group, which might signify repression of traumas or "an inability to forge out of the great diversity of very personal memories a collective memory," for if memory cannot be shared, it will fade or recede into the background.[50] In his assessment, the use of biblical motifs represented part of the conversos' new beginning as well as an expression of their pride in biblical ancestors (heroes), for the biblical past was replacing the nonexistent common past for the group.[51] These motifs can be seen most clearly on the tombstones at the cemeteries in Ouderkerk and Hamburg; the latter have already been mentioned. Use of the biblical past to create an identity resulted in "an ethnic identity neither Iberian nor Jewish." These invented memories were to form the basis of their ethnicity.[52]

Ultimately, seventeenth-century Amsterdam witnessed a unique creation: A Jewish community arose that was composed of former baptized Catholics of Jewish heritage. Their heritage, however, was far more complex than one could imagine. Each had his or her own memory of life as a converso. Some had been hounded by the Inquisition, while others had only lived with the specter of its threat. Others had witnessed family members or friends who had been directly traumatized by this institution. All knew that none of them was completely insulated; only the fool felt secure while on Catholic soil. On the other hand, their education and cultural baggage was totally Iberian. When they left the peninsula, they chose to continue traditions that could be described as aristocratic, and they espoused the notion of leisure time characteristic of the merchant class. These included attending the theater and coffee houses, Spanish literary academies, and gambling.[53] Their spoken language remained Portuguese throughout the seventeenth century; Hebrew was acquired as the liturgical language, and Spanish served as the language of high culture. The Dutch influence slowly infiltrated the realm of manners, but the culture was pure Iberian. These members of the Nation were tied to their fellow members; they were committed to creating a Jewish community, but were not willing to obliterate everything from their past. For example, many of the men had a Hebrew name and a Portuguese name, and the latter would always be used for business purposes. Part of their new identity involved being a "New Jew"[54] with a new approach to being Jewish. This was completely intertwined with their Portuguese pride, and while they abhorred the Inquisition and all it represented, they did not similarly reject their cultural ties to their homeland. These ties included an openness to secularism and modernity, which led many to view them as the first "modern Jews" because they seemed to have managed a peaceful coexistence between secularism and Judaism.[55] It would seem, however, that in order to be a modern Jew, one had to have made the transition from the medieval world into the modern, whereas these individuals had never experienced life as medieval Jews,[56] since in reality they had never been Jews at all.

The newly developed identity of the Dutch Portuguese served them well. They succeeded in creating a viable Sephardi Jewish community with links to other communities. Amsterdam would in turn serve as an example for other developing converso communities, surely the ultimate measure of success. The members of the Nation were devoted to each other; this is reflected in the success of their economic endeavors and the reliability of their partnerships. The occasional aberration was precisely that, the exception to the rule. The typical émigré did not challenge rabbinic authority; he or she was striving to determine what was necessary in order to become a sixteenth-century Jew. These conversos displayed concern for each other and for their poor, although there were cases in which poor coreligionists hoping to settle in Amsterdam were given aid in order to enable them to settle elsewhere, especially in the New World.

A good example of the sense of mutual responsibility in this community is the *dotar* society, which drew ethnic lines but included conversos and ex-conversos as well as Sephardim. The inclusion of Sephardim helped the search for roots come full circle, as it represented ancestral ties, accentuating the fact that the conversos and the Sephardim were not separated by any boundaries.[57] Kaplan points out that the statutes of 1615 of the Sacred Society for Granting Dowries for Orphaned and Poor Brides recognized as "daughters of the Nation" young women living as Christians in Flanders and France as well as from any sector of the crypto-Jewish population.[58] Thus, even the dotar society, with its wide net of activities, usually included Sephardim, namely, descendants of the expulsion of 1492, as well as bona fide conversos who had not left the peninsula. The ethnic identity of these newcomers to Amsterdam was unique, and they were not interested in mingling with the Ashkenazim who arrived in the city.[59] They were "those of the Nation," proud Portuguese who were finally free to define their own lives after so many years of tyranny.

5

France

The Portuguese who chose Amsterdam were able to begin their lives as Jews and to make contributions in various fields such as Hebrew printing, poetry, and apologetics. Their brethren who set forth for France were far more limited in their options, and, as a result, their contributions to spheres other than the economic were less impressive. Ostensibly, France should not have been viewed as a desirable option for the members of the Nation, for unlike Catholic Antwerp and Protestant Holland, this country had expelled its Jews numerous times during the fourteenth century; this act was even reaffirmed in 1615. Nevertheless, its geographical proximity to Iberia made it a logical way station, at the very least. In many ways, the mobility of the conversos was reflected by their presence in France, and newcomers appeared there as late as in the eighteenth century.

The Portuguese and Spaniards began arriving sometime after 1536, most likely due to the establishment of the Portuguese Inquisition, and were joined in the seventeenth century by those who were, for the most part, fleeing the Inquisition.[1] In 1550 Henri II signed a charter known as the *Lettres Patentes*, or Letters of Naturalization and Dispensation, which granted the right of entry, settlement, commerce, and acquisition of property to the Portuguese. The original documents contained the following statement: "Among the Portuguese, known as New Christians, there has arisen a desire, which grows day by day, to take up residence in this our Kingdom and to bring their wives and families, bearing with them money and chattels, in the manner that has been set forth to us by those whom they have sent hither."[2]

In most of the *Lettres Patentes* in future years, a term such as "merchants and other Portuguese" or "Portuguese merchants" or "Spanish and Portuguese" was used, since it was still technically forbidden for a Jew to reside on French soil. Essentially, most of the receptor communities were pleased to have foreigners join them in the hope that they might revitalize the local commerce. The kings who signed *Lettres Patentes* did so for purely self-serving reasons, and their decisions did not always affect local developments. This is because in order to be valid, royal decrees had to be endorsed and registered locally in each province. For example, the city of Bordeaux was not enthusiastic about such privileges and abstained from approving them until 1580. On the other hand, in 1574 a different royal document did affect the conversos in this city, for it guaranteed the Spaniards and Portuguese of Bordeaux that no inquiries would be made into their lives. This was an implication of tacit recognition of their Jewishness, and that their city of residence was a "sure haven."[3] These decrees basically set the tone for life in France; a religious façade was required and maintained fairly consistently until the turn of the following century.

In short, the Jewish community as such did not officially exist in France until the eighteenth century, and these Portuguese conversos, although outside of Iberia, basically continued to live a crypto-Jewish life for generations after they left the peninsula.[4] As Malino states, "That the passage of over one-hundred years had created only a minor change in the privileges of 1550 provided a certain amount of security for the *neuveaux Chrétiens*, who continued throughout this time to live within the framework of Catholicism. . . . Hiding to this extent their supposed religious faith and all that this faith required of them was the price they willingly paid for a temporarily secure existence."[5] A Jewish identity could not really develop under such conditions, and as Portuguese, neither they nor their children or grandchildren could consider themselves bona fide Frenchmen, even if they eventually spoke the language fluently and sounded like natives. For generations, they assumed the guise of Catholics from birth until death, and engaged in the expected life cycle rituals, including baptism and Catholic marital ceremonies. On the other hand, Loker maintains that the Christians were not pedantic observers of the laws of the Church, such as holiday observance and marital ceremonies, and that the conversos who came to Bordeaux maintained a strong desire to become Jews throughout their stay.[6] The conversos could see that their brethren in Holland and Venice were developing serious Jewish communities; this had to have affected them, and there is no doubt that some eventually left France in order to join these Sephardim rather than to continue living a double existence at their first stop outside Iberia.

Demographically speaking, the French Portuguese communities were relatively small and tended to be near the Spanish border. Bordeaux and Bayonne are usually considered to have been the more eminent centers. According to Wilke, in 1625, the largest Judeo-Portuguese colony in the world was not Amsterdam or Venice but either Biarritz (slightly south of Bayonne) or Saint-Esprit-lès-Bayonne, each with a population of 2,000.[7] The major advantage of Bayonne was its proximity to the ports of Spain,[8] although "flight was very difficult in those days of long journeys when to go from Madrid to Bayonne, for example, in a litter or by mule train could take two or three weeks and was expensive because of the nights which had to be spent at inns and the cost of food, not to speak of the peril from bandits and natural disasters."[9]

Peyrehorade, Labastide-Clairence, and Bidache in the Southwest also attracted conversos. Those who settled in Bidache were fortunate, as it was a sovereign principality; as a result, in the seventeenth century, the Portuguese there were already referred to as Jews.[10] By the sixteenth century, small groups had settled in Marseilles, Lyons, and Paris, but prior to the eighteenth century, there were no organized communities there.[11] In addition, there were smaller clusters in Saint Jean de Luz, Rouen, Nantes, La Rochelle, Le Havre, and Toulouse. Saint Jean de Luz served as a first stop for almost all the émigrés until 1618, when the two hundred conversos there fled because of a threat to their lives. In Nantes, the conversos were split into two factions, the Catholics and the Judaizers, but records of the eighteenth century contain no trace of them and thus relatively little is known about these groups or about the identity of their members.[12]

Neither the New Christian identity nor references to these immigrants as New Christians were destined to fade from usage. Thus, the term continued to appear in city ordinances in Bordeaux, Rouen, and elsewhere.[13] As New Christians, these immigrants were usually granted the right of residence, although sometimes this was more or less equivalent to the right not to be evicted. At times the New Christians were asked to leave cities such as Bordeaux due to pressure by the local competing merchants, although on the whole the parliament there seemed to function as a protector of these New Christians. While an expulsion decree for those residing in the city for less than ten years was executed in 1600, the aforementioned expulsion decree of 1615 was never carried out, a reflection of the local ambiguity toward the New Christians. In 1684, ninety-three Portuguese Jewish families of lesser means were evicted. However, the milieu in Bordeaux has generally been portrayed as a positive and receptive environment because of the social climate of the city and the special potential it had for commercial growth.[14]

On the other hand, in Bayonne, the émigrés were not referred to in documents as New Christians or Portuguese merchants, but rather as Jewish merchants or simply as Portuguese. Because Jews were not allowed to settle in the city proper, they were assigned to reside in seclusion in the outskirts, namely, in the aforementioned Saint-Esprit-lès-Bayonne. In retrospect, this proved to be a benefit, as it enabled them to maintain their identity and solidarity. Because of their imposed isolation, this group was not faced with the temptations of assimilation, intermarriage, and conversion that occurred elsewhere in

France. These three options led to the disappearance of conversos whose fate is still a point of contention among scholars. Szajkowski was convinced that "the majority of the first Marranos who came to France at the end of the 15th century, during the entire 16th century, and even at the beginning of the 17th century, became an integral part of the Christian community."[15] He and Révah do not agree at all on this point. Szajkowski also contends that

> many Marranos continued to live apart from the Jewish Nation, openly as Christians, or on the border between the Jews and Christians, unable to make up their minds about their place; even in Bordeaux, where the attitude toward New Christians was more liberal than in other cities; and even after 1723 when the New Christians were allowed to live openly as a *Jewish Nation*. Sometimes Marranos took such a step for economic reasons or because of mixed marriages, but often also because they had lost all ties with Judaism.[16]

Of course, one cannot automatically assume that all of them converted; many of them might have moved elsewhere in France or out of the country, and if so, checking the registers of the Jewish community might not necessarily prove anything decisive. For example, after compiling a list of about three hundred names taken from Jewish and non-Jewish sources, Szajkowski himself admits that many probably left or went abroad and that fifty of them were among those expelled from Bordeaux in 1684.[17] Nevertheless, the temptation of converting was indeed real.

Clearly this was a dilemma that the Jews of Amsterdam did not encounter; their interaction with the Protestant Dutch community was rarely intimate and was not apt to result in intermarriage or conversion. On the other hand, when one attended church, albeit insincerely as did the conversos in France, social interaction with members of the Catholic majority was unavoidable. While the motivation behind some conversions might have been marital, others were the result of parental decisions for their children, and yet others were decisions made by older members of the Nation.[18] As has been noted, in addition to the converts, there seem have been many individuals who simply disappeared into the woodwork.

Nonetheless, other evidence points in a different direction as well. By the late seventeenth century, there were much stronger signs of Jewish life, ranging from cemeteries with Spanish inscriptions on seventeenth-century gravestones[19] to Inquisition trials referring to Judaizers. As a matter of fact, most of the information about the community of Rouen is derived from such trials.[20] Be that as it may, it is difficult to determine the fate of these early immigrants and to know what percentage assimilated and what percentage maintained a crypto-Judaism that would emerge much later in public as Judaism. Nevertheless, evidence of Jewish life from the seventeenth century attests to some level of continuity. Although there was a nearly constant flow of Portuguese and

Spaniards entering France, these newcomers cannot be credited with having initiated Jewish rites and customs on their own. They were either being taught by their brethren who were already in France or being sent to Amsterdam for this purpose. They themselves were not responsible for establishing a stronghold of Jewish observance upon their arrival, for again, they were "New Jews" in need of guidance and direction. In the interim, a significant number of these immigrants were managing to clandestinely observe Judaism, and only later would they feel safe enough to outwardly express their religious preference.

Since more documentation is available for the seventeenth century, a clearer picture of the later development of the communities is provided. Yet as compared to the plentiful documentation for Amsterdam, the French material is neither as abundant nor as consistent; for example, community registers including that of Bayonne have simply disappeared. Nevertheless, many of the researchers of the French Sephardim have examined lists of births, deaths, marriages, and circumcisions in order to see what the members of the Nation were actually doing, voluntarily or involuntarily.[21] One can attempt to assess the situation by examining the contact that existed between the Portuguese and Spaniards of Amsterdam and France. As would be expected, many émigrés first stopped in France before moving on to Holland, in particular those with available funds.[22] At any rate, there are records of a dozen locales where conversos were in touch with their brethren in Amsterdam during this period. This should come as no surprise, since all of the individuals involved were interrelated. These ties might be familial or marital, the result of common commercial enterprises or simply by virtue of the common denominator of being a member of the Nation. Consequently, letters, wills, and other legal documents that have been preserved reveal hitherto unknown information.

For example, at its inception in 1615, the aforementioned *dotar* society of Amsterdam appointed local correspondents in five French communities and had interaction with at least fourteen of the appointees.[23] If these Portuguese were not Judaizing, why would they be affiliating themselves with a Jewish institution and caring for the less fortunate Jewish brides-to-be? This was only one manifestation of the way in which the members of the Nation did not restrict themselves to geographical bounds. There are also examples of legacies in wills where the legator and legatee did not reside in the same city; in addition, matches were made between prospective brides and grooms from both communities. The Bordeaux and Bayonne merchants also supplied kosher wine to the Dutch Portuguese,[24] and both groups engaged in numerous other economic projects. Sometimes the French communities asked the Amsterdam community for help, an act which only strengthened the latter's image of playing a parental role for the smaller communities; it offered aid in various forms, whether financial, spiritual, cultural, or religious.

Amsterdam was naturally viewed as the center, especially in relation to the

French periphery communities; consequently, the level of administration and the services provided by Amsterdam were more sophisticated. Provisions were made for the poor, immigrants from France were helped and educated, help was provided for the purchase of cemeteries such as in Paris (while making sure there would be room there for its poor), and the Amsterdam community was constantly giving advice to its French brethren. Not only did it aim to ensure the survival of these communities, but it strove to include them in the orbit of the Sephardi diaspora. The French logically saw Amsterdam as the source of assistance as well as authority.[25] Because of this relationship, funds for the Holy Land were to be channeled through Holland.[26] In addition, the Dutch rabbis were frequently consulted for their opinions in legal issues. Books and kosher cheese were sent from Amsterdam as well. The community of Bayonne seemed to have had the strongest ties of the French communities to Amsterdam, most likely due to its proximity to Holland. Nahon claims that "the community of Bayonne was largely a creation of that of Amsterdam."[27] The "mother" community strove to unite these geographically disparate locales and hoped that Bayonne would serve as the French center of the associated subordinate groups.[28] This French community had a major role in the Iberian diaspora and helped New Christians emigrating from the peninsula; it provided refuge of either temporary or permanent residence and attempted to prepare the emigrants for their new status as Jews.[29] Nahon contends that the re-Judaization process and the progress of orthopraxy in sixteenth- and seventeenth-century France were partially as a result of constant communication with Amsterdam.[30]

The connection with the larger openly identifying community clearly played an important role in the transition from Christianity to Judaism for the Portuguese in France. The seventeenth-century printing presses of Amsterdam made literature available to the Portuguese and provided a much needed gateway to Judaism for them. There were prayer books in Spanish and wonderful pocket-size manuals, often with an almanac and explanations of holiday and festival observances. It appears that these books were quite accessible and popular and could be found in the possession of many a Portuguese New Christian in France. In actuality, they were published for use by both bona fide Jews and crypto-Jews. What was referred to as the *librito*, or little book, was a major source for learning about Jewish law and observance.[31] It seems that Spanish was the language for accessing Judaism as well as the language of the literati, while Portuguese was the language that most members of the Nation spoke and wrote and even used for delivering sermons as late as the eighteenth century. Nahon, however, deemphasizes the use of Portuguese in France, explaining that because they lived "next to Spain, often receiving immigrants from Spain, maintaining frequent relations with friends and commercial correspondents in Spain, the French Sephardim spoke Spanish within their communities, differing in this from other western Sephardim, whose vernacular was Portuguese."[32]

Conversos in Spain and France as well as in the neighboring communities were publishing literature. A brief comparison of the lives of three seventeenth-century conversos who wrote and published poems in Spanish will demonstrate this fact. Each was born in Spain and educated in the style of "Renaissance men," and it is unclear what role religion actually played in each one's life other than as a negation of Christianity.[33] Each had a different background and path by which he was exposed to Judaism; one experienced crypto-Judaism whereas another faced a crisis which precipitated a change. Nevertheless, each one's collection of poetry has some pieces reflecting an identification with Judaism.

João Pinto Delgado is considered to be the most Spanish and most Jewish of the three. After moving to Rouen where his father was a leader of the early seventeenth-century community, he published a collection of poems with Jewish themes in 1627. He then stopped in Antwerp before settling in Amsterdam, where he remained, Hebraized his name (to Moshe), and eventually died there in 1653.

His colleague Antonio Enríques Gómez, born in Cuenca about twenty years later (1600), was the product of a mixed marriage, namely, an Old Christian mother and a New Christian father; he also had a grandfather who was arrested for Judaizing in 1588. The grandfather, Diego de Mora of Quintanar de la Órden, appears in Inquisition research because he came from a community with an astounding level of Judaizing.[34] Likewise, his father was arrested in 1623–1624, condemned by the Inquisition, and exiled to France, where he settled in Nantes and married a Jewish woman from Amsterdam. His son Antonio chose a different path and married an Old Christian woman in 1618. While still in Spain, he traveled to France for business purposes, eventually moving there in about 1635; he lived temporarily in Peyhorade and Bordeaux and was, by 1644, located in Rouen. Some of his poems contain clear expressions of his identification with Judaism; one pamphlet he published in 1647 even included a condemnation of the Inquisition. Later he returned to Spain, possibly for business purposes; this was a risky affair since it had become known there that he was no longer a faithful Catholic. According to Révah, Enríquez Gómez used the alias of Fernando de Zárate in Spain, and had the traumatic experience of seeing his own effigy burnt in Seville on April 14, 1660.[35] It appears that the Inquisition did not rest in its search for him, and succeeded in arresting him in 1661. He died in prison in 1663.

Miguel de Barrios, the youngest of the three poets, was born in Cordoba in 1635 and chose to leave his homeland after the Inquisition arrested a family member. He first moved to Leghorn, where he was circumcised, and then proceeded to live a double existence, qualifying as a true "cultural commuter."

In Brussels, he lived the life of a Catholic army captain, while in Amsterdam he was known as Levi Daniel, a Jewish family man with three children. In 1672, however, he resigned his army post and decided to make a permanent residence in Amsterdam, where he actively participated in the creation of its literary academy. Although his continued identification with the Sabbatean movement[36] isolated him somewhat from the community, his ultimate life choice and his poetry reveal a total identification with Judaism that might have been originally triggered by fear of the Inquisition.

Each of these three converso poets struggled with his identity, as reflected in the poems he wrote and by his choice of spouse as well as residence. Pinto Delgado had a more direct route, from Antwerp to Amsterdam, where he became Moshe. His saga seems to be the least complicated, perhaps because his crypto-Jewish roots were more clearly delineated or because his father was a leader in Rouen. This French connection did not seem to serve to attract him to France, but after a stop in Antwerp he chose a more established community. Enríques Gómez came from a more problematic background, dotted with observant Judaizers and Old Christian women. He followed in his father's footsteps by first marrying an Old Christian, yet in neither case did this squash the Jewish proclivities of either father or son. While the father eventually chose a Jewish woman as his mate, his son chose Rouen as his residence and was drawn back to Spain. For good reasons, the Amsterdam community advised against visiting the "lands of idolatry." Just as his father and grandfather had been arrested by the Inquisition, so was this poet. While his father managed to create a new life for himself in Nantes, Enríques Gómez was not nearly as fortunate. Although he was not burned at the stake (only in effigy), his death in prison following his arrest ended his literary creativity. The third poet, Miguel de Barrios, did not seem to have a direct connection to France, but nonetheless exemplifies the cultural commuter par excellence. The trigger here was an encounter with the Inquisition that was less close to home than that of de Barrios but apparently no less traumatic. His choice to live a bifurcated life, masquerading as a Catholic while serving in the army in Brussels and as the Jew Levi Daniel while in Amsterdam, reflects the ambivalence of the world of the Portuguese émigré. Enriques Gómez was attracted to Spanish culture and returned to it, only to meet his downfall in his motherland. De Barrios chose an equally risky path, but a bit farther out of the reaches of the Inquisition's tentacles. Unlike some of his Italian compatriots, he was not caught by the Holy Tribunal, and ultimately decided to discontinue his life as a commuter between two worlds. Both he and Pinto Delgado qualified for Jewish burials in the community of Amsterdam; all three were recognized as outstanding literary talents in the diaspora community.

As we have seen, those who chose France rather than Amsterdam did not always have the option of observing Jewish laws and rites as prescribed. What was the community doing in order to continue its rituals before it was recognized? Obviously there were no local rabbis, although knowledgeable guests from abroad would occasionally visit them and legal questions could be sent to rabbis in other communities.[37] During the seventeenth century, it seems that circumcisions were being performed by a ritual circumciser from Amsterdam. Astonishing information came to the fore regarding the dualistic existence of these New Christians from the records of an Inquisition trial. Apparently the rabbi[38] and the priest in Bayonne had reached an accord. After a male child was baptized, the rabbi took the infant to be circumcised. Likewise, when one of the members of the Nation died, the deceased would be washed according to Jewish law, buried in the Christian cemetery, and then mourned halakhically.[39] This cannot be considered cultural commuting, for no real movement was involved; everything occurred in the same location. The religious leaders seemed to have reached a modus vivendi, allowing each to perform what was deemed absolutely necessary. Thus, baptism coexisted with circumcision, while ritual washing and mourning accompanied Christian burial. This was no longer crypto-Judaism,[40] and it stands out in direct contrast to developments in crypto-Jewish life. For example, in Iberia, after the baptismal ceremony, many Judaizing couples would take their infants and wash off the baptismal water, performing what was for them a "debaptism." Clearly this was only a psychological act, for they lacked the ability to prevent these baptisms and were not free to circumcise their sons. By contrast, in seventeenth-century Bayonne, the Catholic priest was aware of the absurdity of the situation and adapted to it to the best of his ability. Until the community was recognized, its members led a dual but openly contradictory existence which was, most likely, an improvement over the clandestine lifestyle previously experienced.

However, once the communities felt secure enough to display their Jewishness, the situation changed. Nahon even refers to the "golden age" of the Portuguese-Jewish Nation, beginning first in Bayonne in the final decade of the seventeenth century and taking place a few decades later in Bordeaux. He insists, however, that they "never really had full freedom of action and their religion was never really recognised by the authorities."[41] Nevertheless, one can even perceive a trend of movement from Amsterdam to France, signifying that the latter locale had become an attractive alternative.[42] This did not detract from the centrality of the Dutch center, which functioned like a converso capital city, but rather provided an alternative for the Portuguese or Spanish Jew.[43] Because there never was an official date for when it was acceptable to be a Jew openly in France, it is a complicated task to try and follow the transition from clandestine to open observance. Nevertheless, there were additional changes in the middle of the seventeenth century, such as the appearance of a cemetery for the Portuguese in Peyrehorade in 1628 and even earlier in neighboring Labastide-Clairence, although the first sign of Jewishness in the latter's cemetery was not until 1659. In Bayonne, by contrast, a priest actually helped the community acquire a cemetery in 1654, being fully aware that Jewish rites would be followed there.[44] There are records of rabbis performing weddings in the 1670s in Bayonne, and during the same decade, in 1679, its synagogue attained public recognition, so to speak, for tourists recorded their visits there.[45]

The attempt to trace this major change in the identity of the Portuguese conversos in France continues in a typically roundabout way.[46] Ironically, discovering the last date for enacting a Catholic rite, such as a baptism, or a wedding in a church, or a burial in a Catholic cemetery, implies that an openly Jewish lifestyle had come into existence. When a cemetery was acquired by the Nation, all its members did not immediately begin to bury their dead according to Jewish rites or with Jewish gravestones, but the way was definitely paved for their entry into the cemetery.[47]

As pointed out earlier, because the community register of Bordeaux is available, more abundant, and at times more precise, information can be provided about this community. For example, there are registers of circumcisions that date to the eighteenth century,[48] although this does not necessarily mean that they were not being carried out beforehand. Because infants were still being baptized as late as the 1690s, serious changes in the community's lifestyle cannot be perceived until the very end of the century. The Nation officially organized itself in 1699, when arrangements were finally made for providing kosher meat and baked goods, for establishing charity organizations as well as an official community. This, of course, included taxation by the community. The tax evader would not be able to use the ritual bath or be married or buried within the community. According to Bordeaux records, Church marriages did not cease until 1711, and by then, marriages could only take place after receiving the syndic's approval. The syndics, or *parnassim* (in Hebrew), essentially governed the community and were selected from among the wealthy by a small group of electors.[49]

The official transition from New Christians to Jews did not occur in Bordeaux until 1723. France had suffered a number of setbacks in the seventeenth century, which included economic disasters, famines, and wars. Although the king had seriously considered expelling the New Christians, he recanted after weighing the economic repercussions of such a decision. Thus, King Louis XV issued *Lettres Patentes* in 1723 that specifically referred to these residents as Jews. "The combination of an undeniable economic *utilité* on the part of the *nouveax Chrétiens*, their capacity to pay a considerable sum of money to the government, and the lesson gained from revoking the Edict of Nantes were sufficiently influential to cause Louis XV to issue the *Lettres Patentes* of 1723."[50] Yet the synagogue there was not inaugurated until 1766, a reflection of the amount of time that passed before a sense of security was manifested by the community.

Now the Jews could finally function as a corporate body, a development that signified "stability, security, and official recognition." Moreover, they prospered and attained a solid economic status, which also added to their sense of security.[51] As they maneuvered their way to normalization, the members of the Nation now regulated their own commerce and finances and simultaneously expressed their commitment to Judaism. Still, as Malino describes, there were problems: "Thus throughout the first half of the 18th century, the *nation* had been faced with a multitude of problems which included an over-abundance of poor, an influx of non-Sephardic Jews, and too few among the wealthy willing to assume responsibility as syndic."[52] These "New Jews" organized their community, but were also aware of their position in a Catholic country whose inhabitants had no love lost for the Jews. While the leaders tried to monitor their members in the tradition of the Amsterdam community, the rabbis never attained a position of prominence; the lay leaders asserted far greater power than they did. Likewise, the type of Jewish education offered was not in keeping with the traditional education available in other communities. The curriculum included Hebrew grammar, Psalms and Prophets and prayers but not Talmud,[53] although Nahon contends that educational standards were higher in Bayonne.[54] As mentioned previously, there was a lack of spirituality, intellectualism, and erudition among the French Sephardim, as well as a tendency to incorporate non-Jewish values; the latter was not a surprising development to have occurred after living there as non-Jews for so many years. As the members of the Nation integrated and adapted to the French reality, they seem to have placed their emphasis mainly on economic achievements.[55]

The story of the Gradis family of Bordeaux effectively demonstrates the centrality of economic activities in the world of the Portuguese conversos as they struggled with their Jewishness and with a means to express it. In the 1660s, the patriarch of the family, Diego, came to Bordeaux from Portugal, resided a short time in Toulouse, and returned to Bordeaux in the 1680s. Of his three sons, only one, David, remained in business with him, and in subsequent generations, a son or nephew managed to continue the firm of "David Gradis et fils." This continuity was considered to be "the equivalent of a noble patrimony."[56]

The Gradis men began their career in the domestic trade of goods such as textiles and expanded to banking, shipping, and colonial trade. Their success was based on their sense of innovation, their international connections with, of course, other members of the Nation, and very carefully arranged marriages. The wealthy converso families viewed marital matches as long-range investments, both of capital and of familial seed.

It is difficult to assess the Jewishness of these individuals. They clearly had an ethnic affiliation with their brethren and were often chosen to publicly represent the community in an unofficial capacity. Presumably it was precisely because of their economic and social status that they were deemed worthy of being spokesmen, but this high degree of interaction with the Christian world often demanded concessions on their part. While David, the founder of the family firm, had strong ties to his family and to the Jewish world, he was nevertheless pulled into the non-Jewish world by his acquaintances. Interestingly, he was depicted as a pious man who provided for the Sephardi poor of his city and of Jerusalem and who encouraged conversos to openly join the Jewish community in formation.[57] He himself played a major role in the community both as a donor and, by 1718, as a syndic and an elder. "In short," writes Richard Menkis, "David Gradis entered the upper echelons of power in the community and became a leader of the Jewish patriciate of Bordeaux."[58]

David's successor, Abraham (1695–1780), was nominally committed to Jewish law, maintaining some semblance of holiday observance, but partaking of nonkosher food in public. His lifestyle appears to be one of contradictions, yet this was characteristic of these noble families. Despite the fact that they were in no way observant Jews, they identified strongly with the Nation. Thus, Abraham served as a syndic of Bordeaux and was asked to intercede on behalf of this community as well as that of Bayonne. These leaders provided for the Jewish poor, but interestingly enough, they also provided for impoverished Catholics.[59] They perceived neither conflict nor contradiction concerning their activities. Although they could not be bona fide noblemen, their lifestyle left the impression that they were; indeed, they were treated with great respect and honor by the titled nobles. Menkis explains that "extending their charitable activities to the non-Jewish world" was for them a reciprocation of this acceptance. This acculturation proved to be difficult to maintain, for once one felt integrated into the outside community, it became more and more difficult to draw the line between the two communities. Ironically enough, the conversos at first lived as Christians with an attachment to Judaism that was dormant or needed to be quietly nurtured. Once they were able to express their Jewishness, the more successful members of the community, like the Gradis men, were accepted socially by the Christians. This acceptance served to blur the distinctions between the two, and usually involved a move away from Judaism. The conversos and their descendants seem to have retained, at the very least, an ethnic tie to the Nation, but the path their lives took created an unstable sense of identity. The men of commerce from Bordeaux, in particular, seem never to have aligned themselves strongly with Jewish law and its demands, emphasizing instead group (ethnic) solidarity, family pride, and commercial success. Apparently, contact with non-Jewish high society served to distract the Jewish elite group as it rose to these heights, although ethnic identity somehow seemed to survive intact among the various levels of the Portuguese converso society in France.

A comparison with a contemporary from Bayonne serves to illustrate the various directions one's life might take in France. Miguel de Robles was born in Bayonne in the second half of the seventeenth century and then chose to move to Iberia. He engaged in tax farming in Castile and in 1714, led a group of Judaizers in Madrid in a Passover Seder. De Robles clearly brought his knowledge of Judaism to Spain and socialized with a group of Judaizers, many

of whom were arrested by the Inquisition between 1716 and 1721. The fact that
he was from Bayonne and that he had been circumcised there "gave him a
certain prestige among the Madrid judaizers."[60] Although his wife and other
relatives were arrested, de Robles managed to escape, perhaps making his way
back to Bayonne. Here was a product of the Bayonne community who moved
to Spain, most likely for economic purposes, but served as a missionary of
sorts in a crypto-Jewish enclave in Madrid. While the Gradis family was assimilating in France, de Robles was endangering his life and that of his family.
The Gradises represented one type of eighteenth-century converso descendant,
who, as we have seen, retained an ethnic identity of sorts; perhaps such persons
could qualify as "fuzzy Jews." De Robles, on the other hand, represented the
other extreme, a native Frenchman of converso ancestry who voluntarily entered Iberia, the "land of idolatry," and experienced life as a crypto-Jew; his
path resembled that of a cultural commuter as he eventually left Spain. No
doubt there were many members of the Nation in France whose life experiences fell somewhere in between these two extremes.[61]

6

England

The trials and tribulations of the Portuguese in France were similar to those of their brethren who settled in England, for the problem of recognition by the authorities hovered over them both. As a matter of fact, the members of the Nation were still referred to as New Christians in the French tax rosters as late as the eve of the French Revolution.[1] In other words, the presence of the Portuguese was tolerated but not officially recognized in France for an inordinate amount of time.

The same can be said regarding the official status of the Portuguese conversos who chose England as their destination. England, like France, had expelled its Jews; this expulsion occurred in 1290, and centuries would pass before a Jew could legally reside there. Thus, the Portuguese who chose this destination had to feign being Catholics, as did their kin who arrived in France. Since France was a Catholic country, posing as a Catholic was a logical and natural option. However, because England was no longer a Catholic country, it was neither as simple nor as appropriate to maintain this façade. The alternative, however, pretending to be Protestant, was never seriously considered. The Portuguese had experience living as Catholics and knew what was required of them by that church, but the high Anglican Church was completely unfamiliar to them. Consequently, the sole realistic possibility was to continue the Catholic façade and to hope that eventually Jews would be granted reentry. Interestingly enough, as practicing Catholics, the only viable option for them in order to observe their "religions" was to attend mass at chapels belonging to the French and Spanish embassies.[2]

It is rather difficult to pinpoint the arrival of the first Iberian conversos in England. A trickle of exiles might have managed to have entered after 1492, but their whereabouts are untraceable. In 1594, a court physician named Rodrigo López was executed as the result of political intrigue; consequently, various kinsmen fled London. It is also believed that a number of Portuguese arrived in Bristol during the sixteenth century. Later, in 1609, King James I expelled some Portuguese merchants whom he suspected of Judaizing, but no community per se had yet been established. As Swetschinski explains, "The Portuguese settlement in London in the days of Elizabeth I and James I never succeeded in gaining a sure foothold. Aside from cloth—which could also be had elsewhere—and fish, the London market offered as yet little opportunity for a substantial exchange to take root. Moreover, from the very first attempts at settlement here, the Portuguese merchants found themselves the target of serious political suspicions of court intrigue and spying for Spain."[3] The first clearly documented record of a Portuguese converso was Antonio Fernández Carvajal, who arrived in 1633 after having lived in the Canary Islands and having fled Rouen. This prosperous international merchant had his own agents, and he owned ships as well as property in the Canary Islands. His personal history is a classic example of an early London Portuguese converso.

Kaplan contends that "the world of the Sephardic Jewish *conversos* was well organized, and the rise of the community in London was the fruit of the combined efforts of highly experienced international merchants from Andalusia, Portugal, southern France, the Canary Islands, and elsewhere."[4] These merchants needed a center from which to continue their commercial ties to the Caribbean islands once the Brazilian settlements were no longer viable; as of 1654, a center was needed to replace Recife. In 1655, Carvajal obtained naturalization along with his three sons, but found himself in a precarious position: If and when England went to war with Spain, now that this merchant was aligned with the British, his goods were liable to seizure by the Spaniards. As a result, he had no recourse but to request the support of Parliament; he subsequently received it a number of times, and because of this allegiance, he was even considered to have been a spy for England.[5] In 1654, when Menasseh ben Israel did not appear although he had received an entry pass to England, David Abravanel Dormido (alias Manuel Martinez Dormido) emigrated from Amsterdam to London after obtaining Cromwell's permission. Soon after, Dormido petitioned Cromwell "as one of his subjects for the readmission of the Jews to England, and Cromwell addressed a letter on his behalf to his ally the King of Portugal, referring to him as a Jew and asking for the return of his goods."[6]

In the following year, as it turns out, Menasseh ben Israel arrived and chose to seek formal approval by the government during a conference at Whitehall.[7] At this time, it became clear that although the Jews were not legally barred from England, Cromwell preferred not to take any action to officially change the status quo, especially in light of the hostility of the competitive merchants of London. Ironically, it turned out to be to the Jews' advantage in the long run that Cromwell did not officially sanction any change; after his downfall they were not subject to the backlash that resulted once the monarchy was reestablished. However, there was an unexpected development the following year because England and Spain went to war and this state of affairs led to the seizure of the property of Antonio Rodríguez Robles. This converso requested restitution from the government on the basis of his being from Portugal and a member of the Hebrew nation who had sought asylum in England. Carvajal and five other crypto-Jews supported the petition. At the same time, after consultation with Menasseh ben Israel, the conversos requested permission to hold private prayer meetings and to purchase a burial ground. The subsequent developments are a bit unclear, but in addition to restoring Robles's property in 1656, the government granted some sort of permission that allowed the Jews to lease a house to be used as a synagogue. In 1657 they purchased land for a cemetery, although many of them feared expressing their Jewishness openly and continued to use Christian graveyards. A Torah scroll was borrowed from Amsterdam for the duration of four years (1656–1660). In 1657 they chose a site for a synagogue and leased a house on Cree Church Lane with a twenty-one-year contract that was renewed until 1701, at which time the community moved to the Bevis Marks Synagogue.[8] Moses Athias, a cousin of Carvajal's, arrived from Hamburg to serve as the *haham* until his retirement in 1664.

The community numbered about 120 in the 1660s, over 400 in the 1680s, and 550 by the end of the century. This was clearly a tiny community; Hamburg was about triple its size, while Amsterdam was probably about ten times as large, although it should be pointed out that these figures are not universally accepted. For example, while Diamond gives approximate figures of 414 Sephardim in 1684 and 663 in 1700, Samuel claims there were a thousand members in the new synagogue in 1701.[9] As Hamburg declined in economic importance in the area, the London Portuguese developed their trade with Portugal and the transatlantic colonies. These businessmen were shippers, shipowners, importers, brokers, financiers (including the Bank of England in 1694), merchants, jewelers, doctors, notaries, army suppliers, and contractors.[10]

The mid-seventeenth century was a period of religious developments including the rise of Puritanism, millenarianism, and a rise in the popularity of Hebrew and the Old Testament, ostensibly creating a (theological) philo-Semitic atmosphere. Barnett describes this environment:

> For a variety of reasons, the climate of opinion was now much more favorable to the Jews. The adoption of the Protestant Christian religion by the English and the introduction and wide availability of English translations of the Bible and the study of the Hebrew original,

especially by the Puritans, combined with the influence of other non-conformists, caused many Englishmen of the new post-renaissance world to look at the problem of the Jews no longer with mediaeval eyes, but in a new light. As fellow targets of the Spanish Catholic Inquisition's hostility, the Jews enjoyed to a considerable extent the sympathy of the English people.[11]

Was this a display of liberal tolerance, and if so how did it affect the development of the community and its identity? According to Swetschinski,

[I]t can be shown that the histories of the New Christian and Jewish communities of Bordeaux, London, and the European settlements in the western hemisphere exhibit some of the same peculiarities encountered in Amsterdam. The same *laissez-faire*, haphazard treatment of problems of Jewish immigration, a comparable reluctance rigorously to define the juridico-political status of Jewish residents, and a similar unwillingness to cater to prejudice, as well as a number of particular regulations (such as the narrower than traditional definition of Jewish autonomy) seem to have prevailed throughout western Europe.[12]

At the same time, Goldish portrays these individuals as having faced various crises as a group while residing in London, ranging from accusations of being enemies and spies in the 1650s to "virulent attacks," mainly of a commercial nature and having survived a period of "near-persecution." The attacks were "quashed by an agile Jewish lobby, which succeeded in getting what amounted to a declaration of indulgence from James."[13] Developments of this nature make one wonder what else affected the formation of identity in this small community.

According to Kaplan, the members of this group varied greatly in their behavior and commitments, most likely because of their unofficial status. Many, if not most, continued to use Christian names in public and Jewish names for rituals and for the synagogue. In 1664, the king made an exception to the prohibition of non-Anglicans to engage in public worship and granted the Jews this right; he also recognized the community in response to a petition he had received the same year. Nevertheless, as Kaplan points out, the "pattern of double life not only failed to vanish at the beginning of the Restoration, when they received official and explicit recognition from Charles II, but it expanded and grew more acute."[14] He contends that from the beginning, this community "was deeply marked by the paths of assimilation."[15] There were some men who refused to be circumcised,[16] others who continued to bury their dead in Christian cemeteries even after the cemetery was available at Mile End, and many who continued to use their Christian names and titles in the public and economic spheres.[17]

Nevertheless, the community began to formally organize itself, basing its statutes on those of Amsterdam and giving the veteran community exclusive authority in London. According to Goldish, "[F]rom the time of Menasseh ben Israel until a rift which occurred in 1704 concerning a legal decision, the London community functioned almost as a satellite of the large and important Portuguese *kehillah* of Amsterdam," which also supplied it with spiritual leaders.[18] Three of the first early leaders came from Amsterdam, namely, Jacob Sasportas, Joshua da Silva, and Jacob Abendana. Oliel-Grausz writes, "Not only did several rabbis come from Amsterdam during those first decades, some of the lower ranking community officers, *rubyssim, hazzanim and bodekim* (teachers, cantors, and meat examiners) were also sent by the Amsterdam *parnassim* following requests from Shaar Hashamayim."[19] All Portuguese Jews in the London area were required to belong to Saar Asamaim.[20] In this community, the presence of rabbinic leaders usually led to conflict because their expectations were not realistic. The rabbis demanded full participation and identification with the community and with Judaism, but they were often disappointed by the reality they encountered and did not always hide their feelings from their congregants. In June 1664, Sasportas, the *haham*, or Sephardi leader, mentioned above, arrived from Amsterdam with his son. He adamantly opposed allowing uncircumcised men to enter the synagogue, and after a six-month period of "toleration," began to harangue five members of the Nation, all of them wealthy men. There was considerable friction between Sasportas and the public officials; the latter perceived this approach as oppressive, and angry denouncements ensued. During this period, some refugees from the Portuguese Inquisition arrived in London as did a number of individuals who were accompanying the entourage of Catherine of Braganza. Not all of them chose to become Jews, and Sasportas wrestled with a number of the non-committed, advocating their eviction. Some considered themselves Jews but did not undergo circumcision. There were those whose children chose an unexpected path to become "proper" Jews, although their parents were already considered marginal Jews.[21] Some of them clearly were not able or willing to commit, yet there is no doubt that they identified with their brethren, at least in an ethnic sense. Apparently, at times it was pure convenience that dictated their actions. Yet during the fourteen months he led the community, Sasportas could not and would not condone this lack of commitment.[22]

Indecision and lack of commitment to Judaism proved to be a thorn in the side of other rabbinic leaders as well. An attempt to comprehend these wavering individuals, their logic or their reasoning, or to learn about them, is not an easy task. Occasionally information emerges about them, as from an incident concerning the five aforementioned men who were reprimanded by Sasportas. An Inquisition trial of a returnee to the peninsula might provide information, but because the non-Jewish names of many of these men were not usually known, it is all the more difficult to trace them.[23] For example, a Christian visitor to the synagogue referred to a friend named Manuel who moved in non-Jewish social circles, but Barnett could not ascertain with definitude who this fellow was. Another converso had wandered from Portugal to Rouen to London to Dublin, was naturalized as an alien Protestant in Dublin, denounced to the Inquisition, and then returned to London.[24] Keeping track of some of them is indeed a challenge.

Yet because their unorthodox lifestyles riled the rabbis of the community, some information can be obtained by studying the activities of these rabbis. Sasportas was not the only haham to be irked by these individuals. The haham da Silva, also emanating from Amsterdam, served the community from 1670 to 1679; he was outraged by the fact that there were members of the congregation who went to the theater on the Sabbath, "carrying money and paying openly for their entertainment."[25] Although he recommended punishment, it seems not to have been executed. In a letter to Sasportas, one of his successors, Solomon Ayllon, who was the haham from 1689 to 1700, invoked against their nonconforming brethren who "transgress in their souls" and "sin with their bodies." He wrote that they refrain from work on Sundays and work on the Sabbath when their stores are open; they do not observe the commandments yet announce to the gentiles that they are Jews. (Interestingly, it appears that some of them did buy meat from kosher butchers.) Ayllon was infuriated that they who live on the "other side" wanted to have their sons circumcised in the community.[26] It is interesting that while these Portuguese were imitating the Christians, there were Christians who sought to attack them. In 1685, forty-eight Jews were accused of not attending church, and most of them were arrested. Fortunately, the leaders of the congregation reacted appropriately, and the king, James II, announced that the harassment of Jews should desist, "that they were to enjoy the same privileges and rights as the King's other citizens so long as they conducted themselves peacefully and in accordance with his Majesty's laws."[27]

As can be seen, the leaders of the community had to deal with a number of serious problems, both external and internal, ranging from attacks by non-Jews to dealing with the blatant eyesore created by their brethren who publicly scoffed Jewish law. At the same time, there were other internal conflicts within the community, beginning with Ayllon and continuing with David Nieto, who came from Leghorn in 1701. The latter gave a controversial sermon; his opponents "probably comprised a varied group of individuals, bringing together devout Jews, genuinely shocked at the sermon, as well as those keen to rebel against the rabbi's authority and that of the Mahamad."[28] An appeal was made to Amsterdam to intervene, but because the resulting decision was not to their liking, the London community vowed never to turn to them again. Perhaps these trials and tribulations helped to strengthen the backbone of those who were already committed and seriously living Jewish lives, but the dilemma of those tempted by the Christian way of life or simply unwilling to succumb to

Jewish dictates was not to be easily solved. As Kaplan points out, "[E]ven those who wholeheartedly affiliated themselves with the new Jewish way of life still retained connections with the Christian frameworks to which they had belonged or with which they had come into contact before declaring their Judaism. At least until the end of the seventeenth century many Sephardic Jews continued to contribute generously to the church of St. Catherine in London, which was close to the synagogue."[29] The haham and the lay leaders did not always agree on policy or on how much pressure to apply to the aberrants (or to the congregants, for that matter), and whether or not they should socialize with them and eat at their homes. "It is clear, then, that while the leaders realized that a marginal Converso could not be allowed to live free of Torah and community authority while maintaining the same communal status as everyone else, they also could not bring themselves to establish a proper fence between kehillah members and their uncommitted brethren."[30]

There was something in the nature of English society at this time that contributed to this "fuzzy" approach. The community had ex-conversos in its midst who were now bona fide Jews, most of them "nouveaux" or "New Jews," together with conversos who were "freewheeling expatriated Catholics."[31] The religious reality did not force the undecided to decide or to commit; they did not have to accept one religion or the other as definitive. This was different from cultural commuting because in this case there was no need to leave either world. On the whole, it entailed a selective process that determined how much and what one would take from each domain, and often left indistinct trails. Essentially there was the perennial problem of deciding the degree to which one would commit oneself; for instance, whether or not one would have a Jewish wedding ceremony, and whether the male should go beyond the point of no return and arrange for a circumcision. Studies of records of marriages of immigrants who arrived between 1703 and 1735 from Portugal as well as Spain, possibly as the result of inquisitorial activity at this time, reveal that some of these couples chose to be married again, this time with a Jewish ceremony. Barnett discovered about sixteen couples whose second wedding ceremonies are recorded.[32] In order to receive aid from the community, circumcision was demanded of the males, yet some hesitated as did their brethren in Holland; they probably still hoped to return to Iberia at a later date for any of a number of reasons, and such an act precluded that possibility. Kaplan points to a poignant example from the seventeenth century, namely, Fernando Mendes da Costa, who lived in London and claimed that many of his brethren were "toying with the idea that many New Christians from Portugal would return to their homeland if it were to change its policy towards them, that is to say, if it ended social discrimination and persecution by the Inquisition."[33]

Nevertheless, the community continued to develop, and various organizations were formed, such as a fund for redeeming Jewish captives (cautivos). There are clear records from 1689–1789 of money sent by the London Portuguese to ransom their brethren, who were often captured by Maltese pirates.[34] Another fund provided support for the Holy Land; records are extant of donations made to Jerusalem, Safed, and Hebron between 1671 and 1790.[35] In the seventeenth and eighteenth centuries, a significant number of poorer members of the Nation appeared in London. Some of these unfortunate souls came from Amsterdam in 1692, and some had fled the Inquisition in 1705.[36] "Between 1720 and 1750," describes Edgar Samuel, "the trickle of refugees from Spain and Portugal became a flood and many of the immigrants were destitute. In contrast to the 17th century, very few rich immigrants came from Portugal to join the community's elite—perhaps only four or five men. Many of the immigrants were sent abroad, including to the American colonies of Georgia and South Carolina."[37] During the second half of the century, impoverished Jews from Mediterranean locales such as Gibraltar, Morocco, Italy, and Morocco flowed in steadily. Apparently the community began to feel overwhelmed and rather upset by the large number of immigrants, yet it managed to organize itself appropriately. In 1748, the Beth Holim Hospital was established, with a special ward for expectant mothers along with another ward for the aged; according to Barnett, this was the first Jewish hospital in Western Europe. The following year heralded the establishment of *Mahasim Tobim* (literally, good deeds), an innovative apprenticing and employment program aimed at helping the less fortunate members of the Nation.[38]

Interestingly, the connections between the communities of France and London were strengthened during the eighteenth century. Evidence of this is most noticeable in two realms: marital ties between families from each locale and commercial ties ranging from investments to providing credit for one another.[39] Similar contacts and marital alliances existed between the Portuguese of Amsterdam and London as well, especially among the wealthier families. Swetschinski perceives a triangular connection between the three aforementioned communities: "To all intents and purposes—socially and economically as well as culturally—Amsterdam-Hamburg-London must be considered one single community."[40] Oleil-Grausz has discovered quite a few interesting examples of contacts in the eighteenth century between London and Amsterdam that included cooperation in "the implementation of social religious ordinances and in preserving order, as with clandestine *kiddushin* and elopements"; exchanges of information about emissaries from the East; methods of dealing with the influx of poor and of supplying *etrogim* (citrons) for Sukkot; and requests for a haham, which were sometimes refused.[41] As we have already seen, the relationship with Amsterdam was rather complex, and the initial dependence on the older community eventually dissipated as the Londoners began to assert themselves and their independence.

Assessing the eighteenth-century community in London reveals a paradox, especially because some scholars, such as Barnett, consider this period to have been a golden age:

[T]he eighteenth century in the life of the Congregation of *Sahar Asamaim* of Bevis Marks may justly in my view be saluted as the Golden Age of Anglo-Sepharad. For in that period for the first time in modern times we may see from the quiet security of England and Holland, in the web of travel and correspondence, a feeling of being woven ever closer of the unity and interdependence of the Jewish communities of the world, in short, of the concept of the brotherhood of Israel.[42]

At the same time, Samuel emphasizes its commercial prowess during this period, pointing to the mercantile prosperity and security in London and elsewhere. In addition, he alludes to the aforementioned charity system, to the educational system, and to the fact that Jews were elected to the Royal Society.

To me a Golden Age means a period of cultural creativity rooted in economic prosperity. The period from 1680 to 1780 seems to me to have been the Golden—or at least Silver Gilt—age of the Portuguese Jewish community of London. It saw the publication of erudite dictionaries, sermons and prayer books, the poems of Daniel Lopes Laguna, with its introductory sonnets by members of the community and Haham David Nieto's remarkable *Matteh Dan y segunda part del Cuzari* in Hebrew and Spanish.[43]

Interestingly, while intellectual prowess rarely is cited as an attribute of these merchants, it seems that there were, nonetheless, some significant minds interested in more than the stock market.[44] Nevertheless, one must also take the arrival of poor immigrants into account, a development which obviously did not contribute to any economic or cultural growth in the community. In addition, there is evidence that some of the former conversos assimilated during this period, clearly leading to a numerical loss of members of the Nation. This phenomenon was compounded by the fact that some of these individuals simply cut themselves off from the community. Taking the above factors into account, it would be difficult to note significant growth in the community.

During the eighteenth century, the Nation gradually became Anglicized. Although English did not replace Spanish as the official language of the community until 1819, there seem to have been changes that reflect various levels of Anglicization that affected the observant and identifying members as well as the nonobservant and nonidentifying. The former, for example, set up a Board of Deputies in 1760 to represent Jewish causes in politics. Moses Montefiore (1784–1885) was the Jewish lobbyist or mediator, the former court Jew par excellence. This was a "purely English-inspired body" but with a deep sense of mutual care and ethnic solidarity that was characteristic of the Nation.[45]

The latter, those who sought to assimilate, did so relatively easily. They had already been exposed to non-Jewish learning and to the non-Jewish world and had by no means been culturally isolated in Iberia. Those who succeeded in trade and finance in London imitated their non-Jewish property-owning neighbors. They subsequently purchased country estates, a move which proved not only to have been a good investment but also was an effective means of climbing the social ladder. Once they owned homes in the country, socializing with neighbors was the next natural step, providing the neighbors had no objections; this led to social integration as well as to a weakening of the ties to the Jewish community. As Endelman points out, "As stock-brokers, government loan contractors, and purveyors of precious stones, male members were already accustomed to mixing with elite landowners in London, to which the latter flocked in growing numbers in the eighteenth century to do business and to be seen. Contacts such as these probably made social integration in the countryside an easier process."[46] Endelman claims that a preference for rural residence was commonplace among those with newly acquired wealth; the decision to leave the city and the community reflected a parallel move away from traditional Jewish values. His research reveals that toward

> the end of the eighteenth century, with an increase in the number of prosperous Sephardi families and the expansion of their social and cultural horizons, intermarriage and conversion became less unusual in other families, appearing generally in the third or fourth anglicized generation. Indeed, by the early nineteenth century they were so common that there was scarcely a well-to-do Sephardi family settled in England for more than two generations in which drift and defection had not made significant progress.[47]

Ultimately, as can be seen, more than a few of these Sephardim intermarried with their neighbors, and at some point some of them converted.

Yet the ties between the members of the Nation were not sundered despite assimilation and intermarriage. While it is difficult to categorize some of these individuals in religious terms, they often continued to seek the company of other former conversos as well as to do business with them. In other words, many members of the Portuguese Nation straddled both worlds, interacting with their brethren as well as with their non-Jewish neighbors. This was not cultural commuting, because they were not putting on airs or pretending to be one type of person in one locale and another type elsewhere. On the contrary, they were assimilating into British society while still maintaining economic and ethnic ties to their brethren, a situation unique to this locale. Kaplan describes this contrast:

> In other Western Sephardic communities, a clear and sharp distinction was made between members of the group who were active within its confines, accepting the authority of Judaism, and those who preferred to remain "outside the walls," refusing to accept the

burden of the commandments and the authority of the leaders and Hakhamim. These recalcitrants and deviants were excommunicated in communities like Amsterdam and Hamburg, but in London the situation was different. While the leadership withdrew its services from those who dwelled at the margins and even forbad marital ties with them, nevertheless, it was careful not to burn all its bridges to that population and, on various levels, it even made sure to maintain ties with them.[48]

Endelman claims that those who eventually abandoned Judaism did so as the result of "a prior process of partial integration into gentile society, rather than an initial attempt to gain access to new worlds or escape onerous restrictions."[49] British society was open in a way unlike any other contemporary society; if one had appropriate wealth and manners, one would be accepted by the upper class. In addition, less wealthy individuals sometimes opted to leave Judaism in order to better their children's access to desirable professions and positions, particularly in London.[50] One famous example was Isaac Disraeli (1766–1848), the father of Benjamin Disraeli. Endelman writes, "That religious conviction was no consideration is clear from Isaac's own repudiation of revealed religion and lack of interest in becoming a Christian himself."[51] Others like him acted similarly in the hope of improving their or their children's lives. The openness of British society was rare (and unexpected) indeed, and the fact that the conversos were not limited in their choice of residence or profession contributed to this phenomenon. Thus, their Anglicization proceeded apace in a surprisingly unproblematic way; as a result, many moved outside the Jewish community to meet their own needs.[52]

An additional component to be taken into account is the nature of the converso experience in London. A larger community like Amsterdam was able to provide a stronger framework for the new arrivals. Traditional Judaism, so alien to the majority of the Portuguese, was not appealing to many of the newcomers, partly because the community was neither strong nor self-sufficient at the time and because most of the leaders were relatively unsuccessful as authority figures.

Attempts were made to thwart or at least to slow down this process. For example, Rephael Meldola, the *haham* from 1804 to 1828, did his utmost to dissuade the members of his flock from leaving. He knew that temptations abounded, including the lure of the Reform platform, and, of course, he was alert to the threat of assimilation. As a result, he took an interest in popular Jewish education and helped publish a prayer book, which he hoped would appeal to his constituents.

At the end of the eighteenth century, there were many Christian scholars and clerics mastering Hebrew and new methods of reading texts, some of whom were also anxious to debate the Jews. For the educated Jews, "the challenge of a new Christian ascendancy of master translators of the biblical text, along with their new prerogatives of claiming exclusive Christian ownership of the text, was felt acutely and painfully by Jewish leaders and educators."[53] While the nineteenth century was a problematic period for the Sephardi community, some of its members actively promoted literature that presented the Jews in a positive vein in an attempt to stem the tide of assimilation. During this time, numerous Protestant "philo-Semites," in the guise of tolerant lovers of the Bible and the Jewish heritage, were actually aiming to convert Jews. Some of these philo-Semites hoped to attract women, pointing out to them that both their religion and their men were oppressing them.

Interestingly enough, a Portuguese writer named Grace Aguilar whose family had only recently arrived in England began to write prolifically, publishing twelve books by the age of thirty-one. The fact that a new arrival was already writing best-sellers in English seems rather remarkable and highly unusual. Ruderman's explanation is that in

> a society that allowed its Jewish minority a relatively higher degree of social integration than anywhere else in Europe, where many professional, educational, and social barriers had practically disappeared by the end of the eighteenth century, despite the failure of the Jew Bill of 1753 and despite a residue of public hostility to both the Jewish upper and lower classes, linguistic assimilation into the English language proceeded rapidly, in the course of one or two generations, across all classes of English Jewish society.[54]

Nonetheless, Aguilar had to have been extremely gifted. Her historical romances and stories were tremendously popular; her books sold hundreds of thousands of copies. In her writings, she presented romanticizations of the crypto-Jewish experience and of relationships between mothers and daughters,[55] for she seemed to feel she was continuing a tradition obtained from her mother, from conversa to conversa.[56] She displayed an impressive knowledge of her people's history as well as an inordinate pride in her heritage. She manifested a strong identity, linked not only to Judaism but to her crypto-Jewish past; through her skilled writing, she emerged as a champion of her people.[57] In Galchinsky's opinion, "Aguilar could see crypto-Jews' history of hiding as an emblem of Anglo-Jewish assimilation."[58] Aguilar hoped to show her readers, both Jewish and non-Jewish, that the period of hiding was over, that one need not be ashamed of the past, for now, as British Jews, they could live without having a cloud of secrecy hanging over them anymore.

Aguilar stands in sharp contrast to the Sephardi presented by Endelman, especially since her novels demonstrate that she was deeply aware of the traumas of the Inquisition. In Endelman's opinion, "[C]rypto-Judaism, while capable of stimulating heroism and steadfastness, could also breed indecision and weakness, religious confusion and philosophical uncertainty. The London

Sephardi community was simply too weak in moral and political authority to counteract the negative impact of the Marrano experience and guide former Marranos and their families back into the bosom of traditional Jewish life."[59] This community suffered a blow in 1841, when a group of eminent families left the Bevis Marks synagogue in order to establish their own synagogue in the West End, where they were residing. Unfortunately, because the outdated statutes gave Saar Asamaim exclusive authority in London, this move or secession created a serious schism in the community.[60]

Attempting to assess the London experience presents conflicting images. On the one hand, there clearly was a trend toward assimilation, intermarriage, and conversion. On the other hand, proud and knowledgeable writers such as Grace Aguilar publicly professed pride in their heritage and sought to strengthen that in their kinsmen as well. Perhaps Aguilar best reflected the complexity and ambiguity of the future of the community; she was clearly fighting what she perceived to be the trends of the time, well aware of the threat of assimilation and of the temptations gentile society held for her fellow Jews. At the same time, there were less well-known Sephardim whose goals were similar, although their techniques differed considerably. For example, David Levi was an erudite spokesman of Judaism who saw himself as an educator, apologist, and defender and "assigned himself the formidable tasks of becoming Anglo-Jewry's primary educator as well as its principal apologist and defender against the verbal attacks of Christian theologians, biblical critics, Evangelicals, deists, and atheists."[61]

Thus, while choosing London for resettlement was a sound decision economically, it ultimately put one's Jewishness at extreme risk. The London community's early years resembled those experienced by its brethren in France, for neither country initially recognized the Jewish presence. The only alternative in each locale was to clandestinely observe Judaism, clearly a learning experience for nearly all of these "New Jews." In both cases, the Jews were eventually permitted to purchase burial grounds and build synagogues, signs that the path to normalization was being paved. Nevertheless, the resemblance between the two experiences ends here. In France, the community maintained its identity until it had to contend with the upheavals of Napoleon and the Revolution. In England, no political development was to have such a powerful effect. On the contrary, it was the nature of British society that appears to have been the decisive factor in the development of the Portuguese community and of the identity of its members.

When the host society tolerates the Jewish presence by allowing it to organize itself, the community uses its autonomy to build a healthy entity, which then enables its members to have a strong Jewish identity. Separatism always played a significant role in the survival of Jews and Judaism. British society did not publicly open its doors to non-Christians, and as we have seen, there were numerous attempts to convert them. Yet the upper class seems to have developed its own set of rules; once one attained the economic prestige required to qualify as a member of this class, a surprising openness to the newcomer was forthcoming, as exemplified by acceptance of these newly gentrified neighbors. Perhaps a sense of the glory of the Sephardi past or a historic memory of the wealthy bankers and court Jews who had been their ancestors enabled the members of the Nation to feel so at ease in Christian circles. For whatever reason, the movement away from observance occurred at a higher level and a faster rate than any of the other communities.

The Portuguese of London were a variegated lot, composed of New Jews, fuzzy Jews, and assorted others. There were those who had hesitated to commit themselves halakhically and others who publicly desecrated the Sabbath and ignored additional laws. By contrast, some devoted themselves to their community as *parnasim*, or as donors and even as regulars at the synagogue. Simultaneously, other Portuguese and Spanish conversos or their descendants purchased homes far from the Jewish residential area, socialized with their Christian neighbors and business associates, and, ultimately, intermarried and converted. They still considered themselves part of the Nation, but they reduced their identification to no more than an ethnic one that could and would easily disappear over the generations.

7

Italy

The fourth diaspora site we will consider is Italy, or rather, the Italian city-states. In this case, the information available about the conversos is quite different. As in France, the conversos were not all in one locale.[1] Residence in a given city invariably led to an experience that differed from that of a neighboring locale. For example, because Sicily was under Spanish rule, the Jews there were expelled or forcibly converted in 1492. At this time, the size of this Judeo-Arabic speaking community was around 30,000, and the edict of 1492 produced, albeit as the result of a prolonged process, somewhere between 5,000 and 8,000 conversos. The Inquisition was also active there, at least until 1550, and involved in what is often claimed to have been economic and political destruction. By the mid-sixteenth century, the *neofiti* were impoverished, and many fled, presumably to Salonika and other cities in the Ottoman Empire. Unfortunately, the protocols of the Inquisition were burned in the eighteenth century, so it is difficult to learn about the lives or the identities of those tried. On the other hand, research reveals that there was a high level of endogamy and a sense of commonality among the conversos, as well as a sense of rejection by some of the Old Christians, which created an identity of sorts for the first generations.[2]

Other Iberian conversos sometimes joined exiles or their descendants or local Italian Jews, although occasionally some of them were the only settlers of Jewish descent. The exiles who came had a difficult time adjusting and adapting to life in Rome as well as in the rest of Italy.[3] While some indeed settled in Rome and Ferrara, there was no overwhelming Jewish immigration to Italy after the expulsion.[4] There were conversos who arrived in the city of Rome before the expulsion, although some of the reports about this phenomenon are rather unclear, mainly because the term "Marrano" was used interchangeably with "Jew." As a result, one must look long and hard in order to determine who arrived when and with what intentions.[5] As Anna Foa has shown, some conversos who were observant Catholics arrived in Rome in the hope of attaining papal absolution. Pope Sixtus himself referred to numerous conversos who had fled Spain and were seeking refuge in Rome. Foa writes, "Those who reached Rome, accordingly, were those who were able to afford an appeal to the Roman Inquisition and who now—however sincere their conversion had been—fully intended to live as Christians, most likely in Rome. Many of them, after all, were ecclesiastics."[6] Nonetheless, there was an auto-da-fé in July 1498, in which numerous sincere converts were reconciled to the Church. In the same year, a Spanish converso named Pedro de Aranda, who had enjoyed papal protection for five years, was arrested as a Judaizer and found guilty. However, this incident did not appear to traumatize those conversos who sought absolution over the course of twenty years.[7]

On the other hand, changes occurred that altered the general papal policy concerning converso immigrants. An influential factor was the eventual establishment of an inquisition in Portugal, especially since Rome was the site of extended negotiations, bribery, and political and economic pressure. As previously mentioned, the converso lobby in Rome was formidable and had spent substantial sums of money for more than two decades, temporarily deferring what they had hoped to avoid. The lobby became defunct in 1536 once the decision was made to deal "appropriately" with the Portuguese heretics and establish an inquisition.[8] Another factor was the challenge of the Protestant reform, which clearly threatened the Church. Nevertheless, even in the 1530s, seemingly unexpected examples of papal toleration can be found, such as the treatment of David Reubeni and Solomon Molkho. The former was a messianic claimant who was accompanied in his travels by the latter, a Portuguese converso who was permitted to live as a Jew in Rome.[9] Whereas the earlier conversos sought absolution, Molkho sought recognition as a Jew!

This "tolerance" more or less dissipated by the middle of the sixteenth century. In addition to the definitive establishment of the Portuguese Inquisition in 1536 and the Roman Inquisition in 1542, the repercussions of the meetings of the Council of Trent (1545–1563) and the rise of the Catholic Reformation (Counter-Reformation) had their effects on the prevailing atmosphere in Italy. Consequently, the experience of the conversos who arrived during this period reflected this changing atmosphere. During the sixteenth century, the local ruler would negotiate with each group that arrived in order to determine how long and under what conditions the group could stay. Papal opinion had to be taken into account, and as long as there was no papal prohibition, the local rulers assumed that what they did was permissible. Needless to say, the determining factor was almost always the economic usefulness of the group; on that basis, the decision was made whether or not to renew its *condotta* (contract). These potential residents, unlike the local Jews, were not primarily moneylenders but rather entrepreneurs, bankers, and industrious merchants, as were their brethren who settled in Holland, France, and England; essentially they helped negate the stereotype of the Jewish moneylender. These Jews would not play a marginal role, but were to become part and parcel of the economic life and development of their new choices of residence. As a result, their presence was desirable, a fact that influenced the bending or breaking of rules on the part of the local rulers, as Bonfil explains: "Unlike the local Jews, they were a significant economic element and could mix with wealthy Christians on an equal footing. For as long as they maintained their outward Christian guise, they could frequent the palaces of the Italian aristocracy and the courts of princes like their Christian counterparts."[10]

Needless to say, the opportunity to cut oneself off from the Christian world was not always perceived positively, and one might prefer to engage in cultural commuting. The converso who declared his Jewishness had fewer options, was socially segregated, and was often limited to residing in the ghetto. On the other hand, those who maintained a Christian façade enjoyed the freedom of social mobility and seemed to have been accepted by the Christians despite the fact that the latter often suspected that this was little more than a guise. Some of these individuals even behaved like Jews yet were not rejected by the Christians, who more or less chose to ignore any displays of Jewishness and to emphasize the positive, namely, their Christian past and Spanish culture.[11] Thus, all the conversos who arrived in various Italian cities did not openly embrace Judaism; although they seemed to have been in the minority, these individuals were tempted by the prospect of the social advantages available to them in the Christian world.

The first three cities to accept conversos who openly reverted to Judaism were Florence, Ferrara, and Ancona; once it became common knowledge that a ruler had opened his gates, a flow of immigrants usually ensued.[12] While most did not appear until after 1536, some conversos began to leave Portugal even prior to the establishment of the Inquisition because they were nervous about the ongoing negotiations in the 1530s and the prospective results. Limited information is available about these three first settlements, particularly Florence, and about the conversos who lived there. The sixteenth-century community was quite small, although in 1549, Duke Cosimo de Medici granted the Portuguese the right to reside as well as to trade in Florence and the duchy. By 1570, most of them were living in the ghetto, and by 1705 there were 453 Jews in Florence. Some of them left the city and moved to nearby villages and quite possibly assimilated with their neighbors.[13] As for Ferrara, according to Rabbi Gedalia Ibn Yehia, conversos arrived there in 1535 and were allowed to perform circumcisions and to return openly to Judaism. This was feasible because Duke Ercole II had issued two *Lettres Patentes*. The first referred to "Spaniards and Portuguese who speak Spanish and Portuguese" who might come to reside or to work in Ferrara and specified that they could live as Christians or as Jews. Less than three months later, this ruler proclaimed that Spaniards and Portuguese, Levantines, and those of other nations, "whether Christians or infidels" who come to live or trade "could continue to live as they had previously."[14] When the plague put lives in jeopardy in 1549, some Jews fled; others were expelled in 1551 also because of the plague. The Abravanels returned to Ferrara in the fall of 1551, while the Mendes family, after leaving this city, chose to relocate in Venice. Various members of the latter family would sporadically reappear in Ferrara. At any rate, most of the others did not return afterward,[15] either because of the plague or due to the Christian victory in Lepanto.[16]

Nonetheless, the Usque family arrived during this period. In 1553, Samuel Usque's *Consolation for the Tribulations of Israel*, promoted by Dona Gracia Mendes, was printed there; this well-known book was intended to provide conversos with encouragement and inspiration.[17] Another Usque named Abraham, who might have been Samuel's brother, set up a printing press that published works in Spanish, Portuguese, and Hebrew.[18] Among its publications were the *Consolation* along with other works written for converso readers, including a translation of the Bible into Spanish in 1553. This Ferrara Bible, financed by and dedicated to Dona Gracia, found a wide audience.

Other interesting figures passed through Ferrara, although they did not always declare their Jewishness during their stay. A Portuguese converso physician named Duarte Gomez who had graduated from the University of Salamanca arrived in about 1550, although he later moved to Venice. Roth referred to him as "a wealthy business-man of Jewish extraction but not of strong Jewish sentiment, with a love of literature and a taste for versification."[19] Roth did not seem to attach importance to this man except for the fact that he associated with certain eminent and wealthy individuals and at times was confused with another converso literati. Brooks informs us that he had been a lecturer in Portugal in the humanities, medicine, and philosophy and was translating Petrarch into Spanish.[20] Amatus Lusitanus, the eminent converso doctor, treated him in Ancona, and considered him to be a "grave, learned person and a poet."[21] Apparently, he was more active in the converso world than Roth originally thought, for he was a senior business representative and an in-house physician for Gracia Mendes, an agent for her nephew Joseph, and was suspected of Judaizing time and again. Most of the accusations against him included his associate, Agostino Enríquez,[22] whose path began in Florence rather than Ferrara but then coincided with that of his colleague in Venice. The two were denounced in 1555 and in 1557 in Ferrara but not convicted; they were denounced by none other than Gracia's business manager, da Costa, who had previously been denounced by them.[23] Testimony against them was then presented to the Tribunal of Venice because they were living the life of upper-class Christians and doing business with Jews. Once again, they escaped the clutches of the Inquisition by presenting impressive evidence of their fidelity to the Church while in Ferrara as well as Venice and producing baptismal certificates for their children; the fact that Enríquez's son was not circumcised proved decisive in the case.[24] In 1574, a third unsuccessful attempt to convict Gomez of Judaizing was made, this time in Lisbon, but the accused had died in the meantime. Another charge materialized postmortem, and Gomez was found guilty of heresy in 1575 because his library contained heretical works.[25] Roth wrote that "after his death, the luke-warmness of his attachment to Christianity became apparent" which, in his opinion, is confirmed by the fact that one of his sons became a Jew. While it is difficult to prove the motivation of either father or son, perhaps the fact that Duarte Gomez was constantly being hounded by the Inquisition convinced his son João, now Samuel Zaboca, that life was safer or somehow preferable as a Jew. While the identity of the father seemed to have been Christian, it was always being tested by the authorities; the fact that his son became a Jew implies the existence of some level of identification with the family's heritage.

A contrasting figure to Gomez is Amatus Lusitanus, also a Portuguese converso physician (known as João Roderigo do Costelo Branco),[26] who likewise studied in Salamanca. Lusitanus, by contrast, was never accused of Judaizing, even in 1533 when he moved to Antwerp. He was about thirty years old in 1540–1541 when he arrived in Ferrara by invitation of the duke, Ercole II de'Este. This member of the Nation was given a position in the university medical school, and because of his impressive reputation, he even attended the pope in Rome. In 1547 he accepted an invitation to Ancona, which proved to be an unfortunate choice for a former Judaizer.[27] While he was not tried by the Inquisition there, his home was looted and he subsequently fled the city, abandoning his belongings.[28] He first went to Pesaro, then to Ragusa in 1556, and in 1558 he finally settled in Salonika, where he lived the last ten years of his life. Lusitanus, clearly a doctor of the highest calibre, never faltered in regard to his orientation. Once he was able to discard the mantle of Christianity in Ferrara, he became an openly loyal Jew, referring to Jewish values and customs in his medical writings.

The arrival of Dona Gracia (Nasi) Mendes (alias Beatriz de Luna) in 1548 must have influenced Ferrara's converso policy. After donning the guise of a practicing Catholic in Portugal (1510–1536), Antwerp (1536–1545) and Venice (1545–1548), this Portuguese member of the Nation had no qualms about declaring herself to be Jewish when she arrived in Ferrara, despite the fact that she recently had an unpleasant encounter with the Inquisition in Venice. She joined the Jewish community in Ferrara that included the extremely wealthy Abravanels, exiled first from Spain and then from Naples in 1541. Some of these double exiles went to Ancona, but the wealthiest were invited to Ferrara

by Hercules II d'Este. Thus, Don Samuel arrived in 1543, when the court secretary told the duke that a group had arrived with "that king of the Jews from
the Kingdom of Naples."[29] This Jew died there three years later, leaving his
widow, Benvenida, as head of the household. While the Spanish Jews and the
Portuguese conversos seemed to have led separate lives in the same city,[30] the
presence of families such as the Abravanels and the Nasis (formerly de Luna)
resulted in contact between the Italian rulers and Sephardi dynasties. As for
the Mendes family, the aforementioned plague of 1551 caused the flight of
Gracia's sister Brianda and her daughter, but they returned to Ferrara in 1555
with a charter of safe conduct from the duke in exchange for a handsome
donation, which was par for the course. According to Segre, this was "not an
agreement involving individual franchises or business matters but a charter
granting the marranos license to dwell in Ferrara for the same number of years
(that is, 'allowing the Portuguese nation to stay and live without any impedi-
ment on the part of the pope or others, and without being expelled, but up-
holding their safe-conduct')."[31] Ferrara was Gracia's last European residence;
in 1552 she finally decided to leave Italy and seek safer shores in Constantinople
after passing through Ragusa in August.[32] Her niece and nephew remained
there until the duke died in 1559; despite their commitment to stay on, they
were being hounded by the authorities, which convinced them that a different
home was necessary, at which point they joined their aunt in the Ottoman
Empire.

In retrospect, one discerns that Dona Gracia's life was permeated by law-
suits, whether initiated by the Inquisition or by members of her own family,
namely, her sister Brianda, who was never satisfied with the fact that Gracia
was guardian of the family fortune and of her niece's inheritance. In addition,
the fact that she was married and widowed in Portugal had implications for
her rights of inheritance as a widow in a Christian land as compared to her
rights as a widow in a Jewish community. These were some of the halakhic
problems resulting from the move from Christian to Jewish society.[33]

This family was comprised of crypto-Jews who consciously decided where
and when they would join the Jewish community. Before making her final
commitment, Gracia was a cultural commuter of the highest order due to the
fact that she was part of the social and economic elite wherever she was to be
found. If she had simply been waiting for the proper moment to return without
maintaining any ties to the Nation, she would not qualify as a commuter.
However, because she devoted herself to her brethren, whether by aiding them
in their flight from Iberia, settling them in Jewish communities, employing
them, and supporting Jewish-converso enterprises of every imaginable sort,
and simultaneously by associating with Catholic high society wherever she was
to be found, she was clearly living in two worlds. According to Segre, "[T]he
attitude of the De Luna sisters toward religion is considerably more uneven

[than that of Jews], for they led a perilous life on the border between the two faiths." Segre points out that Brianda took interesting oaths, swearing on the four gospels in Venice, issuing power of attorney with a Christian oath, and once settling a dispute with her sister by means of an ambiguous allusion.[34] Needless to say, this was a risky path fraught with numerous obstacles along the way, some of which originated in the nature of Jewish law and others which stemmed from the nature of the Catholic Church. Perhaps Italy was the site of the most menacing of these obstacles because the Inquisition took steps to detain Dona Gracia and the women in her family.

Later information on the community of Ferrara was provided by Cecil Roth, who discovered another Judaizer who was so active that the Inquisition simply could not ignore him. Gabriel Henriques was born in Portugal in 1523, thirteen years after Gracia Mendes; he was either born to New Christian parents or converted from Christianity at the age of twenty-three.[35] In 1548 he arrived in Ferrara in order to live as a Jew. In addition to supporting himself as a goldsmith, the Jew Joseph Saralvo became a ritual circumciser and an active proselytzer among the conversos. It was reported in two elegies that he circumcised eight hundred converso males. In 1578, a Portuguese inquisitor general was anxious to locate conversos from Portugal, in particular those from Coimbra, who had fled to Italy, especially to Ferrara; Henriques was on his list. As a result, Henriques alias Saralvo was one of three serious offenders who was sent to Rome to face trial. After being burned at the stake as a heretic in 1583, he was celebrated as a martyr among the conversos, some of whom elegized him poetically. This converso unabashedly joined a Jewish community and devoted his efforts to convincing his brethren to follow suit. Despite the fact that he was no longer living on Portuguese soil, he was treated as a heretic in Ferrara and died as a martyr who never hesitated for a moment vis-à-vis his identity. He, like Dona Gracia, had become a full-fledged Jew, but unlike the latter, Saralvo did not succeed in avoiding the tentacles of the Inquisition. As a result, he faced the ultimate test of his loyalty in Rome; by refusing to be reconciled to the Church, his death was painful and cruel, but his statement was clear.

The third of the early converso settlements was Ancona, where there was a small Jewish presence in the fifteenth and sixteenth centuries. In order to attract business, this city, under direct papal rule as of 1532, was declared a free port in the hope of improving the economy. In the 1530s, various permits were granted to merchants including Iberians, Levantines, and exiles expelled from Sicily and Naples.[36] Pope Paul III (1534–1549) felt that there were revenues to be gained and even granted newcomers the right to build synagogues. As he recorded in the charter, "[T]hey are granted a complete pardon for all crimes perpetrated in the past, including those committed against the Christian faith or the Pope."[37] While the original charter referred to Levantines, the 1547 version was extended and included "Portuguese, also if of Jewish origin called New Christians or of the Jewish nation of whatever origin."[38] This terminology was also used in a charter of privileges by the duke of Urbino.

At any rate, the Portuguese conversos were under the distinct impression that not only were they welcome in Ancona but that they would be forewarned if the terms of the contract were to be changed or terminated. In 1549 an unusual agreement was signed, not only exempting Portuguese bankers from certain taxes but guaranteeing them immunity from inquiries in matters of faith. The incoming pope, Julius III (1549–1555), amended this agreement somewhat, but reiterated that he granted them immunity from charges of apostasy, and, in case of prosecution, he would provide a four-month advance warning.[39] Consequently, a community with a synagogue was organized. In retrospect, one can say that these papal contracts "gave the Portuguese Marranos the false sense of security"[40] that made the shock of the abrupt change of policy by the next pope, Paul IV (1555–1559) all the greater:

> With the enthronement of Pope Paul IV, Rome's policy toward the Jews in general, and the Conversos in particular, took a drastic turn for the worse. It is difficult to say whether objective factors, such as the Catholic Church's struggle against the Reformation and the influence of the policy pursued by the Emperor—who among others sat on the throne of Ferdinand and Isabella—tilted the scales, or whether the main reason was the personality of a senile and idiosyncratic pope whose hatred of the Jews was matched by his religious orthodoxy.[41]

This pope churned out anti-Jewish legislation including the famous *Cum nimis absurdum* in 1555; the various degradations he initiated included the requirement for Jews to reside in a ghetto and to wear a badge of distinction. Essentially, the aforementioned promises were abrogated, the conversos' property was confiscated, and a hundred and two of the converso "rebels" were imprisoned by the papal representative and charged with apostasy.

This incident was extremely traumatic for the conversos of Ancona and, in truth, for those in Italy and its environs as well. These Portuguese members of the Nation had openly become committed Jews with the blessing of a pope. They had never imagined that his successor would overturn this arrangement and create a nightmare for them. While forty of those arrested managed to flee prison, the rest faced trial and had no defense available for themselves. In 1556, twenty-four of the sixty-two prisoners were burned at the stake in an auto-da-fé, and thirty-eight of them succumbed to reconciliation to the Church. The remaining twenty-six recalcitrants were assigned to the galleys in Malta, but they overcame their guard and escaped, mostly to Turkey and Ferrara. The emotional damage incurred upon the community of Ancona was tremendous, but the repercussions of this horror were yet to be manifested.

It is precisely at this point that Dona Gracia, now safely ensconced in her villa in Constantinople, chose to act, and even persuaded the sultan to intervene. Although this converso patroness had attempted to prevent the martyrdom of her brethren, she had not succeeded.[42] In addition to her outrage at such treatment, it should be noted that she had four of her own agents in Ancona, so she was financially vested in this port as well. As a result, she devised a plan to punish the city of Ancona while displaying international Jewish solidarity. The plan involved a ban on the port and replacing it with Pesaro. While in theory it was a viable and ingenious plan, in reality, numerous unforeseen problems arose. Logistically, Pesaro was not quite appropriate as a replacement for the larger neighboring port. Its duke granted the conversos a charter of residence providing they build up the economy, but in 1558, he expelled the newcomers along with those who had resided there prior to the ban.[43] At the same time, Dona Gracia was unable to enlist the support of all the rabbis and merchants who were needed to make the plan effective. Although this patroness attempted to pressure and cajole and apply all her influence, the plan was doomed to failure. Many of the moneylenders and local merchants in Ancona were apprehensive regarding this plan, for fear they would suffer retaliation and financial ruin. At the same time, the rabbis viewed it from various angles, with most of the Sephardim supporting the ban and the Italian, German, and Greek colleagues in opposition. Bonfil recounts one aspect of this opposition:

> In the course of halakhic discussions on the subject, the argument
> was even raised that account should be taken of the fact that the
> Conversos themselves were partially responsible for the fate that had
> befallen them: because of their Christian past, they were not only
> obliged to be more careful; they should also refrain, more so than
> others, from jeopardizing their Judaism in a Catholic land. Some
> even went so far as to say that in fact they had not returned whole-
> heartedly to Judaism, hence their Jewish brethren need not consider
> themselves responsible for their fate.[44]

Little is written about this community after 1559. Those who chose reconciliation must have felt that it was far too dangerous for a converso to live as a Jew directly under the pope's nose. Those whose relatives and neighbors were burned at the stake essentially had an Iberian experience on Italian soil. Fortunately for the conversos, this pope had a relatively short reign, and none of his successors would be as fanatically anti-Semitic. The laments written in memory of these martyrs clearly reflected a Jewish response coupled with a desire to perpetuate the memory of those who died because they were Jews. In 1555, many of the conversos of Ancona fled to Ferrara, and when the pope learned of this, he demanded their expulsion. The demand was not met, but copies of laments of the martyrs were destroyed, and the printing press responsible for its publication was closed.

Thus, growth of the community of Ancona was stunted after 1559. The conversos in Ferrara had dealt with the plague (1549–1551) and later, in the 1580s, with the aforementioned persecution of Saralvo and the other conversos. Roth contended that as a result the converso immigrants turned to Venice,[45] although at the end of the sixteenth century, Portuguese members of the Nation found Leghorn to be an appealing option as well, an option that will be discussed presently.

The Republic of Venice dealt differently with the Jews and the conversos who entered its domain. At the beginning of the sixteenth century, there was local opposition to the presence of Jewish moneylenders. The compromise in 1516 was to relegate the Tedeschi, or German Jews, to the *ghetto nuovo* (new iron foundry) while giving them a contract permitting money lending and dealing in secondhand goods; the hope was that the Jews would provide a source of revenue and aid to the urban poor. In 1541, a second iron foundry, the *ghetto vecchio* (old foundry), was set aside for Levantine merchants, granting them official authorization. The Levantines were technically Ottoman subjects (and were often Sephardi Jews returning with a new affiliation), while the conversos were considered to be Ponentini (westerners) and even had separate graveyards.[46] There were, however, conversos who affiliated themselves with the Levantine group. The latter had their residence rights renewed regularly, probably because they provided needed goods from the East as well as desirable imports from Romania. Renewals continued despite threats of property sequestration and the like when war with Turkey broke out in 1537 and again in 1570.

Venice thus became a center for conversos who were either stopping temporarily on their way to Turkey or who had chosen to join (or not to join) the Jewish community in this port.[47] Roth claimed that the Venetian government tolerated the Jews because it considered the bankers to be an "inexhaustible source of wealth."[48] In 1577, Daniel Rodriga represented the Ottoman Jews and requested long-term residence privileges for them. It seems that Rodriga was persistent; that Venice had commercial difficulties as it was being challenged by Spain, Portugal, France, England, Holland, and the Ottoman Empire; and that the republic was interested in implementing his project in which the Jews could be of help in establishing another port in Spalato. This was an unprecedented concession, giving outsiders rights to overseas trade akin to those of natives; it also included rights for the Ponentine Jews while not advocating any clear-cut policy concerning the converso-Jew phenomenon. The Jews were granted rights of residence and community, freedom of religion, security, and freedom of movement; in addition, they received lower tariff rates and were allowed to trade with the Levant. They had to attain a ten-year residency in order to qualify, and had to wear the yellow hat and reside in the ghetto. They would be dealt with fairly in case of expulsion. However, all new merchants had to be approved.[49] Thus, in 1589, safe conduct was finally granted to the Levantine and Ponentine Jews who were classified as ten-year residents; this meant that the Levantines as well as Ponentines in Venice were now part of the Jewish community.

The native Venetian merchants protested this policy, as did the pope who, for different reasons, was unhappy about having conversos become Jews. An interesting justification of this policy was provided by Fra Paolo Sarpi (1614–1617), who not only pointed to the fact that the previous pope did not object to this phenomenon, but raised the concern that if the conversos were not welcome in Venice, they would leave for Turkey, ultimately strengthening Venice's rival. Apparently this argument was convincing, and their charter was renewed. Despite the fact that the authorities had attempted to banish the crypto-Jews in 1497 and in 1550, "with the charter of 1589 they made it clear that they would in fact tolerate apostasy on the part of all those New Christians who opted to settle in the ghetto openly as Jews, since the charter explicitly stated that Ottoman or Iberian Jewish merchants could settle freely in Venice with their families and practice Judaism, secure in not being molested for matters of religion by any magistracy."[50]

Substantial information about this community was provided by Hector Mendes Bravo, a converso who returned to Lisbon as well as to Catholicism. In 1607 or 1608, Mendes Bravo, who was in his early teens, left Portugal with his mother and headed for Florence. In the following year, they made contact with the conversos in the ghetto of Venice. He emphasized the fact that the majority of the 1,500 Sephardim in the ghetto were Portuguese, although some Castilians were also present. Bravo explained how the rabbis in Venice discussed religion with him, gave him a Spanish Bible, and twenty days later, arranged for a quorum to be present to witness his circumcision. The confession he presented to the Inquisition included descriptions of Jewish holidays, fasts, and other observances and detailed lists of "Judaizers" in Venice, Amsterdam, and Hamburg. He noted the use of Spanish prayerbooks and other literature, and insisted that the Amsterdam Jews were not engaged in sending propaganda to Iberia. This confession was unusual because he described in detail the reception process of these conversos into the Jewish community.[51]

The conversos of Portuguese origin managed to maintain a separate identity even among their Sephardi brethren who were affiliated with the Ottoman Empire. Thus, they maintained their own graveyards and community organizations, such as the *Hebra de casar horphãos* dowry society, which has been likened to a mutual aid society. Their approach to this society is particularly interesting, as the Venetian guidelines emphasized Sephardi identity, and only young women who were Portuguese or Spanish on at least one parent's side were eligible for dowries.[52] It differs from that of Amsterdam, which was quite inclusive and open to Spanish and Portuguese Jews as well as to all crypto-

Jews.[53] The Venetian society, established in 1613, provided for brides not necessarily from Italy and for daughters of crypto-Jewish martyrs but did not create as broad a platform as did the parallel society established in 1615 by its sister community in Amsterdam.

As in Amsterdam, there were also problematic figures in Venice. Whereas those who stood out in the former locale were philosophers and theologians who had difficulty accepting the rabbinic law, this was not the case in Venice. On the contrary, these conversos had not collided with the rabbis nor had they faced excommunication as did da Costa and Spinoza; their fateful encounters were with none other than the Venetian Inquisition.

Ironically enough, the archives of the Inquisition of Venice reveal a number of trials of Portuguese Judaizers accused expressly of heresy or apostasy; in fact, these were conversos who chose to live rather unusual lives. Some of these men were not able to commit themselves to a totally Jewish lifestyle but rather straddled both worlds, caught physically (rather than intellectually) between Catholics and Jews. By choosing Italy, the land of the pope, all conversos faced a certain risk. As has been seen, choosing Ancona proved to be catastrophic for many conversos, while selecting Venice, a republic with its own inquisition, proved to be problematic for a smaller number of the Portuguese émigrés. Pullan explains that the accused were often noted for their intellect and determination: "Detractors of Portuguese New Christians taxed them with conspiracy to accumulate great riches by pretending to be genuine Christians and then to export their wealth to the Ottoman Empire; theirs were no momentary lapses into Judaism. The Inquisition strove to punish not only the act itself, not only the will and the intention behind it, but also the intellect and the sense of responsibility."[54]

In 1547 the Republic attempted to revive its inquisition, and, on the whole, Jews and former Jews were not at the top of this institution's agenda. About 1,550 processes are extant from the sixteenth century, the majority of which are from the second half. About 50 percent dealt with "Lutherans," 150 dealt with sorcery and superstition, and about 70 dealt with Judaism. Some 1,480 processes are extant from the seventeenth century, half deal with witchcraft and magic, nearly two hundred deal with Protestantism, 140 or so concern blasphemy and heretical discourse, a few hundred refer to Islam, and only some thirty-four cases deal with Jews and Judaizers, with an emphasis on Levantines and poor Jews.[55] Zorattini gives slightly different figures for the number of hearings concerned with Judaizing and Judaism. He notes that of thirty cases of Judaizing, all the individuals had been baptized in Italy, so that there was little difficulty proving that they were indeed Catholics and then apostates. These were mostly children of Jews and not of New Christians, who often converted in order to escape poverty and to integrate into Christian society.[56] In addition, most of the hearings did not develop into trials, and there were no autos-da-fé, although the "sentence of banishment for life was imposed on two Jewish physicians of the ghetto, José Naar and Benarogie, who had secretly practiced circumcision on Christians who very likely had been New Christians."[57] In the long run, a republic hoping to attract economic investment would be loath to begin confiscating its residents' property.

Pullan explains that

> by virtue of canon law, of recent papal legislation and of instructions contained in their own manuals, inquisitors were entitled to claim jurisdiction over baptized Christians who flirted with Judaism, who mingled Judaism with Christianity, who alternated between Christianity and Judaism, or who withdrew from Christianity altogether and transferred their allegiance to the Jewish faith.... Charges of heresy and apostasy seem to have been laid against Jews and judaizers only in the second half of the sixteenth century, and it was only in the 1580s that the Inquisition made repeated attempts to judge and punish Jews who had not known baptism. Baptized Jews were convicted of grave spiritual offences in the 1620s and 1630s, but were sentenced for incurring suspicion of heresy rather than for heresy itself.[58]

At the same time, Zorattini refers to the leniency of the Holy Office in Venice, probably due to the government's policy of putting the needs of the state first, whether or not they conflicted with the Church and its rights.[59] As pointed out, the Venetian Inquisition was somewhat reluctant to prosecute members of the Nation as heretics, especially if and when they were wealthy members of the mercantile community. But it was hard to find an excuse in order not to try the wealthy, who were well aware of the consequences of their activities.[60]

Many of the Judaizing conversos in Venice felt safe despite the prospect of facing the Inquisition. Some listed both their Jewish and Christian names in documents such as wills and, in doing so, attested to their double existence; apparently the fact that the notary was Catholic did not faze them. According to Zorattini, "[T]he Inquisition found it almost impossible to prevent the apostasy of these New Christians, who could be quite fearless about revealing their Christian past."[61] The charter of 1589 gave so many assurances to this community that they felt they had no cause for concern. A converso who came to Venice had a strong Jewish community to turn to for guidance and could easily be absorbed into the ghetto; if the newcomer chose to remain a Christian, integration into that community was also feasible.

A look at the lives of some of these Judaizers as reflected in the Venetian Inquisition files provides insight into the complicated existence of some of the Portuguese who passed through or chose to reside in this port city and whose presence was noticed by the local institution. As Pullan aptly notes, there were far more heretics present in the Republic than were tried. "However, its records are extensive enough to contribute to the history of Marranism a number of strange individual stories of ambiguity and indecision. For its attention was devoted to those on the margin between two faiths, to those who embarked on voyages of exploration which took in religions as well as countries new to them."[62] One example was Abraham Habibi, who was born in Portugal in the fateful year of 1497 and baptized as Tristão da Costa. He apparently identified himself with the Judaizing community; this was possible since he grew up during the period when the king had promised not to probe into the conversos' private lives or religious proclivities. Habibi married a New Christian woman, but his family was reluctant to leave Portugal, probably because it owned land. Nevertheless, he and his family set forth for the Low Countries in 1543, eventually arriving in Ferrara. He apparently was afraid to have his sons circumcised there; his less hesitant wife took his children to Salonika where they became clearly identified as Jews. In the meantime, Habibi met Brianda de Luna, the sister of Dona Gracia, and in Venice became her business manager and chief of staff.[63]

Habibi must have lived in the ghetto, since he confessed to having lived in Venice as a Jew for eight years, but it seems that he pretended to be a Christian when necessary, if only for business purposes. He also frequented Brianda's home in Venice at a time when the de Luna sisters had not yet declared their Jewishness. Habibi's Jewishness must have been extremely superficial, for he does not seem to have engaged in any prayers or rituals except for eating kosher food. Pullan describes him as maintaining a "religious neutrality" of sorts, and as being a Jew, "but one who had clung to Europe, balancing loyalty to his faith against the need to make a living, and keeping up, even in Italy, his dual identity on the margins of the Christian and the Jewish worlds."[64] While the de Luna women pretended to be Catholics in Venice, Habibi identified gastronomically and ethnically with the Jews, yet professionally presented himself as a Catholic, wearing the black hat forbidden to the Jews.[65]

The route followed by the de Nis family was similar though not identical to that of the da Costas. In the 1580s, one brother died as a Christian in Venice, another continued to the Ottoman Empire, and the third, Felipe, whose Jewish name was Solomon Marco, faced the Venetian Tribunal. The third branch of the family had assumed the name Filippi and lived outside the ghetto while Judaizing rather indiscretely. When arrested, Solomon, a wealthy merchant, said he had been born a Jew and simply found it more pragmatic to conduct his business as a Christian. Later in the trial, he presented a totally different account of his life, especially after the court proved that he was the son of New Christians from Oporto. He spoke of his mother, who had wanted to return to Portugal, the brother who convinced him to Judaize at age thirteen, his Christian lifestyle in Antwerp and Cologne, and his move to Judaism, which included circumcision that he underwent only after establishing himself in Venice.

While this second confession is somewhat problematic, scholars are convinced that the family "dissimulated to the extent of practicing Judaism outside the Ghetto," for the witnesses in the trial were not Portuguese but rather Venetian, and no denial was made by the defendant.[66]

Perhaps because no outside information corroborated these details, the court did not treat him very severely, "sentencing him to abjuration, some spiritual penalties, and life imprisonment, which they immediately commuted to forced residence under guarantee in Venice; two years later, in view of Nis's [i.e., Solomon's] good conduct, they remitted all material penalties to him."[67] Ultimately he was accepted as a serious repentent and presumably gave up his Jewish affiliation. It seems that the milieu in Venice and its image as a land of liberty tended to promote what was, at times, a false sense of security. The conversos there naively thought that legally they had nothing to fear, and while there were clear delineations of who could reside where, as conversos they made their own personal decisions. Judaizers lived outside the ghetto, while Christian dissemblers lived within the ghetto. While in Iberia such a choice would have been life threatening, in Venice, considerations were very different; consequently, one might choose to commute back and forth between two worlds, even in the very same city.

Other individuals who appeared to have made a choice were sometimes unable to make a clean break with their previous community. Franciscus Hispanus was born in Ferrara in 1552, the son of a Portuguese converso named Abraham de Almeda who had supposedly been circumcised in Lisbon. While in Venice in the 1570s, the son, also known as Isaac, left Judaism; however, when he was in need of financial aid, he turned to his Jewish family. The latter encouraged him to join his aunts in Constantinople, but he had a change of heart en route and confessed to his sins; thus, he was arrested in Venice and sentenced to the galleys. This fellow was connected more strongly to Christianity, but was comfortable maintaining ties of support and succor with the Jewish members of his family. In Pullan's opinion, Hispanus represents "the Marrano who returns to Christianity in Italy, and goes on vacillating helplessly between the two faiths, highly susceptible to pressures from those around him, especially in times of penury and isolation."[68] It is difficult to discern if this connection ran any deeper than a childish reflex to run to one's parents in a moment of distress. Pullan's theory about a number of these bifurcated souls should be mentioned here, for he explains their behavior as a manifestation of teenage rebellion, implying that their choice of religion was not a theological decision of any shape or sort.[69] Some turned to their previous community only when faced with financial distress or illness, while others had questionable ties because they had not spent their formative years together with their families, often for reasons of safety or finance. For instance, a daughter placed in a nunnery for safeguarding would find it difficult to change if and when her family recalled her. Similarly, a son placed in apprenticeship might well feel abandoned and alienated and might not be willing to rejoin his family and change his religion just because the parent insisted upon it.[70]

The two most well-known and well-researched accounts concern Abraham Righetto, known as the Righetto Marrano, and Gaspar Ribeiro, both of whom were tried by the Venetian Inquisition in the second half of the sixteenth century. The story of the Righetto Marrano is complex as well as fascinating. This man has been termed an adolescent rebel[71] and a "restless *picaro* gentleman" who belonged to a frontier-less merchant class and who was hated by Christians and not necessarily loved by Jews.[72] In the words of a contemporary, a Jew from Venice, he was "a ship with two rudders," due to the fact that he was neither Christian nor Jew.[73]

The court records contain two different accounts of Abraham Righetto's life. When first confronted by the court in 1570, he insisted that he was born in Ferrara, that his Portuguese father died in Venice, and that his mother was living in the Levant. His claim was that although a Jew, he had been inside churches and had fraternized with Christians, eating, drinking, and gambling with them.[74] When he later faced the Portuguese Inquisition, that court effectively established that he had been born in 1531 in a village near Lisbon as the son of New Christian victims of the decrees of 1497. In 1536, he was taken to Antwerp, where he was circumcised, and subsequently spent twelve years there with his relatives. His father was arrested in 1547, and after his release the family moved to Venice, where they stayed until the conversos were expelled in 1550. He, his mother, and some other family members moved to Ferrara and maintained a synagogue in their home.[75] The man now known as Abraham Benvenisti stayed in Ferrara for about twelve years. It is interesting to note that in 1552, while living in the Jewish community, his brother wrote a will using his Christian name in which he bequested to his sisters in Christian names. Pullan points out that Jews could not inherit from Christians; therefore, in his opinion, "Righetto must have presented himself as a Christian in order to benefit by the will."[76] At any rate, his mother Violante and two of his sisters eventually moved to Salonika, while two others settled in Constantinople.[77]

Righetto apparently had extragavant taste and enjoyed cavorting with members of high society. The earlier reference to gambling was only part of the story, for he enjoyed this pasttime as well as frequenting Christian courts. In Pullan's opinion, Abraham rebelled against his father by attending non-Jewish festivals in Mantua; upon his return, the son received a beating. The angry reveler stole money from his family to enable him to frequent European courts, including that of Lisbon; it seems that he made three trips to Iberia.[78] Interestingly, witnesses suggested that these risky excursions were undertaken as the result of frivolity, fancy taste, the need to exact debts, or to encourage New Christians to emigrate. However, in Pullan's assessment, his journeys to Spain and Portugal most probably "reflected a patriotic nostalgia of which he could not rid himself and a reluctance to shed the high social role of a rich and spoiled young man which he had seemed born to play."[79] According to witnesses, he was a Christian in Antwerp and Florence, and a Jew in Venice, Padua, and Ferrara. One servant reported that he attended church and mass, ate pork, lodged with Christians and even had an affair with a Christian woman. He was seen walking the streets of Venice, where he alternated two hats. The yellow hat (of the Jew) would emerge when he saw senators and other elite citizens; once these individuals had passed, he would replace it with a black hat under his arm. "Perhaps the tug-of-war in Righetto between his sense of Jewishness and his Hispanicity, between the merchant's heir and the wastrel gentleman, became so strenuous that he began to regard the Catholic and Jewish faiths as mere protective skins, to be donned and discarded at convenience."[80] While he was traveling overland to the Levant, he was arrested, because (Venetian) Cyprus and Lepanto were at war.[81]

This character managed to escape from the Venetian prison twice. After the first escape, carried out during the revelries following news of the victory at Lepanto, he was found in Ferrara a year later, at which time he was returned to the Venetian prison. His second and more successful escape (along with one of his guards) was to Constantinople in August 1573; upon arrival there he made contact with his relative Don Yosef Nasi. Although safe in the Ottoman Empire, he nevertheless hoped to clear his name in Venice and thus was unable to keep a low profile. This seems to be the reason he returned to Christian Europe, only to be arrested again in 1576 by the Inquisition. This time, however, he faced Portuguese inquisitors in Lisbon; his name was known to the Holy Tribunal there because it had received a request in 1572 from Venice. In fact, he was one of many Judaizing conversos tried in that court. In his confession in Lisbon, he provided lists of coreligionists from Bordeaux, Ancona, Florence, Turin, and Ferrara in what served as an attestation to the vast converso network in Europe. Zorattini claims that the list of New Christians in Ferrara was like a census record that helped trace their movements in the second half of the sixteenth century.[82] Righetto himself was condemned as an apostate, but because he was penitent and not in the best of health, his sentence was lightened progressively beginning in 1582. Eventually he moved to Castile and ended his days as a faithful Catholic, most likely gambling and seeking the company of those who had no qualms about his checkered past.

The second well-documented Portuguese family of the Nation that encountered the Venetian Inquisition was the Ribeiro clan. Each member of this family also seemed to go his or her own way; as a result, it was not so simple to establish each one's affiliation. Gaspar Ribeiro was born in Lisbon in 1493 or 1494; he often referred to his past links to the royal family. In 1560, he, his wife Donna Isabella de Medina, and their daughter Violante arrived in Venice. Gaspar was a merchant with ties to Paris and Lyons, and once his son João arrived in 1563, the two men worked together, dealing in pearls, rubies, meat, and other goods and engaging in extensive business with Levantine Jews. They were also in close contact with Gaspar's nieces and nephews, who were Jews residing in Ferrara. The means by which they spread out their interests gave the impression that they too might set forth for the Levant, but this was by no means certain.

Concerning the family's allegiances, Isabella, the mother, was a devout Jewess, known to have kept the dietary laws and the Jewish rites to the best of her abilities. She was no longer alive in 1569 when her daughter Violante announced her refusal to marry a Jew from the Abravanel family. The incident came to the notice of the Inquisition, and Gaspar was convinced to assent to a match for his daughter with a Catholic nobleman who was essentially marrying her for her money; Violante had clearly aligned herself with the Christian world and was rejecting her Jewish past.

In 1574, Gaspar remarried, this time choosing a Christian Venetian lady, and in this way, he, like his daughter, strengthened his ties to the non-Jewish world. Nonetheless, he did not sever his ties to either his relatives or to the community, and he continued to give charity to the Jews. By this time, he had passed on most of his business to his son João. In the meantime, João seemed to have moved in the opposite direction, strengthening his connections to his Jewish roots, although there is no evidence that he had ever been an observant Jew. In 1575, he secretly married Alumbra, a Jewess and a relative of Don Yosef Nasi. She remained in the ghetto of Venice, although the groom had allegedly promised her that he presently would be moving to Constantinople with her. Unfortunately, João died in 1579, and although no last rites were performed, he was buried in Venice as a Catholic.

The bride's family sued for her dowry because they had a Jewish marriage contract as proof of the liaison that was signed by Gaspar. In essence, the groom's father was being sued for having married his Christian son to a Jewess, and in this case, the public prosecutors transferred the case to the inquisitorial court, which was rather perturbed to learn of these developments. Gaspar claimed that the contract containing his signature was a forgery and that Alumbra had been his son's concubine, but there was evidence to the contrary that Gaspar had given her gifts and even invited her to live in his household during his son's illness. As part of his inconsistent testimony, this very difficult man also claimed to be senile. Gaspar died in 1581 at the age of eighty-seven, fourteen months after being arrested, and was condemned as an apostate. No decision could be reached on where to bury him, and it was not until 1586 that the Inquisition surreptitiously buried his remains with the Jews.[83] Thus, the converso who tried to appear Christian would be defined as a Jew after his death, despite the fact that his son had been buried as a Christian. The members of this family were completely at odds with one another, for the Judaizing mother did not succeed in transmitting her commitment to Judaism to her daughter, and the daughter, more devout in her observance than her Catholic husband, had antagonized her own family.[84]

This saga deals with changing locales, but even more so with changing preferences, sometimes on the mere basis of expediency. Gaspar might have had selfish reasons for entering into his second marriage, although accounts concerning the relationship are difficult to assess. João might have aligned himself with Alumbra in case he needed to flee Venice; ties to the Nasi family would certainly have proven to be helpful when in distress. No one really knows which of them, if any, had any serious knowledge of either Hebrew or Judaism. The mother seemed to be the only family member who had an unwavering sense of identity as a Jew. Pullan surmises that women did not have to live double lives as did the men who were coping with business needs, career pressures, or inheritances,[85] although this certainly was not the case with Dona Gracia. At any rate, the other members of this family seemed to have determined their loyalty on the basis of convenience or as a pragmatic reflex, an act of *carpe diem*. Since Gaspar had indeed served as a witness to his son's Jewish wedding contract, all the objections he presented in his own defense seem rather lame. The cultural commuting here was on the basis of expediency and not necessarily in the classic style; rather than moving from one community to another and donning a different guise in each one, these individuals left themselves options for changing their religious or ethnic affiliation in the very same locale. This change might have been due to one's choice of mate, a personal change of life decision, or a calculating economic tactic. In light of the fact that in his senior years Gaspar aligned himself with a Catholic woman whereas his son contracted a Jewish wedding, the official decisions regarding their final resting places seem rather ironic. Gaspar, leaving behind a Catholic widow, was buried in the dead of night as a Jew, while his son, leaving behind a Jewish widow, was buried as a Christian.

While there were conversos who quietly joined the Levantine community in their ghetto, Venice housed others who chose to live close to the ghetto, who were informed about Judaism as well as crypto-Judaism, and who elected to observe or not to observe certain practices.[86] These individuals ranged from dissemblers to those who engaged in simulation and dissimulation. They often had business dealings with Jews and just as often were related to them. For example, Fernão Galindo came from Antwerp to Ferrara, where he changed his name to Moses. He had business contacts with all four of his sons, ranging from the eldest, who lived as a Christian in Venice, to the three younger ones, who lived as Jews in Ferrara.[87]

Here one encounters a type of converso who would play by his own rules and whose behavior would be modified by the environment in which he found himself. While most of the conversos who settled in Ferrara seemed to have joined the Jewish community, this was not necessarily the rule for Venice. The fact that the ghetto was unattractive and crowded and that its inhabitants had curfews probably influenced many a converso's decision. If it was possible to remain outside the ghetto where one could profit from diverse contacts with

Jews and Christians, freely choose one's place of residence, and even travel to Iberia if one so desired, then the attraction or need to opt for living with the Levantine merchants would be nominal at best.

On the other hand, Venice was a major commercial center for Iberian and other Jewish merchants, and it became a center of Jewish publishing, a development attributed to the arrival of Daniel Bomberg from Antwerp. A converso named Felice de Prato convinced Bomberg of the importance of establishing a Hebrew press, and by 1516, it was in operation. Bomberg printed for thirty years, and other presses in the city followed suit for another three hundred years.[88] As we have seen, Venice also became a model community for later converso centers that developed in the West. According to Bonfil, "[I]n their own particular ways, both the Conversos who returned to Judaism and those who behaved publicly as Christians, made a first and extremely important contribution of a conceptual and social bridge between Jews and Christians."[89] This description can be applied aptly to Venice.

The aforementioned charter of 1589, ostensibly allowing for conversos to be included in the Jewish settlement, most certainly influenced the wording and intentions of charters granted in other cities in the following decade.[90] Perhaps the most well known of these charters was granted in 1591 by Ferdinand I (of the House of Medici), the duke of Tuscany.[91] This charter, known as *La Livornina* since it dealt with Leghorn (Italian: Livorno) and Pisa, was reissued and revised in 1593, and a similar charter was granted in Ancona in 1594. *La Livornina* contained the clause akin to that offered in 1538 in Ferrara: "To all ye merchants of whatever nation: Levantines, Ponentines, Spaniards, Portuguese, Greeks, Germans, Italians, Jews, Turks, Moors, Armenians, Persians, and others, Greetings." This particular arrangement was unusual in that it provided for a twenty-five-year term of residence, clearly creating a sense of permanence. It also included numerous tax exemptions and extensive guarantees, such as those of safe conduct and the right to acquire land. In addition, religious rights and protection from the Inquisition were guaranteed. The "Levantine merchants" were even allowed to use their Christian names for trade purposes and were not restricted as to where they could trade. Merchants and manufacturers were the desirable newcomers, as it was assumed that they would help expand industry and trade.[92] There was to be no Jewish badge or ghetto, although by 1604 the Jews would reside in Leghorn in a loosely defined separate area. They could attend university, practice medicine, and have Christian servants. According to Roth, the terms of this charter allowed Leghorn to become "the only place in Italy where Jewish intellectual life was completely untrammeled."[93] The charter allowed for the establishment of a fully independent and competent Jewish court with power over both civil and criminal matters among Jews.[94]

The rulers in Italy were well aware that the Portuguese or Spanish conversos who arrived in their kingdoms had not necessarily chosen their final religious paths. Nevertheless, a clear-cut choice on the part of the immigrants was preferable in their eyes: Either they observe Catholicism seriously or join a Jewish community.[95] However, the potential assets of the presence of an Iberian community of merchants most certainly influenced the more tolerant position. For example, there had been discussions in the Venetian Senate concerning the stance of the New Christians, and the Venetians as well as the Livornese discovered that "it was no easy matter to produce evidence of a return to Judaism, and those governments who wished to welcome Marranos without seeming to infringe on canon law took advantage of this fact."[96] It is quite feasible that the Italian city-states and the raison d'etre of the time played a part in creating some of these new Jewish communities. In the long run, identifying oneself as Jewish proved to be worthwhile for the Iberian member of the Nation.

As a result, the converso coming to Italy at the end of the sixteenth century could continue engaging in his economic activities, and if he became a Jew, he would receive protection and special rights, such as a reduction in overland tariffs. One choice to consider was Leghorn, located on the western shores of Italy, which was a desirable location for trade with Atlantic ports and in competition with Venice as a strategic port. The ships from Holland, England, Spain, and the New World traveled a considerably shorter distance to Leghorn than to Ancona or Venice.[97] Leghorn also seemed to be successful in attracting conversos who were able and willing to declare their loyalty to Judaism; one witness referred to this city as the site of those who can freely observe the true law.[98] Perhaps if Leghorn had had its own active inquisition, its trial records might have unearthed some odd individuals similar to those found in Venice. On the other hand, the indecisive conversos might have realized that communities such as Leghorn and Amsterdam were not appropriate for them. The ban was used in both communities,[99] albeit more frequently in Amsterdam, and ultimately both became organized and committed Jewish communities.

Originally, Pisa had been given the role of the primary community, whereas Leghorn technically had a somewhat secondary role. However, the port of Leghorn proved to be more promising than that of Pisa, and thus the population of the latter grew at a much faster rate. The Jewish population in Pisa was about five hundred in 1615, dropped to 357 in 1632, and by the end of the century was only 250. According to Fratterelli Fischer, "[T]he decline in the Jewish community itself does not seem to be the result of a lack of initiative, as has been claimed; it must rather be ascribed to the growth of commerce in Leghorn and to the process of redistribution of population and resources in the Grand Duchy as a whole."[100] One can see that the Jewish population of Leghorn grew during this period, from 124 in 1601, to 711 in 1622, to 1,250 in 1645. It continued to grow in the next two centuries as well, rising to 3,476 in 1738 and 4,948 in 1833.[101] Essentially, Pisa's community statutes of 1637 were applied to Leghorn, although some variations ensued. The Pisan *massari*, or board of governors, sought to control and influence both Leghorn and Florence but ultimately did not succeed in doing so. Originally, the Pisans had the power of veto over the admission of a newcomer to Leghorn, but after a successful appeal to the grand duke regarding this power, the daughter community achieved its independence.[102] There were also inner struggles in these communities between the Levantine and the Italian Jews, but the Levantines ultimately gained and retained power in Leghorn, which, by 1620, became the main Jewish center in Tuscany and boasted a centrally directed and strictly controlled community.[103]

Leghorn's Jews established the appropriate charitable institutions for the sick, for the poor, for freeing captives, for supporting scholars, and for providing dowries to orphaned girls. All of these institutions were intended to serve Iberian Sephardim.[104] Orfali contends that the dowry society, *Hebra de Casar Orfas e Donzelas*, which was established in 1644, "was undoubtedly one of the most splendid charitable institutions of the Sephardim in that city."[105] There were rules and regulations regarding the members of the society as well as the potential brides. The members, who included women as of 1656, paid entrance fees, which ensured the availability of dowries as well as cash for various types of investments.[106] Members could not convert to Christianity or travel to Iberia; the brides had to marry circumcised Jews. Clearly the founders intended to perpetuate their Spanish-Portuguese Jewish identity outside the peninsula.

Hebrew printing presses were active in Leghorn, particularly in the seventeenth and eighteenth centuries.[107] The community also had a number of eminent physicians, a Talmud Torah (elementary school), and some academies. The most eminent of these was *Los Sitibundos* (The Thirsty), in which members discussed topics from the fields of science, literature, and philosophy. A number of the Iberian conversos who arrived in Italy were also attracted to the art of polemics and apologetics, perhaps a reflection of a preoccupation with their Christian past. One polemicist was Eliahu Montalto, a Portuguese New Christian born in 1567 who had spent time in Antwerp, Bordeaux, Paris, Pisa, Florence, and Venice. He presumably received his most intensive Jewish education in Venice. This physician became a superb polemicist who basically wrote for his fellow conversos.[108] He and his fellow polemicists were troubled by the presence of members of the Nation who remained Christians. Thus, part of their intellectual efforts incorporated appeals in Spanish or Portuguese to their as yet unconvinced brethren. While part of the motivation of these theologians might have originated with challenges by Christians, their true aims were to strengthen those who had already joined them as Jews and to influence the undecided, in particular those who had already left Iberia but might not have chosen their final path.

Montalto represented the converso who had come to terms with his Jewishness and hoped to win over other members of the Nation. There was no ambiguity concerning Montalto's identity; he had clearly made his personal choice and most probably enjoyed his newly found freedom of expression. At the same time, he had decided not to maintain a low profile as a Jew since he felt it was his duty to facilitate the process for others to embrace Judaism. For those conversos who were educated, eloquent, and prolific, the art of polemics or apologetics provided a most appropriate outlet. A well-known example of a publication in this field is "Danielillo," a work that still has not been definitively defined, as it has been characterized as autobiographic, as a literary ploy, or possibly a combination of both.[109] A number of the accounts related in it are extremely similar to real-life occurrences, such as the story of disillusioned New Christians who were rejected from religious or military orders and left Iberia for Rome in the hope of obtaining a more favorable reception there. Ironically, in this story as well as in fact, some of them chose to convert to Judaism.[110]

Conversos like the author of "Danielillo" played an important role in the formation of the identity of conversos in diaspora communities. As a matter of fact, there were numerous intellectuals who sought a means of conveying their message to members of the Nation. Some of them attempted historiographical works, and not a few passed through or settled in Italy.[111] Their writings played a significant role in creating a modern Sephardi diaspora identity, which, by its broadest definition, would come to include conversos and non-conversos, namely, members of the Nation. An outstanding example of a converso with a historical awareness was Samuel Usque, who was previously mentioned in conjunction with Dona Gracia. The fact that his work *The Consolation for the Tribulations of Israel* was written in Portuguese rather than in Hebrew speaks for itself and clearly reveals the nature of the target audience. While written in the form of a dialogue, it attempted to implant a sense of history into the consciousness of the reader.

At the same time, an interesting figure named Alonso Núñez de Reinoso personified a converso intellectual who had left Iberia for Italy by 1550, but was not as certain of his personal path as were some of his fellow authors. Rose claims that the novel contained in the volume he published in Venice in 1552 is parallel to Usque's *Consolation* (1553)[112] but mirrors the author's personal dilemma and reflects "the mental confusion of a man who has left one country and cannot find peace in another."[113] Reinoso moved from Spain to Portugal and then spent time in Rome, Venice, and Ancona. He met up with, served as a tutor for, and was helped by the Nasi family, and he dedicated his poetry and novel to Don Yosef. There is a theory that he chose to dedicate his book to Don Yosef rather than to Dona Gracia because the former was still technically a Christian at this time while Gracia was living in Ferrara as a Jewess.[114] In this book, one perceives "a man of divided loyalties" rather than one of clear-cut faith.[115] Reinoso did not have the conviction of the members of the Mendes family, and his life seems to have been a saga of wandering and suffering.[116] By means of his writing, this converso appeared to be seeking pity and commiseration rather than to be attempting to guide his brethren. Some of his converso readers might have identified with the description of the hardships he faced, but the author did not seem to have attained peace of mind through his writing.[117] He provided neither guidance nor words of wisdom nor historical inspiration for his fellow conversos. While his identity personified a converso in many ways, he somehow seemed destined to continue suffering, using his writing as his mode of self-expression.

The Italian experience differed from that of the other western locales for a number of reasons. Each city offered its own regulations. The pope, whether dormant or active, was always looming in the background, although his proclivities as well as those of the local ruler's could change at a moment's notice depending upon the economic advantages to be gained from the converso presence. This Catholic country differed from its French Catholic neighbor, for the latter was ambivalent about a Jewish presence and dragged its feet as to whether or not to allow the Portuguese to openly profess Judaism. Like England, France struggled with the legal aspect of reentry, and both locales were quite slow to institute any change.

Whether the destination was a Catholic country such as France or Italy, or a Protestant one such as Holland or England, the conversos arriving in each locale faced different choices. In Holland, opting for Judaism was both acceptable and logical, while in England, conversos attended mass at Catholic embassy chapels in order to maintain the façade of Christianity. Although Dutch society was tolerant, the level of assimilation of Jews was rather low; perhaps the fact that the community quickly organized itself and strived to absorb as many of the former conversos as possible was the influential factor here. Although some were unable to adjust to this new lifestyle and its demands, the miracle is that the majority managed, willy-nilly, to conform and create an acceptable modus vivendi.

As we have seen, the fate of the conversos in France was varied; some assimilated, although those in Bayonne and Bordeaux seemed to have inculcated a fairly strong Sephardi identity, at least until the Napoleonic period. By contrast, the small community in London did not succeed in preventing a high rate of assimilation. While many of the members of the Nation retained economic and ethnic ties to their fellow members, they proceeded to socialize with and intermarry their Christian neighbors, steps which often led to conversion.

A look at the Italian experience uncovers a number of storybook characters. While each community history differed, by the end of the sixteenth century it was mostly the major ports that were offering protection and privileges to the Portuguese merchants. As the communities of Venice and Leghorn were achieving eminence, both commercially and as Jewish centers, various individuals were expressing their converso-ness in unusual and creative ways. Some blatantly overstepped the boundaries and found themselves facing the Papal Inquisition or the Venetian Inquisition. Some created literature for themselves or for their fellow conversos in the hope of either redeeming themselves or encouraging their brethren. Some baffled all who came in contact with them—straddling two worlds, dissembling, dissimulating, and simulating religions, lifestyles, and worlds. Others were able to move with relative ease from Judaizing to Judaism and served to inspire, as did the Nasi family.

Traumas were also part of the Italian experience, as in Ancona, although real and promising options eventually opened up to conversos who were seeking religious and commercial freedom. Although Venice saw more than its share of individuals who preferred not to live as ghetto Jews, the government there as well as in Leghorn allowed for clear choices, with no questions asked. Both of these communities were created by individuals who were able to commit themselves to Judaism. The converso identity was multifaceted, multicolored, and, at times, amorphous; yet at other times, commitment and decision accompanied a more clear-cut choice. In Italy in particular, examples can be found of cultural commuters, fuzzy Jews, straddlers, and the undecided alongside the decided. It is hard to imagine that the converso who left Iberia did not pass through at least one stage of uncertainty and/or face a serious dilemma in his or her lifetime. After all, this was the essence of the converso identity.

8

Modern Manifestations

The chronological leap undertaken here is intentional, and serves to allow for an examination of the question of converso identity from the other end of the spectrum through the encounter with modernity. In many respects, a discussion of the contemporary descendants of the conversos or the modern manifestation of converso identity is the most difficult of the topics under discussion. The primary factor at play here is the passage of time, which has resulted in distortions and lacunae in the historical time line. The three cases presented in this chapter have been chosen on the basis of availability of material and the effectiveness of drawing contrasts between them; this is not an exhaustive study of modern manifestations. Each case is different from the other because of separate historical experiences and the difficulties involved in verifying each specific experience. As stated, the goal of this chapter is to extend the investigation of the notion of identity into the twenty-first century, although the resulting product might be akin to a mosaic missing some essential pieces.

Each of these groups can be traced to or claims to have originated with the mass conversions of the fourteenth and fifteenth centuries. The historical developments concerning the first group under discussion, the Chuetas of Majorca, can be outlined fairly accurately. The second group, the conversos of Belmonte, is presumed to be made up of descendants of the victims of the 1497 forced conversions whose ancestors contended with the Portuguese Tribunal in the sixteenth century. The third of these modern manifestations deals with the descendants of conversos in the Southwest region of the United States, whose origins date to sixteenth-century Mexico and the arrival of the Spanish conquistadors and their entourages. This last category is by far the most difficult to define as a group and, as we will see, is also the hardest to characterize. I will attempt, however, to discover how these individuals view themselves as well as how they are perceived by the surrounding society as they engage in their search for identity. This task will prove to be complex and, most probably, not entirely satisfying, but nonetheless extremely interesting, especially as one compares and contrasts these three different experiences.

The history of the conversos of Majorca began with the forced conversions of 1391 but then deviated from the "classic" converso experience, partly because these conversos were not directly affected by the waves of conversion that occurred in the wake of the Disputation of Tortosa or by the final wave of conversions in 1492. Be that as it may, at the end of the fourteenth century, there was tension between the municipal council of the city of Majorca and the villagers, who were heavily in debt at the time. Because the government feared that this unrest would precipitate mass riots and attacks on the Jews, it opted to take preventive measures. Thus, in July 1391, the Jews who lived in villages were evacuated and relocated to urban surroundings. Unfortunately, this proved to be little more than a stopgap measure, for the wrath of the locals was only restrained until August. According to Baer, despite serious attempts to calm the masses and to protect this minority group from attack, about three hundred Jews were killed; some eight hundred managed to escape to a fortress while others fled to Algiers and other African destinations. At the same time, Baer is convinced that "there is reason to believe that the baptisms began on the same day."[1]

As this state of unrest continued, the government feared a general revolt, knowing that the dissatisfaction was directed at itself as well as at the Jews. In October, the masses demanded the release of those Jews who were still being protected in the fortress in order to force them to choose between death and conversion. These demands appear to have been met, since Baer alludes to a list of 111 converts during the month of October, although obtaining precise numbers of martyrs or converts is a nearly impossible task. For example, there were individuals who fled to Algiers and then returned in order to get their families, while others chose to remain there.[2] There are records showing that about 150 from Portugal joined the community a few years later.[3]

After 1391, it appears that some of the converts were able to assimilate into the host society, although the majority remained together as a separate community. Because the conversos were technically Christians, they could consider organizing their own guilds; by 1404 they had successfully done so, and within a decade they received legal and religious approval. According to Kenneth Moore, "The guild allowed the Jews to do publicly and with approval what they had always done by religious tradition and custom: live together communally."[4] Moore, who refers to the conversos as Jews, claims that the guild appeared to be a professional organization but in reality was little more than a replica of the *aljama* (Jewish community) that continued to offer social services. While social benefits were part of any guild's arrangement for its members, in this case the benefits were allotted to all members of "the Nation," even if they were not from Majorca.[5] This is an additional example of a broad definition of membership based solely on the converso experience.

In 1435, as the result of a blood libel-child murder accusation, there occurred a historical aberration unique to Majorca. This accusation created a frenzy on the Balearic island that was overwhelming. The end result was that all of the remaining Jews succumbed to conversion, and Judaism was declared illegal. Consequently, unlike their brethren in Castile and Aragon, the conversos of Majorca had no Jewish community by their side during the fifty-seven years prior to the expulsion. Interestingly enough, Moore claims that as of 1435, both intermarriage with Old Christians and assimilation into Christian society were feasible options for these converts, at least until the end of the seventeenth century.[6]

Despite these historical differences, the conversos of Majorca had to contend with the Inquisition as did their fellow conversos on the mainland. Proceedings against them began in 1488 and continued through 1536. Each time there was a grace period, hundreds of conversos confessed and sought reconciliation. For example, in 1488, 335 penitents appeared before the court; after an incredibly short time, that is to say, between 1491 and 1493, 320 of them reappeared in the court along with 136 "new" penitents. Surprisingly, the members of the first group were not condemned to the stake, although they should have been because they were second-time offenders. During the first two decades of the sixteenth century, nearly a hundred more conversos sought reconciliation with the church. At the same time, between 1488 and 1500, the number of conversos burned alive at the stake appears to have been less than thirty. By contrast, during this same period, those burned in effigy because they had fled and disappeared, namely, 232 conversos, far outnumbered those burned alive. In the following period, between 1500 and 1536, the number of heretics burned alive at the stake increased to more than 50, while those burned in effigy were slightly fewer than before, numbering 219. In the long run, about 15 percent of the victims at autos-da-fé were burned at the stake; the remainder was burned in effigy because they were either deceased or absent. Since the property of all heretics, dead, alive, or in absentia, was subject to confiscation, there was serious property loss involved here.[7] After 1536, the Inquisition did not pursue conversos as heretics again for over a century, until 1675.

What transpired during these interim years? Did the inquisitorial activity against conversos diminish in Majorca because that was the general trend in Spain? Were the Old Christians cognizant of the New Christian presence? Were the New Christians still Judaizing for over a century despite the fact that so many reconciliations were recorded?

Because little information is available concerning these issues other than proceedings of the Holy Tribunal, it is hard to determine what was or was not happening when the courts were not seeking to prosecute conversos suspected of Judaizing. Braunstein is convinced that the revival of trials against Judaizers at the end of the seventeenth century "is conclusive proof of the fact that there remained a considerable group, descendants of those Jews embracing Christianity in 1435, who remembered and observed some of the beliefs and practices of the old Mosaic law which years before they had promised to abjure."[8] It is important to note that in 1624, the inquisitor general issued an Edict of Faith that included detailed descriptions of Judaizing to enable informers to identify heretics and to offer information to the court. Despite this attempt to whet the appetites of prospective informers and enemies of the conversos, no trials ensued, apparently due to lack of information. It is difficult to know if this occurred because the New Christians were indeed good and faithful Christians, or if the social separation between the groups did not allow prospective informers ample access to the world of the Judaizer. In earlier trials on the mainland, the presence of servants proved to be a major source of information on crypto-Jewish life, but because the socioeconomic situation was very different here and the conversos were not as affluent, these in-house informers were not available. The conversos lived in their own section of the city, on the whole married among themselves, and were perceived by many as clannish. Because they resided in a segregated portion of the city, one might have expected to discover intermittent outbreaks of violence as expressions of hostility,[9] but this was not necessarily the case.

Interestingly, because these conversos had been Christian for so long, it has been said that by the seventeenth century, they came to see themselves as "Old Christians" by their own standards and that they were proud of their "purity of blood," their wealth, and their prosperity; if this is so, they might well have been perceived as pretentious.[10] On the other hand, Moore claims that assimilation and intermarriage with Old Christians was not uncommon between 1435 and 1678.[11] While this might have occurred, it does not seem to have been the rule. Braunstein argues that because of their experience with the Inquisition, these conversos developed a group consciousness that paralleled the exclusiveness of the Old Christians, "who increasingly refused to marry with them."[12] Whether the Old Christians refused to marry them or whether they preferred endogamy, the general sense was that in Majorca, "the forced conversion of 1435 changed little in the Jewish community apart from outward appearances."[13]

In other words, the conversos of Majorca remained an identifiable group, living separately and being perceived as well as perceiving themselves as different. The extent of their Judaizing is unknown, and most likely what remained was an atrophied religion at best, although a strong sense of group integrity and common destiny seem to have tied them together. Braunstein writes of their meticulousness in supervising marriage arrangements, their communal mourning when one of their members died, and their basic religious common stance, including a belief in monotheism, the Messiah, dietary laws, fast days, and prayers aiming to communicate with the God of Israel.[14] This common sense of destiny emerged clearly in the 1670s and 1680s, once again as the result of inquisitorial activity.

At this time, information was obtained by the Inquisition that led to a series of developments that were to create a snowball effect. In 1674 and 1675, indictments were drawn up that led to 237 arrests in 1677; these activities resulted in a startling discovery: the realization that a great deal of Judaizing had been occurring in the community; the Inquisition referred to this phenomenon as the "Conspiracy of 1678." There was an auto-da-fé in 1677, followed by five more in 1679, and between 1680 and 1688, a series of posthumous trials were conducted. Some conversos managed to flee, although in 1688 one group was less fortunate. Its doomed flight via an English vessel was thwarted because of terrible weather conditions, and in the interim the Inquisition discovered the plan. This fiasco led to mass arrests and more trials that were concluded by 1691 with the condemnation of eighty-six conversos, over half of whom were women.[15] These trials were characterized by a "vicious circle of confessions and denunciations,"[16] and expanded the dimensions of the "Conspiracy of 1678." Sources of information about this conspiracy range from reports from the Jewish community of Leghorn concerning the Jewishness of the Majorcans to testimonies from informers and traitors. Many of the defendants, hoping to be granted reconciliation, offered streamlined confessions. At the same time, the comprehensive confiscations that took place during this period were rather devastating. Needless to say, this series of persecutions was to have long-lasting effects on the converso community. As a matter of fact, a new nickname for the conversos came into use in 1688. This proud group that had considered itself superior to the Old Christians was now referred to as "the Chuetas of the Street," residents of the neighborhood (*barrio*) of Sagell; according to Selke, pointing to them as New Christians of Jewish descent was equivalent to a "total inversion of their status within the Old-Christian society."[17]

It is not easy to assess the ultimate effect that this bout with the Inquisition had on the community. Moore believes that the confiscations and autos-da-fé "finally broke the will of the Conversos, and organized crypto-Judaism became little more than an awareness of Jewishness among a stigmatized ethnic community."[18] Braunstein, on the other hand, is less fatalistic, concluding that "the Conversos were decisively subdued, but it should not be imagined that they were exterminated."[19] He points to the way in which the Church perpetuated the memory of these martyrs or heretics, literally keeping this memory alive by the display of *sanbenitos* in the Dominican churches and "perpetuating the infamy of the heretics."[20] In the Church of Santo Domingo, there is a picture on canvas of *The Fifteen Ancestral Families of Chuetas*; people would come to this church expressly to see the *sanbenitos* and the portraits of the condemned, even as late as the nineteenth century.[21] Thus, the Chuetas were stigmatized and often perceived as having a pariah status. According to Selke, who describes them as having been pretentious prior to 1691, they now felt despondent and abandoned and had lost their sense of superiority.[22] Yet in Moore's opinion, as "practicing Catholics, the Xuetas [*sic*] continued to play the *role* of Jews."[23] The stigma they bore was a direct result of the numerous condemnations by the Inquisition, and all the Chuetas, whether or not they or their families had been tried or condemned, were actually included in this category.[24]

There is evidence that shows how the stigma was perpetuated in print. An example can be found in the writings of the Jesuit priest P. Francisco Garau, rector of Montesión College, who was an official witness at the four public autos-da-fé in 1691 that ended with the *Cremadissa* (The Great Cremation). His account, entitled *La Fe Triunfante en quatro autos*, was published that very same year and continued to be circulated as late as 1931. This publication contained "a mixture of fanaticism, unctuous pietism and raw sadism together with [such] a perversion of the precepts of Christians ethics,"[25] and succeeded in perpetuating an incredibly negative image of the Chuetas.[26]

As a result, one can establish that the Chuetas as a group represent a creation more or less dating to the end of the seventeenth century; their identity was a given, and whether or not one was a sincere Catholic did not seem to carry weight. The fact that Majorca remained preindustrial despite the technological advances made on the mainland helped to freeze this seemingly medieval state of affairs. In 1773, King Charles III was petitioned by the Chuetas to remove various disabilities and discriminatory statutes from which they suffered. This request agitated their antagonists, who began to circulate anti-Chueta literature and subsequently succeeded in closing the University of Palma to members of this despised group. Oddly enough, the Chuetas never considered leaving their homeland because, despite everything, they viewed themselves as devoted Majorcans. At any rate, between 1782 and 1788, the king finally granted their requests, albeit gradually, in three stages, and in effect officially ended legal discrimination against them.

In 1808, the invasion of Napoleon created problems for the conversos, which included attacks on their neighborhood; the assumption here is that the Chuetas essentially served as a scapegoat.[27] In 1877 a book dealing with the ostracism of the Chuetas was published by a priest named José Taronji who, surprisingly, attempted to criticize and attack existing prejudice.[28] According to Moore, except for a few individuals who were intellectually or commercially integrated, the Chuetas "were at the beginning of the twentieth century still a pariah society, over 95 percent endogamous, occupationally distinctive and the bearers of many traditions of Jewish community life, integrated into the forms of an urban Majorcan neighborhood."[29]

When Braunstein investigated the Chuetas in the 1930s, he stated emphatically, "Nowhere in Spain has the identity of a small group been preserved so tenaciously over such a long period of time as in Majorca."[30] In his opinion, this group was isolated as the long-term result of inquisitorial activity. Braunstein claimed to be able to identify approximately three hundred families in the Chueteria whose members were treated despicably by the rest of society, even called names in the streets at times, and who still rarely intermarried with the Old Christians.[31]

Ultimately, developments in the twentieth century would change Majorcan society and inadvertently improve the status of the Chuetas. The growth of tourism in the 1950s not only improved the economy of the island but led to its modernization.[32] According to Moore, it brought about a reorganization of society and "set the ghetto Xuetas free."[33] The population of Palma more than tripled between 1900 and 1960 due to immigration. Ironically, the presence of these non-Majorcans, unencumbered by ancient prejudices and distinctions, precipitated serious changes in Majorcan society. Marriage was no longer based on whether one was Chueta or non-Chueta, but rather on modern criteria. Thus, the community that in 1910 had been characterized by 85–90 percent endogamous marriages underwent drastic changes: By 1960, only 20 percent of the Chuetas were marrying fellow Chuetas. Unofficial statistics refer to the presence of 10,000–15,000 Chuetas on the island in 1978 out of a total population of 525,000, but these numbers are hard to verify. Fifteen family names are considered to be pure Chueta, forming the main reference base of the community, based on the "Quince Linajes,"[34] the fifteen ancestral families on the island. Moore insists that they no longer suffer from stigmas, public insults, or residence restrictions. "However, the awareness of Chueta identity is vivid, and is still of enormous consequence in day-to-day interaction in the city and throughout the island."[35]

If outside forces are no longer at work, how can this identity be expressed? These Chuetas are by no means practicing Jews, but they still retain a sense of Jewishness. Some are proud of their past while others are ashamed, but either stance reflects an awareness of who their ancestors were. Moore refers to "Jewish cultural patterns" and kinship ties that express a "Chueta-ness."[36]

Thus, despite changes that seem to have precipitated due to the rising rate of intermarriage with non-Chuetas, a "Chueta-ness" remains in the consciousness of the descendants of the conversos of Majorca. Despite the passage of centuries, a sense of membership in the Nation is deeply ingrained in their being. The fifteen family lineages are still known and can be identified in modern Majorca; the repercussions of the Inquisition succeeded in outlasting the institution itself. While the Chuetas are not Jews, they still identify with the Jewish people and see themselves as different, although they prefer not to reveal themselves or to discuss their origins. Nevertheless, Gloria Mound, the founder of *Casa Shalom*, the Institute for Marrano-Anusim Studies, has established contacts with descendants of conversos on the Balearic Islands. In addition to discovering secret synagogues and some documents, she has been organizing an annual Passover *Seder* for *Chuetas* (or descendants of conversos) on the island of Ibiza. In the long run, the product of a enforced separateness and a voluntary separateness has resulted in an odd phenomenon. Moore writes, "Chuetas do have great pride in their origins. They are very defensive and protective of their own. At the same time they want to see the designation Chueta disappear in Majorcan society."[37] This conflict accurately reflects their continuing problem concerning their identity as well as the internal and external conflicts that have been perpetuated in Majorca over the centuries.

The descendants of conversos in Belmonte, Portugal, were also perceived as an identifiable group, both from within and from without, although they rarely openly admitted their roots. Like the Chuetas, they too have been considered as outsiders, and even the sincere Catholics among them were relegated to this status. Likewise, their religious observances would be classified as atrophied, again due to the passage of time and the difficulty involved in maintaining secrecy for so many centuries. Nevertheless, a sense of common destiny and identification with the Jewish people somehow has prevailed in both groups. In addition, the role of the Inquisition was significant in each case. In Majorca the stigma of Judaizing in the past kept the Chuetas apart from the others, while in Belmonte the fear of the Inquisition played a major psychological role that was central to the formation of the identity and religion of the crypto-Jews there. However, the encounter with modernity was to have very different consequences for each group: In Majorca it facilitated the disintegration of endogamy, while in Belmonte new and unexpected directions were taken.

Relatively little is known of the early history of this community other than the existence of a stone from a synagogue with Hebrew inscriptions that can be dated to 1297.[38] Presumably, Spanish exiles crossing the border settled in this northern village at the end of the fifteenth century, increasing the size of the local Jewish community, which would soon be transformed by the forced conversions of 1497. There are records of trials of the Portuguese Inquisition of Judaizers from Belmonte as well as from the neighboring villages; these trials created a deep-seated fear of the Inquisition, which influenced the lives of these crypto-Jews for centuries to follow. One can discern an awareness of the danger of observing that was incorporated into many of the observances themselves. Thus, for example, when the women prayed inside their homes, the men stationed themselves outside as guards, playing cards so that no one would suspect any unusual activity.[39] Likewise, Yom Kippur and Passover were intentionally observed on the wrong day, after the prescribed date, on the assumption that no one would suspect or anticipate such a ploy.

In Portugal, the legal power of the Inquisition was ended between 1768 and 1774 by the Marquis of Pombal (supposedly of New Christian descent), and the Inquisition was officially abolished in 1821. In a report published in 1926, Lucien Wolf concluded, "The truth is that the Pombal reforms found the Marranos exhausted by their long struggle and quite satisfied to be relieved of the daily terror of the Inquisition, even at the cost of being still condemned to the secret observance of their religion. The exhaustion was both spiritual and material."[40] Thus, at the end of the eighteenth century, the lives of these descendants were characterized by the same crypto-Judaism and the same in-grained fears as before, for the psychological mindset of these individuals had not undergone any change.

Although the Jews of Lisbon received permission to build a synagogue in 1902, they clearly were not interested in the New Christians, whom they considered to be more or less like other baptized Catholics. The truth is that any interference on the part of the Jews would have been risky, for the Church would not have appreciated meddling with its Catholic population, and the Jewish community was not strong enough to consider such ventures. At this time, some publications made references to descendants of Jews,[41] and after the establishment of the Republic in 1910, there was evidence of some interest in the Portuguese conversos.[42] After Nahum Slouscz's visits to the area, in 1912 and again in 1925, he wrote a Hebrew book on the topic in which he mentioned New Christians from Belmonte who joined the community in Amsterdam in the seventeenth century.[43]

Crypto-Jews made a great impression upon Samuel Schwarz, a Polish mining engineer living and working in Portugal, after he met some of them in 1917. His book about them, a mixture of serious research and apologetics, was published in Portuguese in 1926 and created a surge of interest in these crypto-Jews.[44] Yet the crypto-Jewish tradition of Belmonte was jealously guarded and revealed only after gaining the complete trust of the outsider. Schwartz wrote that the crypto-Jews' "knowledge of Judaism has been transmitted throughout the generations orally and secretly; and secrecy has come to be endowed with the same sanction and sanctity as any other detail of their rites and ceremonies. Consequently they consider it now as an essential element in the Jewish faith, and they are astounded to learn of Jews who make no profession of hiding their faith from their non-Jewish neighbors."[45] The engineer found it difficult to study them and their customs, despite the fact that he was a Jew in their eyes, because of their deep sense of distrust, fear, and secrecy.[46] As we will see, this insistence upon secrecy proved hard to relinquish.

At any rate, Schwarz recorded the surviving customs and prayers to which he had been made privy only after he had succeeded in proving his Jewishness to them.[47] The women leaders were loath to acknowledge that anyone unknown to them might be Jewish. However, once Schwarz recited the *Shema* prayer ("Hear, O Israel") for them, they recognized the word *Adonay* ("the Lord"), apparently the only Hebrew word they knew; this word magically opened their doors for him. It should be noted that the Judaizers' encounter with this "genuine" Jew precipitated a period of turmoil, exposure, and substantial outside interest. For example, a plan for a school for Jews and crypto-Jews in Lisbon was suggested, although there were those who claimed that the Lisbon Jews, seeking outside aid, added the converso element only because they lacked funding for their own children's education.[48] It turns out that in 1925, the two chief rabbis of Israel considered how to determine the legal status of the New Christians. They ruled that technically they were to be recognized as Jews, but this ruling applied only to those who were ready to become Jews, although each case was to be adjudicated on an individual basis. Most were as yet unwilling to expose themselves to the outside world.[49]

Schwarz and others noted that most of their observances centered on the Sabbath, Yom Kippur, and Passover; there were also some secret marriage and burial rites. Little to no Hebrew knowledge had survived except for a few key words, although numerous Portuguese prayers were recited by heart by the women. The engineer commented, "I was surprised, however, to learn that it was the women-folk, especially the old women, who knew the prayers in their entirety by heart, who recited them in the communal gathering, and who in fact presided over their Jewish religious rites and ceremonies."[50] Canelo refers to them as "women-priestesses" who "nourish the religion of the community" and who served as "faithful guardians of the tradition."[51] In fact, all those who gained access to this world commented upon the unusual role of the women. In the film made by Fredric Brenner, *The Last Marranos* (1991), one can clearly see them in charge of the Passover preparations, and only they knew and recited all the prayers in the Belmonte repertoire.[52]

The Sabbath was marked by lighting lamps in which only pure olive oil was used. The lamps contained special linen "prayer wicks" made of seven strands that had been painstakingly prepared by the older women; the wicks were also prepared for Yom Kippur as well. During preparation, the name of God was mentioned seventy-two times while the special prayer itself was recited seventy-three times![53] The only Sabbath days when they did not work were the four prior to the holidays of Yom Kippur and Passover. During the Sabbath day, meals were usually cold and meatless, so that cooking was avoided. No meat would be eaten for thirty days before Yom Kippur. Prior to this fast, which they called the *Dia Grande* or *Dia Puro*, they rinsed their mouths three times, asked forgiveness of one another, and prepared the breakfast meal that ended this day. As in normative Judaism, most of the day was devoted to prayer, although in Belmonte, the women generally led the prayers; a leader chanted out loud while the others whispered in response.

Another observance, the fast of Esther, was no longer related to the forgotten holiday of Purim, but rather marked a month before Passover. The Jewish heroine had been transformed into Saint Esther and was considered to be a pillar of their religion.[54] Here is the first of many examples of syncretism and unusual combinations of Catholicism and Judaism that occurred in this community. Passover, the most elaborate of the celebrations, was observed a month after the actual holiday in order not to be detected. During this festival, no bread, pork, meat, or coffee was consumed. The unleavened bread intentionally was not prepared until the third night; presumably no one would suspect them of baking it at such a late date. The women recited prayers as they baked thick matzoh which was to be eaten only during the holiday. (Each year, a ball of cooked dough would be set aside and saved along with those of previous years.) At this time, the Judaizers were barefoot, and the men and women dressed in white robes and sheets respectively. A traditional picnic would be held on the last day of Passover at which time the whole community would take olive branches down to the river. They used the branches to beat the water as part of the symbolic reenactment of the parting of the Red Sea, while reciting the "Water Prayer"; dancing would follow. This was the only organized communal activity throughout the year.[55]

When a member of the community died, the body was washed as per Jewish law. The family of mourners gave alms en route to the cemetery, discarded the water in the house, covered mirrors, sat on low benches, burned an oil lamp for seven days, and prayed three times a day. They also gave alms after the funeral as well as throughout the year, refrained from eating meat, and fasted on the eighth and thirtieth days and then every three months.[56] At wedding ceremonies, an old woman placed the hand of the groom on that of the bride and tied a kerchief around them while she offered a blessing. Preceding the ceremony, provided the groom and bride were of Jewish heritage, a fast was observed by the bride and two of her friends as well as the groom and two of his friends.

As we have seen, their lifestyle also reflects manifestations of syncretism to which they were oblivious and that they never viewed as contradictory or threatening. In addition to their veneration of the aforementioned Saint or Holy Queen Esther, they recited the Pater Noster, albeit without the christological ending, included a prayer for Saint Rafael, and turned to the angel of protection in many of their own prayers. They decorated the Torah scroll with artificial flowers, clearly a Church-influenced innovation.[57] They loved and venerated "holy little Moses" and the Holy Queen Esther and displayed pictures of these figures and the "Guardian Angel" in their homes.[58] They observed Ascension Thursday, the Feast of Corpus Christi, and *Natalinho* (Minor Christmas). (This last holiday was celebrated "eleven days from the new moon of December" and seems to be connected to Christmas or possibly Hanukkah.) Yet they never seriously considered immersing themselves in Catholicism, basically because they harbored a deep hatred for the church.[59]

This brief survey of Belmonte observances leaves questions as well as many gaping holes concerning observance of the wide spectrum of Jewish customs and laws. For instance, dietary laws and kosher slaughtering practices seem to have fallen by the wayside.[60] The prayers in their repertoire were far removed from those in any Jewish prayer book, and many holidays, such as Sukkot, Shavuot, Rosh Hashana, Tisha B'Av, Hanukah, and Purim, did not survive the test of time. As Lucien Wolf reported, after meeting crypto-Jews from various villages in Portugal, there was "no evidence that they have any very definite idea of Jewish doctrine and ethics, and it is certain that they know nothing of Jewish history outside the Bible and certain stories of the Inquisition."[61]

In short, from the end of the fifteenth century until the twentieth century, it is not known if these individuals had contact with Jews, with Jewish literature, or with any other manifestations of normative Judaism. The above descriptions by their "discoverer" Samuel Schwarz or by others who managed to infiltrate their world in the 1920s and 1930s or even in the 1960s reflect the presence of a closed, endogamic, and somewhat paranoid group that considered itself to be the paragon of Judaism. Schwarz began to envision himself as a godfather of sorts and aspired to bring them back to Judaism. Although he had ties to the community in Lisbon, the two groups made no real connection. The urban Jews were very concerned about their own precarious position as the first recognized Jewish entity in Portuguese society since the end of the fifteenth century, and in 1925 the Lisbon community refused to bury a New Christian in its cemetery, for fear of Church reprisal. In 1928, the chief rabbi of Israel approved the burial of another descendant in a separate area, but again there was opposition.[62] No real integration into the Jewish world had as yet taken place.

Essentially the Belmonte community had mastered the art of living in two worlds simultaneously, adopting two mentalities, both of which were normative for them. This was not a case of cultural commuting, nor was it an example of a ship with two rudders. This cognitive dissonance did not perturb them, for they were able to separate the Catholic world from the crypto-Jewish one without apparent difficulty. The twentieth-century Judaizers, like their brethren of the seventeenth and eighteenth centuries, had assimilated into and were involved in Portuguese society on many levels. Yet the Old Christians still knew precisely who the New Christians were, and often referred to them as Jews despite the fact that they knew they were baptized Catholics who prayed in Church alongside them for centuries. As a result, they maintained a culture among themselves that was both transmitted by memory and influenced by trauma.[63]

At this time, Professor Adolfo Benarus of the Lisbon community appealed to the Anglo-Jewish Association to help them arrest the deterioration of this community and to help restore its former glory. A proposal was suggested to set up a boarding school for the "Marrano" youth in Lisbon, since the older generation was considered to be "hopeless."[64] The Alliance Israélite Universelle and the Spanish-Portuguese Jews' Congregation in London were included in the deliberations; a decision was made to finance a four-week exploratory visit for Lucien Wolf, who set forth for Portugal in January 1926. This British Jew visited six villages and met with Jews in Lisbon as well as with the president and prime minister of Portugal.[65] In his assessment, Wolf was not as pessimistic regarding the fate of the older generation and recommended investing in institutions in Porto rather than in Lisbon because of the distance of the capital (at least 150 miles) from these villages; in this way access to them as well as to an education would be more realistic.[66]

The appearance on the scene of Arthur Carlos Barros Basto at this time serves to accentuate the complexity of the situation. Basto's grandfather revealed his Jewish roots to his grandson at the age of nine, but this boy, born in Porto in 1887, had essentially grown up outside the converso community.[67] He had attained the status of hero as a captain in the army of the Revolution of 1910 and eventually chose to be circumcised in Tangier (Spanish Morocco), where he continued the study of Hebrew and Judaism that he had begun in Lisbon. Upon his return as Ben-Rosh, he married a Jewish woman from Lisbon, and in 1923 he established a Jewish community in Porto. Four years later, he began to publish Ha-Lapid (The Torch) in Portuguese; this publication represented an attempt to introduce and expose the conversos to general Jewish knowledge and to assorted related topics of interest. This newsletter was the editor's personal publication and had a Zionist angle; some felt it also had a messianic egocentric overtone.[68] Concurrently, Ben-Rosh adapted Menasseh Ben Israel's Tesouro dos Dinim in order to provide his brethren with access to the halakhic world. He also made available a Brazilian book, The Rudiments of Judaism, and Paul Goodman's The History of the Jews.[69] He took it upon himself to translate prayers as well as the Haggadah into Portuguese, for it was clear to him "that the times of fear and dissembling of the inquisitorial and clerical eras having passed, an overt, normative Judaism without reservations or fear should be embraced."[70] Cecil Roth referred to him as an "apostle" of the Marranos, a term that Basto adopted, most likely, as Stuczynski suspects, because of his Catholic upbringing and the "anthroposophical leaning of his youth."[71]

Barros Basto was a proselytizer who called his work "redemption." He estimated the number of potential returnees to Judaism to be in the tens of thousands.[72] This number probably included every descendant of every New Christian, regardless of whether that descendant had any awareness of or interest in his or her ancestry. Schwarz tossed out some figures as well. For example, he claimed that half of the 20,000 residents of Covilhan and that 6,000 of Belmonte's residents were New Christians; he referred to the existence of 10,000 families in Portugal in 1926.[73] Whereas Schwarz advocated turning Lisbon into an educational center with the expectation that the younger generation would then return home as "missionaries," Basto was not convinced that this was the wisest path to take. In truth, the relationship between the two men was complex and not always clear, but Stuczynski refers to an unspoken division of labor between them. In other words, Basto dealt with the northernmost villages such as Porto and Tras Os Montes, while Schwarz moved in the eastern region, which included Belmonte. In this particular case, Wolf decided to support Basto's preference for a local center, a decision that was not received kindly in Lisbon.[74]

At this time, Basto was already ensconced in Porto, where there was a one-room synagogue serving the seventeen European families already there along with four New Christian families. This leader hoped to convert Porto into "the religious lighthouse of the Portuguese Marranos," and in 1927, he traveled about in the company of ritual circumcisers in the hope of gaining new recruits. The Church and various Christian organizations were not happy about these developments.[75] In addition, Salazar, the dictator who came to power in 1927, was not pleased to learn about the activities of this war hero decorated by the republic that he had toppled.[76] Yet according to Canelo, "[A]ll seemed to be well on its way for the conversion, en masse, of the Crypto-Jews scattered throughout Portugal."[77] Two Torah scrolls were sent to Porto in 1926, and twenty-five Portuguese prayer books arrived there in 1927. In 1928, a plot of land was bought in order to construct a more serious synagogue, and the cornerstone of *Mekor Haim* was laid the following year. Funding came from the three aforementioned organizations as well as from other communities such as Vienna, Manchester, New York, Philadelphia, Berlin, and Munich.[78] At first, a good portion of the funding was provided by Baron Edmond de Rothschild of Paris; the Kadoories of Shanghai, who came to visit in 1933, facilitated the completion of the synagogue in 1938. It should be noted that at the opening ceremony, most of the three hundred people in attendance were not New Christians.

Basto also requested the establishment of a theological institute for training Jewish religious teachers, and he opened a yeshiva named *Rosh Pinah* with five students, three of whom were from Belmonte. Stampfer points out that most of the students came from towns in the north, including Belmonte, Braganza, Covilha, and Lagoaca.[79] Amilcar Paulo, who published in *Ha-Lapid*, collected prayers and descriptions of observances in the Tras-os Monte area, and later researched and published about this community, was also a student in this institute. This yeshiva, however, proved to be the downfall of Basto, for his methods were rather unorthodox, to say the least. There is no doubt that Basto's style was somewhat egocentric and rather authoritative. His emphasis was not exactly halakhic, and many visitors to the yeshiva received the impression that he was functioning as the leader of a sect. This was not the aim or intent of the investors, although one must keep in mind the fact that all the outsiders had their own interpretations of what constituted "authentic Judaism." Objections were raised both on the local scene and from afar, mostly due to disagreement over how to implement changes in the world of the conversos. Most likely the fact that these New Christians were from remote villages, often illiterate and deeply rooted in Portuguese society, did not help.[80]

In 1933, Leon Cassuto, who was to become president of the congregation, arrived from Hamburg together with his son, Afonso, who became a teacher at the theological institute. This was, at first, a positive development, as long as Basto worked together with them. Eventually, however, problems and frictions ensued and created a schism in a community that already suffered from a lack of sufficient funds and inconsistent leadership.[81] There were problems with the Dutch pro-Marranos committee, including its appointment of a cantor-teacher named Jacob Shebabo whom the committee moved from place to place. A feud erupted between London and Amsterdam, and the president of the committee, Van Son, attacked Basto and the London committee in circulars.[82] This divisiveness prepared the way for destructiveness; Basto was brought to trial in 1935 on charges of inappropriate conduct at his own yeshiva. There are those who claim that the trial was the direct outcome of a visit by a priest to the yeshiva, for this visitor later reported that Basto supposedly engaged in homosexual activity and performed circumcisions without a license. Others are convinced that internal enemies within the community fabricated these accusations.

These claims were never proven, yet Basto was never acquitted nor was his name cleared. The army became involved and court-martialed him on the grounds of immorality; consequently, the proud captain was demoted. Stuczynski summarizes his demise: "Attacked and discredited for his arbitrary religious-educational conduct by certain influential members of the Lisbon Jewish community, by the Dutch pro-Marrano Committee (1929) in the person of Mordechai Van Son and by several rabbinical authorities who observed the 'Obra de Resgate' in person, he was finally judged on the basis of accusations by members of his own communal milieu."[83] This sad chapter in converso history has been compared to that of Dreyfus, but the comparison is not really applicable since those who stirred up the trouble were Barro's own kinsmen.[84] Unfortunately, most if not all of the yeshiva students left Portugal for Brazil, where they eventually married Catholic wives. Although discredited, dishonored, and bankrupt, Basto continued to visit various New Christian communities until 1946. He managed to continue the publication of Ha-Lapid until 1958, when the last issue, number 156, appeared. He died three years later.

The political situation in Europe before and after the trial—namely, the rise of the dictator Salazar in Portugal and the troubling developments in Germany—seriously affected the fate of these crypto-Jews. It was as though the attention of world Jewry was now demanded elsewhere, and as a result, the community that had never sought attention or recognition almost naturally reverted to its previous modus vivendi. As Stuczynski explains, "The rise of Nazism, the Holocaust and the creation of the State of Israel, together with the fear of displaying any religious difference in Salazar's Portugal, brought with them a thick veil of silence and voluntary forgetfulness, as if nothing had occurred years before."[85] From 1939 until 1948, the community seems to have been cut off from outside contact. According to Canelo, the rural mentality, the active role of the Catholic Church, and the perpetuation of the "religious fear," together with the anti-Semitism of the 1930s and a distrust of the Barros Basto movement in Porto, made these individuals "even more" crypto-Jewish.[86] The three decades to follow, however, would see some renewed attempts to strengthen the community.

For example, in 1963, Steinhardt noted the presence of a few Belmonte conversos who had come to the Lisbon synagogue for services on Yom Kippur. During their conversation, the Judaizers unexpectedly invited him to visit them and to meet other "members of the Nation" in their village.[87] The use of this particular term by Judaizers in twentieth-century Iberia clearly demonstrates that this community still used the frame of reference identical to that of their ancestors of the sixteenth and seventeenth centuries. The identity of the descendants of these conversos continued to be a function of belonging to the Nation, regardless of historical developments and changes.

After his visit, Steinhardt realized that the turmoil following the activities of Schwarz and Barros Basto had created considerable confusion and tension in the community, especially in terms of how to relate to the old versus the new. He emphasized that extreme care must be taken on the part of anyone hoping to introduce or reintroduce the Portuguese conversos to normative Judaism.[88] The complexity of the converso identity in Belmonte made it difficult to define the religious status of these Judaizers and presented an even greater challenge to anyone hoping to lead them into the Judaism of modernity.

At this time, Novinsky, a Brazilian historian, and Paulo, the former student, also visited Belmonte.[89] From their comments one can surmise that the crypto-Jewish observance and lifestyle there had barely changed in thirty years. As before, the old women still knew all the prayers by rote. "They consider themselves purer than the Jews from Porto or Lisbon, who, according to what they have heard, practice the religion of Moses in a 'falsified' manner."[90] Beginning in 1974, some contact with outside Jews was made, perhaps as the result of a newly acquired sense of security vis-à-vis religious freedom in Portugal. This contact consisted of an occasional visit to the Lisbon synagogue and a visit by a few of the younger members of the community to Israel in the 1970s, yet no substantive changes or influences seemed to have transpired.

In 1988, however, a change did occur when a group of young men from Belmonte became very enthusiastic about the State of Israel. Molho contends that they were not Zionists but rather perceived Israel as akin to the celestial Jerusalem. Although it is somewhat odd that their epiphany came about forty years after the establishment of the state, this appears to have been the moving force.[91] Consequently, they decided to form a non-profit organization in order to obtain a legal status for themselves; eventually this would evolve into recognition of a bona fide community. These changes were the result of the exposure to modern communication, which came rather late to these remote villages. In addition, once democratic rule replaced Salazar's dictatorship and Portugal entered the European Union, conditions were created that allowed for the establishment of a normative community.[92]

These young men were interested in having some type of solid backing, such as that of a consul or a representative of the Jewish state, convinced that this would give them "ethnic power."[93] The new government's stance was reflected in the unprecedented speech by President Soares in March 1989 when he asked forgiveness of the Jews of Portugal for the persecutions they had suffered.[94] More requests were made by the Belmonte conversos of the outside Jewish community, such as being provided with a rabbi, who appeared in 1990. In the meantime, a representative from the Jewish Agency arrived, as did a ritual slaughterer, whose salary was provided by a private donor. Because the project to bring Judaism to Belmonte was financed privately, it seems that corners were cut in order to reduce costs. The Belmonte community had to contend with a number of less than scrupulous ritual slaughterers; some were simply unskilled, while others were mere opportunists. However, the Judaizers as well as those who expressed interest in converting were serious about eating kosher food, especially kosher meat. Unfortunately, the Portuguese had difficulty discerning who was qualified and who was not, for they had no familiarity with the laws of ritual slaughter.[95] Nevertheless, it should be noted that before embarking on this enterprise to bring ritual slaughterers from the outside, the men in Belmonte consulted with the women about their initiative and obtained their consent. One cannot but assume, however, that this path of regaining traditional Judaism was destined to enable the men to regain "their lost authority."[96]

The older generation was, nonetheless, understandably skeptical and doubted that these other Jews were Jewish enough, so they continued their traditions, while the younger men brought with them the winds of change. Mea and Steinhardt describe this generation gap: "The Marrano population of Belmonte survived the decline of the Work of Redemption [Bastos] and never abandoned their ritual tradition; they maintained their spirit of being a 'family' and a 'nation' in intermarriages, and in their midst there grew up a new generation that decided to enter mainstream Judaism, bringing their parents and grandparents with them, and opening a synagogue."[97] The dedication ceremony for the new synagogue building in 1996 was not quite appropriate for this community. Despite the fact that there was next to no knowledge of Hebrew in Belmonte at the time, the scene was set in a most traditional manner, with books and rabbis present, creating a false impression of the presence of rabbbinic leadership and scholarship. The transition was going to be very difficult, especially for the older generation.[98]

The older generation felt that after all the sacrifices it had made for its religion, it had no reason to seek change. After all, this is what had survived, and the fact that it had been maintained in secret was seen to be the ultimate proof of its authenticity.[99] When presented with the option of conversion, which included circumcision for the males as well as the study of prayers and immersion in the ritual bath, each member of the community weighed his or her options before deciding upon a course of action. For example, because the mother's religion is the determining factor by Jewish law, a New Christian man married to an Old Christian woman would not take this path because his children would not be part of the Nation; this stands in contrast to the children of a New Christian woman married to an Old Christian husband. At the same time, the established merchants in the community faced a quandary: The large number of Jewish holidays to be observed would require them to lose many workdays. Such a loss was viewed as too great a luxury for these hardworking breadwinners, although the option of deferring conversion until retirement was considered to be viable.[100]

Nevertheless, the groundwork was laid for the reentry of these Judaizers into the modern Jewish world. At the end of the twentieth century, Belmonte, comprised of between 2,600 and 3,000 inhabitants, had about 120 New Christians in its midst. Belmonte is considered to be a village without overt anti-Semitism or any records of persecution.[101] However, Yerushalmi contends that the locals in villages like Belmonte are still very biased and anti-Semitic and tend to think in terms of stereotypes.[102] At any rate, this village received Israeli rabbis of Moroccan origin to enable the transition from one world to the other; each one was present for two to three years, from 1990 to 1992, and from 1993 to 1996. During this time, they succeeded in converting the majority of the conversos. In 1992 seventy of the Belmonte Judaizers became official Jews, and in 1993 another fifteen joined them; about thirty-five chose not to convert. A *mohel*, or ritual circumciser, came from Lisbon together with a nurse to perform the ceremonies. Once the *mikveh*, or ritual bath, was built, a fee was collected to cover the cost of the immersion, although some Judaizers resented this payment. Rabbis now perform weddings, and the *mohel*, also a physician and community leader, comes in from Lisbon.[103] This is more or less the status of the community today.

Essentially, the conversions had an interesting effect on the members of the community. A major division between the converted and nonconverted did not occur, most likely because they are all related to one another. When the Moroccan rabbis were present, they were shocked by the nature of the Judaizing customs observed there. They were extremely anxious to inculcate their version of Jewish laws and rites, even if they included various Kabbalistic customs as part and parcel of normative halakhic Judaism, such as dabbing wine from the Sabbath kiddush cup on one's neck. The truth is that they did not succeed in educating most of the converts, who had also suffered from exposure to confusing information that had been provided by some of the ritual slaughterers. For example, one of the less than pious slaughterers changed the time of Sabbath prayers for his own convenience, and thus these services were finished before the Sabbath had even begun. Moreover, once the rabbis departed, no one was on hand to monitor the community's activities or to provide it with direction; apparently the older women are still asked for guidance in the rabbi's stead.[104] In addition, unsanctioned intermarriage continues to take place, as there is no rabbi to object to such an unacceptable activity for a Jew.[105] On the whole, the men choose a democratic approach to community decision making, although, at times, changes are introduced on an arbitrary basis. Because there are no rabbinic leaders, newly learned observances are not always remembered or remembered correctly from year to year. For instance, only three years after learning about Rosh Hashana, some of the families could not recall what they were supposed to do.

The result is a fascinating syncretism of the old and the new. For example, the community devised a Jewish way to bury a nonconverted member: A member circumcises the deceased, who is then given a Hebrew name, and the problem is "solved."[106] Each family still has its own set of traditions and system of decision making. Molho refers to the group as a "quasi-community" that is mostly informal and voluntary and cannot effectively carry out sanctions. In her opinion, the most effective means of continuity is through endogamy and social supervision, especially by means of the rampant gossip that is characteristic of a small town.[107] The older women seem to have absorbed some of the new traditions, which they have promptly juxtaposed to the old. For example, before they had access to the Jewish calendar, a council of elders made up of the older women would meet and fix the dates of the holidays; today the Jewish calendar is used. While the ancient tradition of preparing the prayer wicks has not been relinquished, the men now wear skullcaps. At the synagogue, prayers from the new prayer books might be recited alongside traditional prayers, or possibly a combination of both might result. In addition, those who have formally converted are joined there by those who have not.[108] The crypto-Jewish traditions that survived for five hundred years will not easily be replaced. A family might return from Sabbath services at the synagogue and recite the blessing over wine or, for that matter, the woman of the house might recite the traditional crypto-Jewish prayers.[109]

The older members of the community who did not convert still consider themselves to be authentic Jews. While kosher food and the calendar were incorporated into the daily agenda, the ancient traditions that held these people together for so long cannot easily be discarded. One's identity as a member of the Nation is one and the same. Those who converted and those who did not are members of the same family and of the same Nation. This is highly reminiscent of the seventeenth-century definition of a member of the Nation, when those who had become Jews and those yet living as New Christians in Iberia had an equal status in the newly founded communities. Perhaps the outcome might have been different if a better education and a higher rate of literacy had been achieved in the community, but this is not the case.

While the men now have an institution of their own, namely, the syna-gogue, the women have not relinquished all their "traditional" roles. The women still marry within and without the fold, and the Passover picnic is still the annual community affair. Perhaps it is only a matter of time until a more "Jewish" community emerges, but perhaps not. The crypto-Jewish identity has remained an integral part of the newly acquired Jewish identity of the descen-dants of the Portuguese conversos. While it was unexpected to discover a com-munity still identifying itself as Jewish after half a millennium, it should not be assumed that the identities of its members would change so easily just because circumcision, ritual immersion, or even conversion had taken place. Despite the fact by the standards of the outside world, two-thirds of them converted and are full-fledged Jews, the "Last Marranos" seem determined to retain the Marrano part of their identity as well. Molho contends that they are still hiding from the rabbis and from the outsiders who pry into their lives.[110] She insists that the tradition of maintaining a façade regarding one's religion created a sense of paranoia and a tradition of deception and lying that is deeply instilled. Despite modern developments and the recognition of the Jewish com-munity and of Judaism in Portugal, this proclivity seems to be an ingrained and learned behavior pattern that has not yet changed. The New Christians of Belmonte are essentially unable to cut their ties with their ancient traditions or to alter a mindset that was responsible for successfully preserving their identity for an incredibly long time.

The third modern manifestation of converso identity is by far the most problematic, particularly in terms of definition and self-definition of both the group and of the individuals. As we have seen in the case of the Chuetas, today it is the continuity of their identity that is at stake; endogamy had preserved their group identity, if only as the result of centuries of isolation and discrim-ination. The transformation of modern Majorcan society has led to a high rate of intermarriage, and the future identity of the Chuetas is at stake. The Bel-monte Judaizers, on the other hand, are now coping with exposure to and entry into modern-day Judaism that is, on the whole, characterized by a lack of rab-binic leaders and sanctions; thus, they seem to be creating a new lifestyle for themselves that is riddled with syncretism but that serves a deep-seated need to maintain cherished traditions. The third situation differs from both of these because the very status of the descendants of the conversos in the Southwest—that is, New Mexico, Arizona, Colorado, and Texas—is the subject of vigorous debate, mainly because their roots cannot be traced as clearly and their identity cannot be defined with any degree of certainty.[111]

An attempt to chart their origins reveals that conversos arrived in New Mexico along with the conquistadors, but it is very difficult to know which of them secretly observed Judaism. A large wave of immigrants of converso back-ground arrived in Mexico in the sixteenth century, and these newcomers lived in relative peace until 1585. After 1580, the number of Portuguese immigrants increased because the unification of Spain and Portugal facilitated access to lands in the Spanish Empire for them. As one would expect, this group had a better knowledge of Judaism than the converso group of Spanish origin that preceded it. This very fact came to the notice of the Inquisition, whose investigators quickly began some two hundred proceedings against Judaizers between 1585 and 1601.[112] As a result, the crypto-Jewish community was severely weakened, and its leaders and their activities received a great deal of unsolicited attention.

During the same period, a number of expeditions headed north, mostly in search of mining opportunities. In 1590, despite the fact that he had no official permission, the lieutenant governor, Castaño de Sosa, took 170 people to what is now northern New Mexico; it seems likely that among them were crypto-Jews hoping to escape the tentacles of the Inquisition.[113] The leaders of these expeditions usually had *encomiendas*, or grants of land, giving them the right to coerce the locals to work for them. In 1598, although he did not have permission, Governor Juan de Oñate set forth with 135 individuals; among them were descendants of Jews who joined him in order to establish the first permanent colony in New Mexico.[114] Despite the difficult conditions there, these particular settlers benefited from the fact that there were very few priests in the vicinity.[115]

The following period, between 1610 and 1642, was calm and uneventful for the conversos of Mexico and its environs, especially in terms of inquisitorial activity; essentially, none is recorded at this time. However, between 1642 and 1649, the Holy Tribunal once again turned its attention to the descendants of the Portuguese conversos residing in New Spain, particularly because Portugal had declared its independence from Spain in 1640. The fact that the viceroy of Mexico at the time, Escalona, had been sympathetic to these residents was no longer to their advantage. After he was deposed in 1642, they lost their protection and suffered from their affiliation with him. Because of these political developments, all colonists of Portuguese origin became suspect, and a hundred conversos were subsequently arrested. Thirteen were burned at the stake, many were reconciled to the Church, and some were sentenced to exile.[116] Consequently, any previously existing sense of security on the part of the community was seriously undermined.

The community living in Santa Fe, the central site of the early colonial settlement in the Southwest, suffered a setback in 1689. The Pueblo Indians there rebelled because of the oppression they had suffered, especially at the hands of the Franciscans; most of the settlers fled at the time of the attack.[117] Governor Diego de Vargas then attempted to resettle the area as part of the reconquest of New Mexico and eventually convinced two groups to recolonize. By 1694, nearly 140 families had returned to the upper Rio Grande valley.[118]

After 1701, there was no significant inquisitorial activity in Mexico itself or in New Mexico that pertained to Judaizers. While this was obviously a favorable situation for the crypto-Jewish settlers, the result for the researcher is that information regarding the lives of these colonists after this time is almost nonexistent. It is precisely because of this formidable lacuna that the sudden appearance of the descendants of these settlers who claimed to have maintained a direct link to Judaizing after nearly three centuries is all the more surprising.

These descendants did not appear in the public sphere until the end of the twentieth century. In 1987, a documentary was broadcast by National Public Radio concerning an exciting discovery: In the state of New Mexico, there were some 1,500 families whose members were described as descendants of the conversos who settled in the Spanish colony of New Spain (Mexico) in the sixteenth and seventeenth centuries.[119] This information that had been so well concealed within this community for so long was being revealed to Stanley Hordes, ostensibly because he had gained their confidence while serving as state historian of New Mexico from 1981 until 1985. It seems that his expertise in the history of the converso community of sixteenth-century Mexico convinced them that he would honor their request not to divulge names and specific details that would identify specific individuals; this request was honored but created skepticism regarding Hordes's reliability in the outside world.[120]

One of the interesting by-products of this discovery was the creation of a number of societies of crypto-Judaism in the West and the Southwest, for example, in Portland, Oregon, and Denver, Colorado. Some consider these societies to be proof of a growing and strengthening communal identity.[121] They assumed names such as the (National) Society for Crypto-Judaic Studies and the Hispano Crypto-Jewish Research Center in Denver and organized bulletins and assorted activities. Likewise, on August 7, 1998, notices were sent out on the Internet by two additional societies. The first, the Society for Crypto-Judaic Studies, has a bulletin entitled the *Lapid*, coincidentally, the same name as Barros Basto's publication. Its members declare that the "SCJS serves the following purposes: The fostering of research and networking of information and ideas into the contemporary development of Crypto-Jews of Iberian origins."[122] The second society is based in Washington, D.C., emanating from the Library of Congress. "There is a new list for people who think, know, suspect or are interested in the descendants of the Spanish and Portuguese Jews who were forced to convert in order to stay in the Iberian Peninsula. . . . The list is called *Anusim*. . . . If you believe your ancestors were Iberian Jews, please join us!"[123] Note the wording here; it is almost reminiscent of a call by the Inquisition for informers during the grace periods in order to amass information about Judaizers: again, if you "believe" your ancestors were Iberian Jews—not if you know or if you are a descendant. It suffices simply to believe.

It is impossible to imagine such a call emanating from either Majorca or Belmonte. As we have seen, in Majorca everyone knew who the Chuetas were, despite the fact that this was not a topic of public discourse. As for Belmonte, Schwarz and Barros Basto took the initiative and set forth to seek and identify conversos, realizing that they were unlikely to get many volunteers to identify themselves. Obviously, the Southwest experience took a separate route. Bulletins were published, conferences were organized and a network of identifying individuals and supporters was created.[124]

These developments created a great deal of confusion among the descendants themselves. A few converted, although the vast majority of them did not and were not being encouraged to do so; many have never seriously considered this option. In addition, they were not accustomed to behaving publicly as Jews or as Judaizers or of even thinking of themselves as Jewish. Their public exposure even created a number of rifts within individual families, as many of them took opposing personal stances. At the same time, anthropologists and other researchers began to examine and elaborate upon what had at first gained exposure solely in the popular realm. The discovery was an attention getter, gaining popularity and a certain power of its own.[125]

The confusion exists on many levels and not only among these families; the most basic issues have not yet been clarified, such as how to determine the characteristics of a crypto-Jew or his or her descendants. It is unclear whether one should seek cultural manifestations, remnants, or aberrations, for the criteria have yet to be determined and those being suggested differ depending upon who is suggesting them. For example, four components of crypto-Jewish identity have been singled out by Kunin: self-identification, practice, genealogy, and beliefs. He also differentiates between born crypto-Jews, potential crypto-Jews, and those that are self-identifying.[126] At the same time, Jacobs, another anthropologist, lists three indicators of crypto-Jewish heritage: Jewish-based rituals in the family of origin, Inquisition records bearing Jewish family names, and oral transmission of Jewish ancestry by family members.[127] By contrast, Halevy categorizes the information at her disposal as "family customs that can be reasonably explained as of Jewish origin." In this instance, a differentiation is made between those who had been told they were Jews and were subsequently instructed, those who were told they were special and would observe ancient customs, and those who became aware that they were "different."[128] The fact that such a categorization could be made reflects the murkiness surrounding the identity of these individuals. A sense of feeling "different" can hardly qualify as a characteristic. At the same time, the notion of "ancient customs" needs to be analyzed; there are certain to be disagreements over which reported observances are legitimate or not. Halevy, for example, did not consider as conclusive numerous reports such as of a quick burial after death, covering mirrors in a house of mourning, maintaining a year of mourning, or the tradition of putting stones on graves, because these practices are too commonly found in New Mexico. Other researchers, however, distinctly mention putting small pebbles on cemetery headstones as well as covering mirrors as being clear-cut Jewish observances.[129] Clearly there is no consensus regarding criteria among the various researchers.

Nevertheless, some practices are more or less universally accepted as Jewish; they include lighting candles on Friday nights, refraining from eating pork or bacon, and some attempt to use separate dishes along with other semblances of dietary law observances. Trimming nails and even burning or burying them is sometimes included. Sweeping the dirt from the house to the middle of the room rather than out the front door is a practice considered to be the sign of a Judaizer rather than a custom derived from Jewish law.[130]

Hordes recorded instances of individuals engaging in Sabbath observance, male circumcision, and the use of the *pon y saca*, the dreidel equivalent. The use of the dreidel is quite problematic, for it was nonexistent in the Spanish and Portuguese communities prior to the modern era. On the contrary, the Ashkenazic community has historically engaged in this game, and the local Sephardim might have encountered this tradition when Ashkenazi immigrants settled in the Southwest in the mid-nineteenth century. Thus, owning or playing with a top would be totally inappropriate as proof of a Judaizing heritage! Kunin, however, has an interesting take on the dreidel: Since, in his eyes, crypto-Judaism is in the process of developing and negotiating its identity, the act of borrowing from the Jewish community that it had encountered, in this case Ashkenazi, is totally acceptable to him. His is an example of an anthropological, antihistorical approach to crypto-Judaism.[131]

One of the longer lists of "proof" of Jewish ancestry is provided by Hernández, herself a professed descendant of conversos. This list is erratic, containing clear Jewish observances alongside traditions and customs that are hard to characterize as Jewish. More traditional observances include prayers on Rosh Hashana, fasting on Yom Kippur, bathing and changing linen in honor of the Sabbath, making little huts in the fall (akin to Sukkot booths), and eating unleavened bread in the spring. Prayer leaders would copy Ladino prayers and psalms and teach some of them to their followers. There is also mention of certain customs such as turning the body of the deceased toward the wall, eating meals of eggs and cheese after funerals, and requiring a postpartum mother to rest or be secluded for forty days after birth. The new month was sometimes acknowledged by women by placing two glasses on the household altar, one containing coins and the other a stalk of grass, an obscure observance unrelated to any Jewish legal requirement or custom.[132]

Various behavior patterns such as endogamy are considered by some to characterize these descendants. These patterns include not encouraging one's child to engage in sports on the Sabbath, bathing regularly, pride in reading and education, eating special foods on the Saturday before Easter or Good Friday, and baking a lard-free bread called "Semitic bread." There are medieval linguistic carryovers reminiscent of Ladino in ceremonies at vigils and wakes, there are tombstones with the Star of David on them, and there are families that will not hang pictures on the walls of their homes or kneel during church services. Likewise, there are individuals who harbor an antipathy toward the church and a deep-rooted fear of priests, attitudes that supposedly link them to a Judaizing past.

Syncretistic as well as totally unrelated customs abound. As in Belmonte, Queen Esther became a saint along with Saint Moses; candles are lit in their honor. The "Day of Esther" developed as a women's holiday when daughters receive explanations from their mothers about domestic tasks and make *empañadas*. The attempt to compare this triangular pastry to the triangular *hamantaschen* (pastries) that were not eaten by Sephardi Jews is, quite frankly, far-fetched. Richard Santos points to the use of what he terms "crypto-Jewish ingredients" such as raisins, pecans, and mineral or vegetable oils when preparing pastries, as well as eating cactus egg omelets during Lent, and drinking mint tea, fruit juice, or chocolate during Holy Week or on Easter Sunday. There are references to a women's society that cared for the poor and provided dowries, somewhat reminiscent of the Chueta community charity organization or even of the Amsterdam or Leghorn *dotar* society. Some individuals slaughtered fowl by wringing the neck by hand or by chopping off the head with one stroke and draining the blood and washing it.[133] While draining the blood from fowl appears to have a correlation to Jewish law, this same rite seems to be a local practice enacted by those without any Sephardi ancestry.

One report refers to visits by Jewish cousins from Portugal, in itself a surprising comment. Unfortunately, there was no attempt to trace this connection or to determine how contact had been made between the relatives. Of all the "evidence" of ties to the Iberian Peninsula, this is potentially the most poignant, but no one seems to have bothered to try to follow it up.[134]

Claims to be descendants are also made on a far less tangible level. The historian Santos contends that his ancestry originates with the original Sephardi immigrant families but that most of the group assimilated due to the threat of the Inquisition,[135] the presence of the Indians, and the difficult living conditions. Those who had not been arrested, tried, or punished tended to blend into the Christian and pagan populations.[136] In his opinion, the fate of the original sixteenth-century "keepers of the faith" was subject to the factors of time, politics, and geography. As a result, their descendants essentially became "keepers of the family secret."[137] Present-day descendants have little more than a memory or a well-guarded secret and "certain cultural traits, practices, attitudes and riddles which go about begging for an explanation."[138] Their lives are described as taking place in a "marginal cultural milieu" whose participants suffer from a "severe lack of identity" and lack of knowledge of their history and culture.[139] If someone lacks an identity, can it be assigned to him nevertheless? What is the value of a secret that is so well kept that there is little to substantiate it? Which remnants of Judaism serve to substantiate a Jewish tie and which remnants have either lost their significance or cannot be substantiated?

The various sociologists, anthropologists, and ethnographers attracted to these phenomena have encountered precisely these difficulties. For example, Atencio discusses crypto-Jewish influences in Manito society, pointing to endogamy, life-cycle rites, mobility patterns, Iberian roots, and other rites and practices that he believes coincide with crypto-Jewish traits.[140] These claims, however, are hard to prove, and even if there is a grain of truth to them, it is questionable if a descendant of crypto-Jews who has no awareness of his ancestry is comparable to one who claims to be continuing ancient observances. On the other hand, Halevy claims that "the more obscure the rabbinic practices observed, the more compelling the evidence of an unbroken Jewish tradition."[141]

At the same time, Jacobs refers to a "sense of separation and alienation from the cultural roots of Judaism" that exists among modern descendants "who speak regretfully of the loss they have experienced as a result of historical oppression and familial secrecy."[142] She discusses the generations of denial, fear, trauma, and a history of a hidden ethnicity. The cultural loss, in her opinion, is not irreversible, but involves a strenuous effort to recover roots, reclaim Jewish spirituality, and reinvent an ethnic and religious self.[143] As the result of her fieldwork, particularly among women in the Southwest, she concludes that a crypto-Jewish heritage exists if there was Jewish ritual in the family of origin, if Jewish ancestry was revealed by parents or grandparents, and if one can trace Jewish ancestry to Inquisition records in Mexico City.[144] The second possibility, the revelation, often consists of a deathbed confession by a parent or grandparent.[145] As dramatic as this seems, such a declaration weakens any chance of effectively transmitting anything more than nostalgia to the younger generation. Obviously, the third of these criteria is the most convincing. In addition to what appear to be clear-cut ties to the past, she lists other characteristics of modern crypto-Judaism, such as a consciousness of fear and persecution, the practice of Jewish-originated rituals and customs in secret,[146] the development of a syncretistic religious culture, and the influence of secrecy on the actual transmission of knowledge.[147]

Some of these manifestations have been noted elsewhere. A consciousness of fear is clearly part of the Belmonte mentality, just as syncretism is part of their lifestyle, the latter being exemplified by the transformation of Esther into a saint in both locales. The influence of secrecy on practice is exemplified in the Southwest by the fact that women light oil lamps in churches on Friday nights. Secrecy also changed the Belmonte lifestyle but somehow allowed more significant portions of the past to be retained. While Jacobs is aware that in the past, crypto-Jewish women transmitted their religion as they did throughout the years in Belmonte, it is much harder to accept many of the statements that were made by the women of the Southwest as evidence of Jewish continuity. When Jacobs refers to a woman whose grandmother insisted that nail clippings or hair be burned, this is a clear-cut Jewish ritual. However, she then cites the ritual bath as a means for women to create a bridge between the present and the past, even for the woman who is not converting.[148] This is a move to the symbolic and the imaginary that seems oblivious to Jewish law. She believes that some women "have chosen this rite of purification for their reentry into the imagined community of their persecuted ancestors."[149] Perhaps it is precisely this "imagined community" that is so problematic for the historian.

The discovery of Belmonte's crypto-Jews led to an involvement on the part of twentieth-century world Jewry in the 1920s and 1930s and again in the 1990s, ultimately resulting in the conversion of two-thirds of the community's members. The rabbinic stance concerning the descendants in the Southwest has also been that in order to be accepted as Jews, either these individuals prove matrilineal descent or convert. As we have seen, the researchers interested in this phenomenon vary greatly in their assessments, and those who consider themselves to be part of this heritage are anxious to prove the validity of their findings. Clearly this is no easy task; it is hard not to be skeptical about the veracity of this discovery. Halevy affirms that this is a problem: "Research is hampered by the difficulty crypto-Jews have in identifying what may be Jewish among customs remembered from home, and the proclivity some have to attach Jewish meanings to customs or foods, without serious investigation. The mixture of fact and fantasy in reports remains a serious problem."[150]

This is precisely what triggered the extreme reaction of the ethnographer Neulander, who claimed that the academic promotion of crypto-Jewish survival is an example of "an ersatz marrano survival."[151] In her opinion, the claim of Jewish origins by these individuals is a means of attaining upward mobility that is motivated by a desire to beat the Anglo hegemony. According to this interpretation, these individuals are "choosing to be chosen" in an interesting variant of the blood purity laws. Once New Christian ancestry was a source of shame and exclusion; now it serves to promote social standing.[152] In the mind of this researcher, the crypto-Jewish past is being "intuited, or deduced, according to demonstrably unfounded perceptions" of crypto-Jewishness in local folkways. She calls the result a "canon" or body of "demonstrably unfounded beliefs about the cultural past."[153]

A great deal of the scholarship in this field is far from impeccable; the enthusiasm and ease with which the media as well as members of certain academic disciplines accepted this phenomenon at face value and romanticized it is clearly problematic. Is this an imagined community? How does one assess a deathbed revelation? For her entire lifetime, a particular individual guards a powerful secret attesting to her Jewish heritage, and when her days are numbered, she feels compelled to pass it on to the next generation. Such a declaration must shock the recipient who has been brought up as a faithful Christian; perhaps after scrutinizing his life, he then might begin to comprehend various aberrations and oddities in behavior and family tradition. But is this a heritage? The identity this individual had formed is challenged and ostensibly turned topsy-turvy as he is brought into what is no more than a vague semblance of crypto-Judaism characterized by a long tradition of silence, secrecy, and isolation.

The task of assessing this group's identity is no easier once one has analyzed its development. While the Chuetas and Belmonte Judaizers were identifiable, this third entity did not even vaguely resemble a group until the end of the twentieth century, and it is still questionable if there is a bona fide group in existence. According to Kunin, there "is little or no documentary evidence to demonstrate the existence of formal structures or group identity prior to the last ten years."[154] By contrast, the roots of the conversos in Iberia have been acknowledged by the outsiders as well as the insiders, whether reluctantly or enthusiastically. As we have seen, concerning the Southwest, no agreement seems to have been reached by either the descendants themselves or by those studying them. It is almost impossible to find a common denominator among the various individuals, and they do not seem to have the shared sense of destiny or peoplehood one encounters in other Iberian communities.

A look at what survived might help to define their identity. As in Majorca and Belmonte, there is evidence of some atrophied observances and of syncretism. The elements of secrecy and fear united the Belmonte community and determined the nature of its observance. The descendants of the Southwest retained the element of secrecy and quite possibly the fear, but more in the realm of a memory or a feeling. Jacobs claims that this family secrecy was meant to protect its members and to create a collective memory, which serves as a basic component of their crypto-Jewish identity.[155] This collective memory might exist, but it is questionable whether or not it can form the basis of a group identity. The Southwest Judaizers did not live with a stigma as did the Chuetas, for the former had assimilated and intermarried to such a high degree that there was nothing identifiable to stigmatize. This group had no institutions, whereas the Chuetas had a communal help organization and the Portuguese of Belmonte had their halakhically based traditions, especially during the Passover season.

The Chuetas had no pretensions; they knew they were descendants of conversos as did their Old Christian neighbors, at least until recently. The Judaizers in Belmonte never doubted their identity for a moment, and members of both Iberian groups preferred endogamous marriages. Each of these communities has dealt with modernity differently: The Chuetas seem to be assimilating, while most of the Portuguese Judaizers have become Jews or developed a syncretistic lifestyle based on Judaism and crypto-Judaism. Most of the descendants of the Southwest have no such inner strength from which to draw because their roots were severely weakened over the passage of time.

While a few of these individuals have begun to study Judaism in recent years, the majority of them are in a quandary over how to proceed. The truth is that most of the material available regarding the Southwest descendants has been provided either by scholars committed to their legitimacy or by self-declared and self-identified descendants. Some of the latter are certain of their ancestry because they were bequeathed a Jewish rite or two; others are convinced of their Jewish roots because of a deathbed confession; yet others are anxious to prove their ancestry through genealogy or inquisitorial investigation. There is no doubt that among them are descendants of conversos and of Judaizing conversos who settled in the Southwest region. The history of this group, unlike the two contemporary groups in Iberia, did not allow it to be continuously identifiable. The means by which its members might or might not have identified themselves over the years are somewhat obscure, yet the determination of some of the modern descendants leads one to believe that some semblance of identity survived the secrecy and the atrophy. As Ward comments, "No doubt many claims of heritage, of survival of tradition, or of genealogical purity, are too grandiose, but the primacy given Judaic heritage and identity are striking."[156]

The nature of the research dealing with this phenomenon is also problematic, for, as we have seen, most of the material available regarding the Southwest descendants has been provided by scholars committed to their legitimacy. At the same time, it has become clear that anthropologists have a different agenda from historians. The former are, on the whole, more accepting and willing to redefine crypto-Judaism as these individuals rediscover and even imagine their past. The historians are anxious to find documentation to link them directly to their converso ancestors. While conclusive evidence is lacking at this time, one can only hope that serious and knowledgeable researchers will be able to unravel the secret of the identity of the converso descendants in the Southwest, ostensibly the most recent link, albeit controversial, to the Iberian conversos of the fifteenth and sixteenth centuries.

Conclusion

In effect, according to Abravanel, religious conversion cannot bring about the ethnic assimilation of the Jews, and the Conversos are by no means removed from the collective destiny of the Jewish people. That destiny continues to be shared by all who are of Jewish *origin*.
—Yosef Hayim Yerushalmi

Abravanel had witnessed the expulsion of the Jews of Spain and was well aware of the uniqueness of Spanish Jewry and of Spanish Jewish history. While he himself had not converted, he was deeply concerned with the fate of his brethren who had done so.[1] Although these comments stemmed from his interest in messianism, his assessment is striking because of its accuracy as well as its prophetic nature. The feasibility of ethnic assimilation following conversion plays a central role in the history of the conversos and their collective destiny which is "shared by all those who are of Jewish origin." This sense of collective destiny remained in the converso consciousness for centuries. Not only was Abravanel pondering the question of converso identity, but, in retrospect, his analysis was surprisingly accurate from a historical perspective.

The history of the Iberian conversos reflects an ever changing reality that was significant in their identity formation. Forces from within and from without played crucial roles in this process and would likewise influence the process of assimilation. In Spain the forced conversions of 1391 precipitated this chain of events, initiating the creation of the converso group; various historical events in Spain would eventually increase the number of Jews who underwent religious conversion. In the interim, however, Spanish society had found a means of preventing the assimilation of former Jews. Acceptance would no longer be determined on the basis of religion; ethnicity or origin would be its new criteria. Purity of blood statutes and anticonverso sentiments and legislation would serve to separate the New Christians from the Old Christians and to perpetuate the former's sense of otherness despite church policy to the contrary. Thus, ethnicity was to play a part in the processes of discrimination as well as of self-identification.

The Spanish Inquisition, created in order to eradicate the heresy of crypto-Judaism, also managed to further the development of the converso identity, albeit unintentionally. Sometimes it inadvertently provided the conversos with knowledge of Judaism by publishing edicts of Faith. The *sanbenito* hanging in the churches for generations was a sign of shame that perpetuated the memory of those who had been martyred. At the same time, the threat of the Inquisition sometimes backfired; the converso might seek out his roots rather than abandon or reject them, curious to know what could be so threatening to the Church and state. In addition, fear of the Inquisition proved to be a factor in the formation of crypto-Jewish religion and practices as well as of the converso identity. The power of this fear was so long lasting that even after the Inquisition had been disbanded, crypto-Jewish communities did not relinquish their secret observances.

The next step in dealing with the converso problem was the expulsion of the Jews in 1492, which, ironically, did not succeed as planned. While it did manage to technically remove the Jews from Spanish soil, it did not succeed in removing Judaism from Spain. On the contrary, the fact that so many knowledgeable Jews chose to convert rather than to leave their homeland actually infused the converso community with new blood and knowledge. In addition, those who chose exile and later regretted their decision could return to Spain within seven years, ultimately opting to convert and to join their converso brethren.

One cannot help but be struck by the heterogeneity of the Spanish converso community. As of 1391, new converts would continue to appear for over a hundred years, and while some Judaized, others were anxious to assimilate. Still others chose more checkered paths, sometimes changing their stances drastically during the course of their lives. As we have seen, even the most avid converso assimilationists would be constantly reminded of their ethnic background and of their origins, sometimes accounting for a change of heart.

By contrast, the Portuguese converso community was far more homogeneous. While there were cruel and disastrous incidents such as the saga of the Saõ Tomé children, the majority of the Jews in Portugal were forcibly converted during the course of 1497. The fact that a large portion of this group was composed of Spanish Jews was significant; these exiles had chosen to remain faithful to Judaism and not to convert, only to befall the dreaded fate in exile.

The Portuguese converso group was formed as the result of a collective traumatic experience that would reinforce a sense of collective destiny on their part. Thus, it is not surprising to find them appealing to the king for special privileges or organizing and financing a lobby sent to negotiate with the pope in Rome in the hope of preventing the establishment of a Portuguese Inquisition.

The riots of 1506 in Lisbon and the visit of David Reubeni in 1525 also illustrate this sense of collective destiny. The conversos formed their own networks and displayed a sense of unity that continued well after the Portuguese Inquisition was established in 1536. The ethno-religious affiliations between them served to strengthen this sense of unity. The lives of those who came to be known as "men of affairs" were based on extensive and comprehensive ties of marriage, business, and other economic interests as well as having experienced trauma. They also exhibited a collective memory that served to prevent ethnic assimilation. They were "members of the Nation," and their origin was clear both to them and to those around them. They had a solid economic base in Portugal, and once Spain and Portugal united in 1580, they settled in important trade centers such as Seville and Madrid. Nonetheless, this unity and otherness was not viewed positively by the nonconversos; by the beginning of the seventeenth century, the Inquisition in Spain redoubled its efforts to extirpate the Judaizing heresy revitalized by the Portuguese immigrants.

The Portuguese conversos looked beyond Iberia in search of alternatives. Those who arrived in Amsterdam had to contend with creating a community without ever having experienced the Jewish world themselves. The basis of their identity was nationhood, as they were all members of "the Nation," whose roots to Iberia ran deep and included cultural, linguistic, educational, and psychological manifestations. This identity was based on ethnicity and pride; while it included elements of the traumatic and the emotional, the sense of a common heritage was both strong and long lasting.

Because the Dutch had successfully rebelled against Catholic Spain, they were more apt to welcome Jewish Iberians as opposed to Catholics, who, more importantly, could significantly contribute to Dutch trade and commerce. The Iberians themselves were seeking a way to be Jewish, for they could not return to something they had never been. Thus, they organized a community and made ritual and halakhic demands of their members; a small number of them were unable to meet these demands. Nonetheless, the marvel here is the fact that the majority of these conversos were able to juggle their two worlds and create a modus vivendi for themselves. Life in Iberia had exposed them to secular culture and to modernity, but their sense of belonging to the Nation helped most of them navigate their way to Judaism. Thus, institutions of mutual aid, where they cared for their poor and for their unmarried brides, were fairly easy to organize. On the whole, there was relatively little assimilation into the larger Dutch society, for the new community provided a sense of belonging to a larger whole, to the Nation. One's ethnic roots did not have to be denied, although in the religious realm, males had to undergo circumcision and all were expected to accept the rabbinic heritage and authority. As we have seen, the interesting part of this identity was that instead of identifying with the Jewish people as a whole, they basically identified with those of the Nation, those of Iberian heritage. This larger group was defined expansively and included the conversos who were still living as Catholics on the peninsula as well as the Sephardi Jews who had left Spain in 1492.

Of the four Western European communities, the majority of the Dutch Sephardim seemed to have had the least traumatic transitions, although some of them might be classified as "troubled" or "fuzzy" because they felt Jewish but were somehow unable to accept either Judaism or Christianity as the definitive religion or culture. Moving from Catholic Iberia to any non-Iberian country presented a challenge unto itself, especially since the émigrés were so quintissentially Iberian. However, the move to Holland allowed them the means of expressing their cultural heritage in a Protestant country where the shadow of the Inquisition was nonexistent. Their brethren who chose alternate destinations were not always as fortunate.

For example, the choice of France precluded the option of forming a Jewish community until the seventeenth century. All the Portuguese merchants who settled in various French locales had to maintain the façade of Catholicism, just as they had done in Iberia. Needless to say, this clandestine existence also created difficulties for the researcher attempting to reconstruct the lives of these immigrants; it is even harder to trace the development of their identities. Some of them clearly assimilated and intermarried, while others maintained close contact with their brethren in Amsterdam, obtaining printed matter from them for guidance. There were, no doubt, some "fuzzy" Jews among them as well as cultural commuters who essentially lived double lives. When a community was finally formed, the emphasis on Jewish education was somewhat low-key, yet this is understandable since the group was so thoroughly French by this time. Nevertheless, organized communities were formed and led by lay leaders, many of whom had achieved considerable commercial success. Again, it is precisely because of this success that the French rulers and cities tolerated the converso presence; the Portuguese merchants had justified their existence.

Strong ethnic ties can be discerned among the French Iberian conversos, and their strength and longevity were impressive. Ties to Jewish law were far less impressive, yet this too is understandable. The conversos adapted to life in France by creating a crypto-Jewish existence that was appropriate to the French reality. When the restrictions were lifted, a variety of lifestyles was found among their descendants, although a sense of group solidarity and family pride had somehow survived intact. The Inquisition managed to lurk in the shadows for some time in this Catholic country, as spies were sent from Iberia to report on their activities; at the same time, those who dared to travel to Iberia on business as cultural or as "economic" commuters might have been detained and even tried in court. The conversos in France miraculously managed to retain a strong sense of identity despite the formidable obstacles of secrecy and time. The fact that their Iberian pride remained relatively unscathed is evidenced by their detachment from the Ashkenazim who arrived in northeastern France and by the fact that they received rights as a group in 1790 separately and prior to the non-Sephardi Jews.

A third variation is reflected in the experience encountered by the conversos who settled in England. Like France, England had expelled its Jews, and the option of forming a Jewish community was nonexistent there as well. On the other hand, England was no longer Catholic, and the spectre of the Inquisition was never a threat. As in France, the immigrants had no choice but to live a double life, often choosing to attend Catholic services in the chapels of Iberian consulates. As in France, these newcomers adapted to their new environment and mores, imitating and benefiting from the open nature of British society. This might well account for the fact that when a community did form, it did not have a strong Jewish backbone. As we have seen, many of its members were criticized by visiting rabbis for their laxity of observance. While there were marital and communal ties with both Amsterdam and France, there were similar connections with the British themselves. By the eighteenth century, the Anglicized and wealthier among them were buying estates and living in the style of the British upper class. Interestingly, even those who intermarried did not necessarily cut themselves off from their brethren. At this point, however, their identity was solely of an ethnic nature. While abandoning Iberia should have enabled the creation of a new Iberian converso diaspora, not all chose to identify themselves as Jews despite the fact that most were proud to be Iberians and members of the Nation.

A fourth destination for these immigrants was Italy, where the converso experience varied depending upon the time and place under discussion. Here was a Catholic country, where the pope himself resided, linked to the threat of an inquisition emanating directly from Rome. A convert opting to practice Judaism could be arrested at any time if the authorities chose to pursue the path of persecution. At the same time, choosing the Jewish path led to social segregation as compared to social mobility for the former Catholic; thus, in Italy there were a number of "cultural commuters" par excellence who could not choose one single path. The temptation to forego the freedom granted to Catholics in a Catholic country was too great for a number of the more colorful figures who arrived there. Some lived marginal lives, perhaps akin to the "fuzzy" Jews, while some never made up their minds. Others were simply pragmatic in their decision making process, and yet others harbored sincere dual loyalties. Thus, one finds Christian dissemblers appearing alongside the Jews in the ghetto, men like the Righetto Marrano or "a ship with two rudders," and characters such as Gaspar Ribeiro in whose family each member took a different stance. The identity of these conversos was so complex that one is not certain if they themselves understood what and why they were doing what they were doing, whether they were truly being pragmatic, and whether they were caught between two worlds or if they were actually able to live in both without encountering contradictions in their own existence.

Toward the end of the sixteenth century, cities such as Leghorn and Venice sought out the converso merchants, offering them commercial preference and rights as well as religious freedom. In such locales, normative Jewish communities could establish themselves religiously as well as economically without the fear of an inquisition. In the long run, the Iberian conversos in Italy were a multifaceted group whose members espoused every imaginable permutation and combination of lifestyle. The cultural commuters lived alongside the straddlers, the decided, and the undecided. All had a sense of being Iberian members of the Nation, but the personal choices they made often reflected the options available to them.

The popes were similarly inconsistent in their persecution of the conversos. The trauma of Ancona (1555) was not easily forgotten, especially by illustrious figures such as Amatus Lusitanus and Dona Gracia; the latter had lived both as a Catholic and as a Jew while sojourning in Italy. Once again, regardless of one's affiliation with standard Jewish institutions, the Iberian conversos in exile were aware of their heritage and of their strong ties to fellow Iberian conversos. If one could live in two worlds without encountering inner or outer conflict, so be it. When analyzing the types of choices made by these immigrants, especially concerning those in Italy, one can only strive to list all the options that were available to them.

By the twentieth century, the encounter with modernity had left its mark on the lives of the identifiable converso communities. For example, in Iberia, the conversos of Majorca had maintained an endogamous community for more than half a millenium. The persecution by the Inquisition appeared to have instilled a group consciousness more effectively than could ever have been imagined, especially after the intensive trials of the 1670s. The Majorcan conversos, probably because they were stigmatized, developed a strong sense of group identity and of a common destiny. While the original group was formed in the fateful year of 1391, its members did not necessarily identify with the other Iberian conversos. This was most likely the result of both their geographic and historic isolation, for the historical developments in Majorca after 1391 were not parallel to those of the mainland conversos, a factor that surely contributed to this separateness.

The fact that the Chuetas maintained a separate identity for so long that was separate from the other Majorcans stands in sharp contrast to other converso communities, both inside and outside of Iberia. The restrictions and social isolation imposed on them were clearly as effective as were the inquisitorial persecutions. Once these social barriers broke down in the twentieth century, the restrictions and insults began to disappear. The enforced separateness was no longer a social requirement, although some of the Chuetas still prefer a voluntary separateness in order to ensure survival. These proud Majorcans, who rarely if ever considered leaving their homeland despite the discrimination and prejudice they encountered for hundreds of years, had an identity that had essentially been thrust upon them. They accepted this distinction and created a strong sense of interdependence in the community. Internal and external forces were at work in creating the Chueta identity, which, ironically, now that the discrimination and prejudice are largely a thing of the past, may well dissipate in the twenty-first century; only time will tell.

The other Iberian converso group we examined was that of Belmonte; this group is often referred to as the "Last Marranos." These conversos also represent an identifiable group with a strong sense of a common destiny. However, much clearer signs of crypto-Judaism exist in Belmonte than in Majorca, despite the fact that there has been significant atrophy over time. This crypto-Judaism is ingrained with fear and secrecy; the fact that the Inquisition has been disbanded has scarcely affected the mindset of these individuals. In many ways, they became a closed endogamic and somewhat paranoid group that managed to live in two worlds and to balance two mentalities. The world for them is either Jewish or Catholic, and they have successfully lived in both of them.

The changes that transpired in this community during the first half of the twentieth century were unusual. Once the outside world was alerted to their existence, they were exposed to normative Judaism for the first time in centuries. Each of the individuals involved, such as Schwarz, Wolf, and Barros Basto, had his own agenda. The reports that startled the pre-World War II Jewish world created a great deal of interest and were followed by attempts to educate the neglected Portuguese communities. Yet the demise of the proselytizer Barros Basto and other historical circumstances brought these activities to an end and to the creation of a time warp of sorts. Thus, in the long run, time seems to have stood still or to have gone backward because this particular exposure to modernity had few, if any, long-term effects.

The identity of these crypto-Jews was centered on the family and the Nation; one was a member of both. Everything was transmitted by memory along with the notion of trauma that shaped the very essence of the community. When the second and more lasting encounter with modern and normative Judaism began toward the end of the twentieth century, the subsequent developments were unexpected. The old as well as the new were embraced, and at varying times, one might outweigh the other. The synagogue suddenly became the central location for prayers, while the home remained the site of the older women's prayers. An interesting syncretism of the old and the new emerged. While the gospel of the rabbis who visited Belmonte was respected, the old crypto-Jewish tradition has manifested an amazing inherent tenacity. Although two-thirds of the community have made a commitment to modern Judaism by converting, others still intermarry despite the fact that the children of non-Jewish women are not accepted as members of the community. When there are no rabbis present, which is usually the norm, the older women are consulted as ritual experts. The identity of these individuals has always been "Jewish" according to their perceptions of Judaism. Today their identity remains Jewish, and while it has been influenced by normative Judaism, there has not really been any abandoning of the ancient customs and traditions.

The final contemporary phenomenon is not to be found in Iberia, but is the result of the Iberian conquest, namely, of Spain's conquest of Mexico. This group is the most difficult to pin down, for many of the members are themselves uncertain of who they are and the significance of self-identification. The descendants of the conversos who arrived in Mexico and then moved north to the Southwest region of the United States claim to have lived in isolation and in fear for centuries. Although the communities of Majorca and Belmonte both lived in fear and isolation, these two groups were unable to avoid notice and identification by outsiders. Consequently, they were defined from without as well as from within. However, the converso descendants of the Southwest have lost so much of their essence due to secrecy and lack of outside contact that it is extremely difficult to substantiate their claims.

Their observances are far from unified and by no means easy to ascertain. There are no groups or communal organizations, not even for charity or similar purposes. It is almost impossible to define who they are, and it is similarly difficult for them to define themselves. Criteria are mostly the subject of debate rather than tangible or scientific data, and thus confusion abounds. At the same time, changes occurred once this phenomenon came to the public eye. This stands out in contrast to Belmonte, where the first round of attention resulted in outside intervention that mainly produced reports; some fifty years later, however, renewed attention brought rabbis there to teach and convert. By comparison, in New Mexico and environs, attention seems mainly to have brought about confusion and conflict, both among the members of this group as well as among the researchers examining them. This case is the most difficult one to characterize; it is equally difficult to ascertain who is a descendant and what, if any, identity survived. It is unclear if any sense of the Nation survived or if any bona fide Jewish observances were directly transmitted from their ancestors. Only further delving into this puzzle might produce satisfactory answers.

As elusive as any identity seems to be, and as complex as the conversos and their history may be, it is interesting to reflect upon the question of identity in the realm of Iberian converso history. Religious conversion was the first step in the creation of this identity, but the way in which the larger society dealt with these conversions determined the subsequent stages of converso history. Once the Old Christians aligned themselves against the New Christians, whether in Toledo in 1449 or in Majorca in the seventeenth century, the stigmatization and isolation processes were set into motion. Even those conversos desperate to be absorbed into Old Christian society were denied full access. Ethnic assimilation became an impossibility or a near impossibility; this fact would determine the destiny of the converso identity.

Every converso, whether in Spain or in Portugal, was aware of his or her origin. Almost every attempt to deny this fact was met with a reminder. The Inquisition was a successful Iberian institution that seemed to be constantly perpetuating itself and its power. It made use of direct confrontation, such as a trial, as well as indirect confrontation, such as the threat of arrest. It also exploited visual and psychological reminders by utilizing public forums such as the auto-da-fé and, of course, the haunting image of the *sanbenito* clearly displaying the embossed family name of the deceased heretic; the latter had a long-lasting effect on all who attended church and, above all, on their memories.

Those Iberian conversos who chose to leave their homelands carried a tremendous amount of baggage with them, which was emotional and cultural as well as national. They continued to identify as proud Iberians, but of a special breed: They were "members of the Nation" or Portuguese merchants or the like. This uniqueness enabled them to retain their Iberian heritage and to reclaim their Jewish one if they so chose.

As we have seen, not all who left Iberia elected to combine these worlds or succeeded in combining them. Some preferred not to attempt, while others, such as the "fuzzy" Jews, were psychologically or philosophically unable to do so. Others straddled both worlds without committing themselves, and yet others "commuted" culturally between them with finesse and comfort. The image of the converso "returning" to Judaism was more a fantasy than a reality; because they had not experienced Judaism, they could not return to it. The term "new Jew" was applicable to many of them, as Kaplan has aptly noted. There were those in Amsterdam who became highly respected Sephardi scholars and yet others who were successful merchants and who maintained a strong affiliation to the community.[2] In France and England, the choice was deferred, and the time that passed in the interim critically affected the way in which Judaism was embraced when it became a viable option. Thus, the French community could not compete with that of Amsterdam, and ultimately, contending with the demands of Napoleon and the effects of the French Revolution would also take their toll. The British Sephardim established a small community that would witness the intermarriage and assimilation of many of its members, yet oddly enough, these members retained a sense of solidarity with their brethren. In Italy, the experience was so variegated that it is all the more impressive that a number of solid communities such as Venice and Leghorn succeeded in organizing themselves and that they flourished.

The contemporary experience enables a comparison of the effect of modernity on converso history and the converso identity. The Chuetas seem to be slowly disappearing as the result of intermarriage, but the longevity of their group consciousness is astounding. The existence of the crypto-Jews in Belmonte and other Portuguese communities in the 1930s surprised the Jewish world. Now, although modern Jewish leaders have attempted to make demands of these individuals, the tenacity of their crypto-Jewish traditions is admirable. While the accoutrements of rabbinic Judaism have been espoused, the transmitted traditions have impressive weight and staying power. Lastly, while the confounding phenomenon of the descendants of conversos residing in the southwestern United States suggests a longevity of the converso identity, it also points clearly to the deterioration that can transpire over time and to the dangers of making claims that can be so hard to validate. This difficulty is exacerbated by the fact that no references to these individuals or to any group during the interim years have been found. In addition, the reluctance of these individuals to convert points to a much weaker tie to the Jewish heritage than in Belmonte, and perhaps informs us that their pride is in the Iberian versus the Jewish aspect of their heritage. While this group may or may not be composed of members of the Nation, it is worthwhile to examine their backgrounds and attempt to verify or deny these claims. The strength of the converso identity has proven to be long lasting and powerful; it is doubtful if their fourteenth- and fifteenth-century ancestors ever dreamed that in the twenty-first century the question of converso identity would still be a matter of debate.

Notes

PREFACE

1. Some new works have come to my attention. See Jonathan I. Israel, *Diaspora within a Diaspora: Jews, Crypto-Jews, and the World Maritime Empires, 1540–1740* (Leiden: Brill, 2002); Gretchen D. Starr-Lebeau, *In the Shadow of the Virgin: Inquisition, Friars, and Conversos in Guadalupe, Spain* (Princeton, N.J.: Princeton University Press, 2003); and David L. Graizbord, *Souls in Dispute: Converso Identities in Iberia and the Jewish Diaspora, 1580–1700* (Philadelphia: University of Pennsylvania Press, 2004).

2. "We introduce the word and the concept of 'fuzzy Jews' to cover the kinds of individuals who, either converting to Christianity themselves or being the children or grandchildren of converts, still feel themselves to be Jewish, although, for a variety of reasons, they can neither bring themselves to accept either Christianity or Judaism as their defining religion—or culture. We use this odd expression because none of the alternatives seem pertinent to all the situations involved." See Charles Meyers and Norman Simms, eds., *Troubled Souls: Conversos, Crypto-Jews, and Other Confused Jewish Intellectuals from the Fourteenth through the Eighteenth Century* (Hamilton, New Zealand: Outrigger Publishers, 2001), 1.

3. Thomas F. Glick, "On Converso and Marrano Ethnicity," in *Crisis and Creativity in the Sephardic World, 1391–1648*, ed. Benjamin R. Gampel (New York: Columbia University Press, 1997), 71, quoted from Benjamin N. Colby and Pierre L. van den Berghe, *Ixil Country: A Plural Society in Highland Guatemala* (Berkeley: University of California Press, 1969), 20. Glick refines the term by stating that the "cultural commuter was a well-known social type in the Spanish world of the sixteenth and seventeenth centuries. Here I define a commuter as someone who changes in cultural guise, including religions, if not habitually, then at least more than just once; he can switch back and forth" (71).

INTRODUCTION

1. Yerushalmi made these comments during a lecture at Harvard University in the spring of 1975 in a course on the history of the Jews in Christian Spain, a course that provided me with a synthetic and balanced perspective of Spanish Jewish history.

2. For an in-depth study of the Islamic period, see Eliyahu Ashtor, *The Jews of Moslem Spain*, 3 vols. (Philadelphia: Jewish Publication Society, 1973).

3. This was true for many other groups as well; see Elana Lourie, "A Society Organized for War: Medieval Spain," *Past and Present* 35 (1966): 54–76.

4. More information on the reconquest can be found in Derek W. Lomax, *The Reconquest of Spain* (London: Longman, 1978). Concerning the early period, see Bernard F. Reilly, *The Contest of Christian and Muslim Spain 1031–1157* (Cambridge, Mass.: Blackwell, 1992).

5. For information concerning guilds, albeit somewhat dated, see Julius Klein, "Medieval Spanish Guilds," in *Facts and Factors in Economic History* (New York: A. M. Kelley, 1967), 164–188.

6. For examples of friction between the king and other groups, see Yitzhak Baer, *A History of the Jews in Christian Spain*, 2d ed. (Philadelphia: Jewish Publication Society, 1992), 1:117, 126, 133, 176, 180, 365; 2:249.

7. For details of the development of the Jewish community during the reconquest, see Baer, *History of the Jews*, 1:1–186.

8. See Jeremy Cohen, *The Friars and the Jews: The Evolution of Medieval Anti-Judaism* (Ithaca, N.Y.: Cornell University Press, 1982).

9. See Cohen, *Friars and the Jews*, 103–108.

10. Numerous examples appear in Cohen, *Friars and the Jews*, 109–264.

11. See the review essay by John Edwards, "Was the Spanish Inquisition Truthful?" *JQR* 87, nos. 3–4 (1997): 357.

12. Scarlett Freund and Teofilo F. Ruiz, "Jews, Conversos, and the Inquisition in Spain, 1391–1492: The Ambiguities of History," in *Jewish-Christian Encounters over the Centuries*, ed. Marvin Perry and Frederick M. Schweitzer (New York: Peter Lang, 1994), 174.

13. Freund and Ruiz, "Jews, Conversos," 172, 175. See also Angus MacKay, "Popular Movements and Pogroms in Fifteenth-Century Castile," *Past and Present* 55 (1972): 33–67; and Philippe Wolff, "The 1391 Pogrom in Spain: Social Crisis or Not," *Past and Present* 50 (1971): 4–18.

14. Baer, *History of the Jews*, 2:97.

15. See Haim Beinart, "The Jews in Castile," in *Moreshet Sepharad = The Sephardi Legacy*, ed. Haim Beinart (Jerusalem: Magnes Press, 1992), 1:27–31.

16. Yom Tov Assis, "The Crown of Aragon," in Beinart, *Sephardi Legacy*, 98.

17. Baer, *History of the Jews*, 2:100–101.

18. For more intricate details of the events in each community, see Baer, *History of the Jews*, 2:95–110.

19. Anyone who reads Baer's rendition cannot help but notice his biases. He believes that the community was divided into the faithful—namely, the poor and modest lower class plus the artisans—and the less faithful, highly corrupt oligarchy. The latter group had deteriorated morally due to its exposure to philosophy, in particular

Averroism, which was responsible for the catastrophe that befell the Jewish community. He can not understand why the Jews made no attempts to protect themselves; he firmly believes that the moral degeneration he discerned was so prevalent that it had to be the clear-cut explanation for all the travails that followed.

20. See Ángel Alcalá, "Tres cuestiones en busca de respuesta: Invalidez del bautismo 'forzado,' 'conversión' de judíos, trato 'cristiano' al converso," in *Judíos. Sefarditas. Conversos. La expulsión de 1492 y sus consecuencias*, ed. Ángel Alcalá (Valladolid: Ámbito Ediciones, 1995), 537.

21. See Jacob Barnai, "The Jews of Spain in North Africa," in Beinart, *Sephardi Legacy*, 2:68. The grandfather of Isaac Abravanel had lived in Seville and was forced to convert in 1391; he or his son eventually fled to Portugal and returned to Judaism there. This explains the Portuguese origin of the famous Isaac Abravanel, who in 1482 fled Portugal for political reasons, only to spend ten years in Castile before joining the exiles and relocating in Italy. See Elias Lipiner, *Two Portuguese Exiles in Castile: Dom David Negro and Dom Isaac Abravanel* (Jerusalem: Magnes Press, 1997), 76.

22. Fragments from this letter appear in Baer, *History of the Jews*, 2:104–105.

23. See the introduction by Benjamin R. Gampel, "Yitzhak Baer's *A History of the Jews in Christian Spain*," in Baer, *History of the Jews*, 1:xv–lvii.

24. Yosef Hayim Yerushalmi, class lecture, Harvard University, April 8, 1975.

25. See Moisés Orfali, "El judeoconverso hispano: Historia de una mentalidad," in *Xudeus e Conversos na Historia*, ed. Carlos Barros (Santiago de Compostela: Editorial de la Historia, 1994), 1:117–134.

26. See B. Netanyahu, *The Marranos of Spain: From the Late 14th to the Early 16th Century according to Contemporary Hebrew Sources*, 3d ed. (Ithaca, N.Y.: Cornell University Press, 1999), 251–53. Regarding Portugal, see Maria José Pimenta Ferro Tavares, "Expulsion or Integration? The Portuguese Jewish Problem," in *Crisis and Creativity in the Sephardic World, 1391–1648*, ed. Benjamin R. Gampel (New York: Columbia University Press, 1997), 95–96.

27. E. Marín Padilla, "Relación judeoconversa durante la segunda mitad del siglo XV en Aragón: Enfermedades y muertes," *Sefarad* 43 (1983): 253.

28. For detailed examples, see Renée Levine Melammed, *Heretics or Daughters of Israel? The Crypto-Jewish Women of Castile* (New York: Oxford University Press, 1999), 16–30.

CHAPTER ONE   THE AFTERMATH AND A NEW REALITY

1. Yirmiyahu Yovel, "The New Otherness: Marrano Dualities in the First Generation," The 1999 Swig Lecture, University of San Francisco, September 13, 1999, 3.

2. Stephen Haliczer, *Inquisition and Society in the Kingdom of Valencia, 1478–1834* (Berkeley: University of California Press, 1990), 210.

3. B. Netanyahu, *The Marranos of Spain: From the Late 14th to the Early 16th Century according to Contemporary Hebrew Sources*, 3d ed. (Ithaca, N.Y.: Cornell University Press, 1999), 21.

4. Yovel, "New Otherness," 3.

5. See Michael Glatzer, "Pablo de Santa Maria on the Events of 1391," in *Antisemitism through the Ages*, ed. Shmuel Almog (Oxford: Pergamon Press, 1988), 127–

137; and Glatzer, "Between Yehoshua Halorki and Shelomo Halevi—Towards an Examination of the Causes of Conversion among Jews in Spain in the Fourteenth Century" (in Hebrew), *Pe'amim* 54 (1993): 103–115.

6. Ángel Alcalá, "Tres cuestiones en busca de respuesta: Invalidez del bautismo 'forzado,' 'conversión' de judíos, trato 'cristiano' al converso," in *Judíos. Sefarditas. Conversos. La expulsión de 1492 y sus consecuencias*, ed. Ángel Alcalá (Valladolid: Ambito Ediciones, 1995), 533–535.

7. See Bath Sheva Albert, *The Case of Baruch: The Earliest Report of the Trial of a Jew by the Inquisition, 1320* (in Hebrew) (Ramat Gan: Bar Ilan University, 1974), for a fascinating case of a French Jew who claimed he was baptized by force and the criterion applied to his case, namely, whether he had expressed vocal objection at the time of baptism.

8. See Carlos Carrete Parrondo, *El judaísmo español y la Inquisición* (Madrid: Editorial MAPFRE, 1992), 22, 25.

9. Luis Coronas Tejada, *Conversos and Inquisition in Jaén* (Jerusalem: Magnes Press, 1988), 16. See also Linda Martz, "Conversos Families in Fifteenth- and Sixteenth-Century Toledo: The Significance of Lineage," *Sefarad* 48 (1988): 117–196.

10. Regarding Ferrer, see Francisca Vendrell, "La actividad proselitista de Vicente Ferrer durante el reinado de Fernando I de Aragon," *Sefarad* 13 (1943): 87–104.

11. See Yitzhak Baer, *A History of the Jews in Christian Spain*, 2d ed. (Philadelphia: Jewish Publication Society, 1992), 2:167–169.

12. For information on the royal policy, see Francisca Vendrell, "La política proselitista del Rey Don Fernando I de Aragón," *Sefarad* 10 (1950): 349–366.

13. For a very detailed account of the debates and their repercussions, see Baer, *History of the Jews*, 2:170–243.

14. See Angus MacKay, "The Hispanic-*Converso* Predicament," *Transactions of the Royal Historical Society* 35 (1985): 162–63.

15. B. Netanyahu, *The Origins of the Inquisition in Fifteenth-Century Spain* (New York: Random House, 1994), 1095–1102, 1313–1315.

16. See also Scarlett Freund and Teofilo F. Ruíz, "Jews, Conversos, and the Inquisition in Spain, 1391–1492: The Ambiguities of History," in *Jewish-Christian Encounters over the Centuries*, ed. Marvin Perry and Frederick M. Schweitzer (New York: Peter Lang, 1994), 176; and Baer, *History of the Jews*, 2:231.

17. Haim Beinart, *Conversos on Trial: The Inquisition in Ciudad Real* (Jerusalem: Magnes Press, 1981), 8.

18. Haim Beinart, "Great Conversion and Conversion Problem," in *Moreshet Sepharad = The Sephardi Legacy*, ed. Haim Beinart (Jerusalem: Magnes Press, 1993), 1: 350–351.

19. See Alcalá, "Tres cuestiones," 536.

20. See Marc Shell, "Marranos (Pigs), or From Coexistence to Toleration," *Critical Inquiry* 17, no. 2 (1991): 310–311; and I. S. Révah, "La Controverse sur les statuts de pureté de sang—Un document inédit," *Bulletin Hispanique* 73 (1971): 263–306.

21. Regarding the statutes, see Albert A. Sicroff, *Les controverses des statuts de pureté de sang en Espagne du XVe au XVIIe siècle* (Paris: Didier, 1960), who, among other things, refutes the notion that these statutes have their origin in Jewish sources as claimed by Américo Castro in *The Structure of Spanish History* (Princeton, N.J.: Princeton University Press, 1954). B. Netanyahu discusses this notion in "Américo

Castro and His View of the Origins of the Pureza de Sangre," in *American Academy for Jewish Research Jubilee Volume*, ed. Salo W. Baron and Isaac E. Barzilay (Jerusalem: American Academy for Jewish Research, 1980), 397–457.

22. A discussion of this progression also appears in Yosef Hayim Yerushalmi, *From Spanish Court to Italian Ghetto: Issac Cardoso: A Study in Seventeenth-Century Marranism and Jewish Apologetics* (New York: Columbia University Press, 1971), 12–16.

23. David Gitlitz attempts an interesting taxonomy of New Christians that divides the conversos into types. The first type are Christians, which includes conversionist zealots, Christian reformers, heterodox Catholics, Christian professionals, and low-profile Christians. The second type includes observant Judaizers, accommodationist Judaizers and anti-Catholic Judaizers. The third group has vacillators and syncretists, while the final type is basically comprised of skeptics. The premise here is based on commitment to each or to both religions. David M. Gitlitz, *Secrecy and Deceit: The Religion of the Crypto-Jews* (Philadelphia: Jewish Publication Society, 1996), 82–90.

24. A detailed discussion appears in Beinart, "Great Conversion," 351–368.

25. Coronas Tejada, *Conversos and Inquisition*, 20–21; and Coronas Tejada, "El motín antijudío de 1473 en Jaén," in *Proceedings of the Seventh World Congress of Jewish Studies*, vol. 2 (Jerusalem: World Union of Jewish Studies, 1981), 141–177.

26. Coronas Tejada, *Conversos and Inquisition*, 19.

27. Beinart, *Conversos on Trial*, 9; B. Netanyahu, "Alonso de Espina—Was He a New Christian?" *PAAJR* 43 (1976): 107–165.

28. See Alisa Meyuhas Ginio, "The Fortress of Faith—At the End of the West: Alonso de Espina and His *Fortalitium Fidei*," in *Contra Iudaeos*, ed. Ora Limor and Guy B. Stroumsa (Tübingen: J. C. B. Mohr, 1996), 234–236; and Meyuhas Ginio, *La forteresse de la foi* (Paris: Ediciones du Cerf, 1998).

29. MacKay, "Hispanic-*Converso* Predicament," 165.

30. Meyuhas Ginio, "Fortress of Faith," 229–230.

31. See the trial information that appears in C. Carrete Parrondo, *Fontes Iudaeorum Regni Castellae, III Proceso inquisitorial contra los Arias Dávila segovianos* (Salamanca: Universidad Pontifica de Salamanca, 1986).

32. See Edward Peters, *Inquisition* (Berkeley: University of California Press, 1988), 84.

33. Ibid., 97.

34. Beinart, *Conversos on Trial*, 240.

35. See MacKay, "Hispanic-*Converso* Predicament," 169.

36. See William Monter, *Frontiers of Heresy* (Cambridge: Cambridge University Press, 1990), 4–15.

37. For detailed information concerning the archives, see Gustav Henningsen, "The Archives and the Historiography of the Spanish Inquisition," in *The Inquisition in Early Modern Europe: Studies on Sources and Methods*, ed. Gustav Henningsen, John Tedeschi, and Charles Amiel (DeKalb, Ill.: Northern Illinois University Press, 1986), 54–78.

38. Haliczer, *Inquisition and Society*, 225.

39. For statistics from the second and third periods, see Jaime Contreras and Gustav Henningsen, "Forty-Four Thousand Cases of The Spanish Inquisition (1540–1700): Analysis of a Historical Data Bank," in Henningsen et al., *Inquisition in Early Modern Europe*, 100–129.

40. Details of this fascinating case appear in Haliczer, *Inquisition and Society*, 215, 394 n. 20. The original trial records are from 1490 and 1496 and can be found at the AHN archives in Madrid.

41. Ibid., 221, 395 n. 38.

42. Jaime Contreras, "Judíos, judaizantes y conversos en la península Iberíca en los tiempos de la Expulsión," in Alcalá, *Judíos. Sefarditas. Conversos*, 461.

43. See Haliczer, *Inquisition and Society*, 216, 394 n. 21; the records are located in the AHN.

44. Ibid., 217, 394 n. 24.

45. See Haim Beinart, *Records of the Trials of the Spanish Inquisition in Ciudad Real* (Jerusalem: Israel Academy of Sciences and Humanities, 1974), 1:57–58; and Beinart, *Conversos on Trial*, 69–70.

46. Andrés Bernáldez, *Historia de los Reyes Católicos* (Madrid, 1953), 70:600–602, as cited in Coronas Tejada, *Conversos and Inquisition*, 31. This phenomenon will be discussed in more detail in the following chapter.

47. Beinart, *Conversos on Trial*, 60.

48. See Beinart, *Records of the Trials*.

49. His trial is leg. 184, nº 11 (1515–1527) in Beinart, *Records of the Trials*, 3:536–584. His mother's trial is leg. 154, nº 22 (1484–1492) in ibid., 3:315–334. For a detailed analysis of the family history, see also Haim Beinart, "Three Generations, Members of One Family Tried by the Inquisition" (in Hebrew), *Tarbiz* 30 (1960): 46–61.

50. See Beinart, *Records of the Trials*, 1:36.

51. Coronas Tejada, *Conversos and Inquisition*, 31–32.

52. Beinart, *Conversos on Trial*, 191–192.

53. There were probably conversos who arrived after the forced conversions of 1391; those who fled in the 1480s were perceived to be "false Christians." See Maria José Pimenta Ferro Tavares, "Expulsion or Integration? The Portuguese Jewish Problem," in *Crisis and Creativity in the Sephardic World, 1391–1648*, ed. Benjamin R. Gampel (New York: Columbia University Press, 1997), 95–96.

54. See Francisco Cantera, "Fernando de Pulgar y los Conversos," *Sefarad* 4 (1944): 339. The land of the Muslims, according to Norman Roth, is Granada; see his *Conversos, Inquisition, and the Expulsion of the Jews from Spain* (Madison: University of Wisconsin Press, 1995), 227.

55. For an example, see the chapter on the trial of Beatriz Rodríguez, a midwife, in Renée Levine Melammed, *Heretics or Daughters of Israel? The Crypto-Jewish Women of Castile* (New York: Oxford University Press, 1999), 140–149.

56. See Coronas Tejada, *Conversos and Inquisition*, 34.

57. Regarding opposition to use of the sanbenito, see Haliczer, *Inquisition and Society*, 236–238.

58. Jean-Pierre Dedieu, "The Archives of the Holy Office of Toledo as a Source for Historical Anthropology," in Henningsen et al., *Inquisition in Early Modern Europe*, 169.

59. Ibid., 168–169.

60. Ibid., 171.

61. John Edwards, "Was the Spanish Inquisition Truthful?" *JQR* 87, nos. 3–4 (1997): 365.

62. Yerushalmi, *From Spanish Court to Italian Ghetto*, 23–24.

63. These two factors were also supposed to be considered by the Church since, technically, it was forbidden to convert by force.

64. A classic and still excellent article on the topic is that of Simha Assaf, "The Conversos of Spain and Portugal in Rabbinic Literature" (in Hebrew), *Zion* 5 (1933): 19–60.

65. Actually, this is not so different from the factors responsible for variations in inquisitorial judgments. Although there were guidelines for the courts, the judgment rendered (as well as whether or not there would be torture) often depended upon the judge himself, his proclivities, the make-up of the court, the time and location of the trial, and the fanaticism or levelheadedness of those involved.

Concerning the responsa, a number of cases decided by North African rabbis can be found in Netanyahu, *Marranos of Spain*, 5–76. This scholar published important and interesting responsa, but thought that they proved his contention that the conversos were almost completely assimilated by the time the Inquisition was established. The classic critique of this book appears in Gershon Cohen, review of *The Marranos of Spain*, *Jewish Social Studies* 29 (1967): 178–184. As Edwards points out, in Netanyahu's later work, "the voluminous records of the post–1478 Inquisition are, however, dismissed out of hand as evidence." See Edwards, "Was the Spanish Inquisition Truthful?" (review of Netanyahu's *The Origins of the Inquisition in Fifteenth-Century Spain* and Norman Roth's *Conversos, Inquisition, and the Expulsion of the Jews from Spain*), 354. In this marvelous review, Edwards asserts that "there are, in fact, problems with all the alternatives to Inquisition evidence, including the rabbinic sources on which both these authors mainly rely for their interpretation of the issue" (360–361).

66. *Resp. Rashdam*, sect. "Hoshen Mishpat," no. 215 (Lemberg, 1822), p. 43b.

67. See Libby Garshowitz, "Gracia Mendes: Power Influence and Intrigue," in *Power of the Weak: Studies on Medieval Women*, ed. Jennifer Carpenter and Sally-Beth MacLean (Champaign: University of Illinois Press, 1995), 94–125. See also Andrée Aelion Brooks, *The Woman Who Defied Kings: The Life and Times of Doña Gracia Nasi* (St. Paul, Minn.: Paragon House, 2002), 369–375.

CHAPTER TWO   THE EXPULSION AND ITS CONSEQUENCES

1. Yosef Hayim Yerushalmi, "Exile and Expulsion in Jewish History," in *Crisis and Creativity in the Sephardic World, 1391–1648*, ed. Benjamin R. Gampel (New York: Columbia University Press, 1997), 17.

2. Ibid., 19.

3. Norman Roth, *Conversos, Inquisition, and the Expulsion of the Jews from Spain* (Madison: University of Wisconsin Press, 1995), 313–314.

4. Jane Gerber, *The Jews of Spain* (New York: Free Press, 1992), 137.

5. Haim Beinart, "The Expulsion from Spain," in *Moreshet Sepharad = The Sephardi Legacy*, ed. Haim Beinart (Jerusalem: Magnes Press, 1992), 2:38. For an extensive survey with documentation of the expulsion and its effect on the Jewish community, see Haim Beinart, *The Expulsion of the Jews from Spain*, trans. Jeffrey M. Green (Oxford: Littman Library of Jewish Civilization, 2002).

6. Regarding developments in Murviedro, see Mark D. Meyerson, "The Jewish Community of Murviedro (1391–1492)," in *The Jews of Spain and the Expulsion of 1492,* ed. Moshe Lazar and Stephen Haliczer (Lancaster, Calif.: Labyrinthos, 1997), 129.

7. Eleazar Gutwirth, "Jewish-Converso Relations in XVth Century Segovia," in *Proceedings of the Eighth World Congress of Jewish Studies,* vol. 2 (Jerusalem: World Union of Jewish Studies, 1982), 52.

8. Encarnación Marín Padilla, "Relación judeoconversa durante la segunda mitad del siglo XV en Aragón: Nacimiento, hadas, circuncisiones," *Sefarad* 41, no.2 (1981): 273, 275. Regarding *hadas,* see Renée Levine Melammed, "Noticias sobre los ritos de los nacimientos y de la pureza de las judeo-conversas castellanas del siglo XVI," *El Olivo* 13, nos. 29–30 (1989): 235–243.

9. Marín Padilla, "Relación judeoconversa . . . : Nacimiento," 274–275.

10. Ibid., 288.

11. Ibid., 290–293.

12. See Encarnación Marín Padilla, "Relación judeoconversa durante la segunda mitad del siglo XV en Aragón: Matrimonio," *Sefarad* 42, no. 2 (1982): 249–250.

13. Ibid., 266–293.

14. Stephen Haliczer, *Inquisition and Society in the Kingdom of Valencia, 1478–1834* (Berkeley: University of California Press, 1990), 218.

15. Marín Padilla, "Relación judeoconversa . . . : Matrimonio," 265. I should comment here about mixed marriages. There are numerous cases of conversos and conversas who chose Old Christians as mates. Some of the New Christians were seeking to improve their status through matches with the nobility, and often Old Christian noblemen were willing to consider matches with New Christians of substantial means. However, not all intermarriages were among the wealthy. The converso who rejected endogamy might have done so for romantic reasons or in search of some security, hoping his or her children would be accepted by society. At any rate, problems arose when one mate was a Judaizer and the other was not. There are examples of conversos who Judaized until their marriage and then began again when the mate died. There are Judaizers who hid their activities from their partners, and others whose partners knew and disapproved, often vociferously. See Renée Levine Melammed, *Heretics or Daughters of Israel? The Crypto-Jewish Women of Castile* (New York: Oxford University Press, 1999), 66, 154. Regarding a surprising situation whereby, after discovering that her husband was a Judaizer, an Old Christian wife requested lessons in Judaism, see Melammed, *Heretics or Daughters,* 160–161. See also David M. Gitlitz, "Divided Families in *Converso* Spain," *Shofar* 11, no. 3 (1993): 5–14. One of his conclusions is "that the frequency of divided families in the record suggests that religious division often led to dysfunctionality and to destruction of the family. . . . [D]ivided families ran disproportionate risks and all too frequently fell into the public record" (19).

16. This is one of the main reasons, if not the main one, that prevented the king of Portugal from expelling the Jews in 1497. There had been no forced or voluntary conversions in Portugal in the fourteenth or fifteenth centuries as in Spain, and thus no converso middle class existed. If he were to expel all the Jews, he would not be left with a substantial middle class, and thus he would endanger the economy of his kingdom.

17. See Máximo Diago Hernando, "Los judeoconversos en Soria después de 1492," *Sefarad* 51 (1991): 259–297.

18. Linda Martz, "Converso Families in Fifteenth- and Sixteenth-Century Toledo: The Significance of Lineage," *Sefarad* 48 (1988): 119.

19. Henry Kamen, *Inquisition and Society in Spain* (London: Weidenfeld & Nicolson, 1985), 15.

20. Stephen Haliczer, "The Expulsion of the Jews as Social Process," in Lazar and Haliczer, *Jews of Spain and the Expulsion of 1492*, 246.

21. Regarding contact between Jews and conversas, see Levine Melammed, *Heretics or Daughters*, 18–30, 34–39, 209–215.

22. David M. Gitlitz, *Secrecy and Deceit: The Religion of the Crypto-Jews* (Philadelphia: Jewish Publication Society, 1996), 591.

23. See Carlos Carrete Parrondo, "Jews, Castilian Conversos, and the Inquisition," in Lazar and Haliczer, *Jews of Spain and the Expulsion of 1492*, 148.

24. Meyerson, "Jewish Community of Murviedro," 133.

25. Gitlitz, "Divided Families," 2–3.

26. Encarnación Marín Padilla, "Relación judeoconversa durante la segunda mitad del siglo XV en Aragón: enfermedades y muertes," *Sefarad* 43, no. 2 (1983): 251–285.

27. Marín Padilla, "Relación judeoconversa . . . : Enfermedades," 269–285.

28. Ibid., 283. The document, from a trial in 1488, is found in the Archive of the Territorial Audience (Z.AAT), 283 n. 114.

29. Ibid., 285 n. 124.

30. For additional references to death and mourning, see Renée Levine Melammed, "Some Death and Mourning Customs of Castilian Conversas," in *Exile and Diaspora*, ed. Aharon Mirsky, Avraham Grossman, and Yosef Kaplan (Jerusalem: Ben Zvi Institute, 1991), 157–167.

31. Ibid., 290–292 nn. 144–147. The trial is also recorded in the Z.AAT.

32. Ibid., 297 nn. 174–176. The trial took place in 1487 and is found in the Z.AAT.

33. Ibid., 299 n. 178. The file is also in the Z.AAT.

34. Ibid., 314.

35. Ibid., 316 n. 233. The original is in the Z.AAT.

36. This accusation is found in José Cabezudo Astrain, "Los conversos aragoneses según los procesos de la Inquisición," *Sefarad* 18 (1958): 276, but without a reference to which file contains this trial.

37. See the trial of Juan González Pintado, leg. 154, nº 10, as transcribed in Haim Beinart, *Records of the Trials of the Spanish Inquisition in Ciudad Real* (Jerusalem: Israel National Academy of Sciences and Humanities, 1974), 1:123. See also Beinart, *Conversos on Trial: The Inquisition in Cuidad Real* (Jerusalem: Magnes Press, 1981), 61.

38. Yitzhak Baer, *A History of the Jews in Christian Spain* (Philadelphia: Jewish Publication Society, 1961), 2:297–98. Portions of the original appear in Fritz Baer, *Die Juden im christlichen Spanien*, (Berlin: Schocken, 1936), 2:484–509; the trial transpired from 1489 to 1490. See also the interpretation of Encarnación Marín Padilla in part 2 of "Relación judeoconversa durante la segunda mitad del siglo XV en Aragón: Nacimiento, hadas, circuncisiones," *Sefarad* 42, no. 1 (1982): 59–77.

39. Baer, *History of the Jews*, 2:299; and Baer, *Juden in christlichen Spanien*, interspersed in the aforementioned trial.

40. Haliczer, *Inquisition and Society*, 213, 394 n. 15. These trials are located in the Archivo Histórico Nacional.

41. Ibid.

42. Yolanda Moreno Koch, "La Comunidad Judaizante de Castillo de Garcimuñoz," *Sefarad* 37, nos. 1–2 (1977): 369. The information about Judaizers from this Castilian town is from Inquisition files in the Archivo Diocesano de Cuenca (ADC). Other examples of Jewish wet nurses can be found in Marín Padilla, "Relación judeo-conversa . . . : Nacimiento," (part 1), 280–281. See also Renée Levine Melammed, "Sephardi Women in the Medieval and Early Modern Periods," in *Jewish Women in Historical Perspective*, 2d ed., ed. Judith R. Baskin (Detroit: Wayne State University Press, 1998), 133, 144 n. 44.

43. Moreno Koch, "Comunidad Judaizante," 370.

44. Ibid., 364.

45. Beinart, *Conversos on Trial*, 69. It is ironic that they chose Cordoba, for riots had occurred there in 1473, as pointed out in the previous chapter.

46. Beinart, *Records of the Trials*, 1:57–58. The original trial is leg. 143, n° 11 (1483–1484).

47. Ibid., 52–53.

48. The file is found in the National Historical Archives of Valencia and was cited by Manuel Sánchez Moya, "El Ayuno del Yom Kippur entre los judaizantes turolenses del siglo XV," *Sefarad* 26 (1966): 273–274.

49. Ibid., 283 n. 23. The trial is from the Teruel files in the AHN in Madrid.

50. Ibid., 288.

51. See, for example, ibid., 290, 291, 292.

52. Ibid., 292–293.

53. Ibid., 291.

54. Haliczer, *Inquisition and Society*, 218–219.

55. Ángel Alcalá contends that converso writers assimilated to the point that they often expressed anti-Jewish opinions. See "Jews and Conversos in Spanish Literature," in *Jews and Conversos at the Time of the Expulsion*, ed. Yom Tov Assis and Yosef Kaplan (Jerusalem: Zalman Shazar Center for Jewish History, 1999), 111–116.

56. Meyerson, "Jewish Community of Murviedro," 136, 141, 145 n. 50.

57. Beinart, *Conversos on Trial*, 102 n. 53.

58. Ibid., 134–135.

59. Carrete Parrondo, "Jews, Castilian Conversos," 149.

60. Ibid., 151.

61. Haliczer, "Expulsion of the Jews," 240; see also Jocelyn N. Hillgarth, "The Reactions of Catholic Intellectuals to the Jewish Presence in Spain during the Reign of the Catholic Monarchs," in Assis and Kaplan, *Jews and Conversos*, 53–64.

62. See Joseph Hacker, "New Chronicles on the Expulsion of the Jews from Spain, Its Causes and Results" (in Hebrew), *Zion* 44 (1979) = *Yitzhak F. Baer Memorial Volume*, 219–223.

63. Ibid., 242.

64. Meyerson, "Jewish Community of Murviedro," 132–133, 143 n. 21.

65. Beinart, *Conversos on Trial*, 226; and Beinart, *Records of the Trials*, 1:54.

66. Beinart, *Conversos on Trial*, 59.

67. Ibid., 59 n. 45; and Beinart, *Records of the Trials*, 2:50.

68. See Miguel Angel Motis Dolader, "Aplicación efectiva del Edicto de Expulsión," *Proceedings of the Ninth World Congress of Jewish Studies*, vol. 2 (Jerusalem: World Union of Jewish Studies, 1986), 126.

69. Benjamin R. Gampel, *The Last Jews on Iberian Soil* (Berkeley: University of California Press, 1989), 110. The term "native" appeared in a tax register to separate the two communities.

70. See ibid., 120–134, for a discussion of this event.

71. For a translation into English of his description of the expulsion in *Historia de los reyes Católicos Don Fernando y Isabel (Seville, 1869)*, see *The Expulsion 1492 Chronicles*, ed. David Raphael (North Hollywood, Calif.: Carmi House Press, 1992), 69–73.

72. Baer, *History of the Jews*, 2:436.

73. Jerome Friedman, "New Christian Religious Alternatives," in *The Expulsion of the Jews 1492 and After*, ed. Raymond B. Waddington and Arthur H. Williamson (New York: Garland Publishing, 1994), 20–21.

74. For details, see Beinart, *Expulsion of the Jews*, 413–500.

75. How did the veteran conversos of 1391 or their brethren view the new 1492 converts? An amazing idea was propounded by Constance Rose, that the newer New Christians might be unacceptable to the older vintage New Christians, who were further removed from Jewish origins. Was there a nouveax New Christian suffering from discrimination by the established New Christian? See Rose, *Alonso Núñez de Reinoso: The Lament of a Sixteenth-Century Exile* (Rutherford, N.J.: Fairleigh Dickinson University Press, 1971), 34–35.

76. Gitlitz, *Secrecy and Deceit*, 26.

77. See, for example, Yolanda Moreno Koch, "Las Deudas de los Judíos de Segovia después de la Expulsión," in *Hispano-Jewish Civilization after 1492*, ed. Michel Abitbol, Yom-Tov Assis, and Galit Hassan-Rokem (Jerusalem: Misgav Yerushalayim, 1997), 3–13. See also Moreno Koch, "De la diáspora hacia Sefarad: La primera carta de regreso de un judio convertido?" *Michael* 11 (1989): 257–265.

78. Gampel, *Last Jews*, 71, 76–77.

79. See Luis Coronas Tejada, *Conversos and Inquisition in Jaén* (Jerusalem: Magnes Press, 1988), 21.

80. Luis Suarez Fernández, *Documentos acerca de la Expulsión de los judios* (Valladolid: Ediciones Aldecoa, 1964), 487–489. See also Beinart, *Expulsion of the Jews*, 329–331, 403–406.

81. Ibid., 495. Atienza is in Castile, north of Madrid.

82. Ibid., 508–509. Cuéllar is also in Castile, due north of Madrid.

83. This permit was issued on February 15, 1493; see ibid., 504–505.

84. Enrique Cantera Montenegro, "Judios de Torrelaguna: Retorno de Algunos Expulsados entre 1493 y 1495," *Sefarad* 39, no. 2 (1979): 334–336.

85. Ibid., 336. His documentation is from the Archivo General de Simancas, nn. 12–13; see also pp. 340–342.

86. Ibid., 337 n. 14; for documentation, see 342–343.

87. Ibid., 337–338 n. 17; for documentation, see 343–344. See Mary Elizabeth Perry, "Beatas and the Inquisition in Early Modern Seville," in *Inquisition and Society in Early Modern Europe*, ed. Stephen Haliczer (London: Croom Helm, 1987), 147–167.

88. For details, see Máximo Diago Hernando, "El ascenso sociopolítico de los ju-

deoconversos en la Castilla del siglo XVI: El Ejemplo de la Familia Beltrán en Soria," *Sefarad* 56 (1996): 221–250.

89. See Rebecca Winer, "Family, Community, and Motherhood: Caring for Fatherless Children in the Jewish Community of Thirteenth-Century Perpignan," *Jewish History* 16 (2002): 15–48; and Winer, *Women, Wealth, and Community in Thirteenth-Century Perpignan* (Aldershot, England: Ashgate, 2004).

90. See Robert I. Burns, *Jews in the Notarial Culture: Latinate Wills in Mediterranean Spain, 1250–1350* (Berkeley: University of California Press, 1996), 30.

91. Suarez Fernández, *Documentos acerca de la Expulsión*, 509–510.

92. For further details, see Libby Garshowitz, "Gracia Mendes: Power, Influence and Intrigue," in *Power of the Weak: Studies on Medieval Women*, ed. Jennifer Carpenter and Sally-Beth MacLean (Champaign: University of Illinois Press, 1995), 94–125.

93. Beinart, *Conversos on Trial*, 169.

94. This is probably Osma, located in the province of Soria in Castile.

95. Suarez Fernández, *Documentos acerca de la Expulsión*, 528–529.

96. Benjamin R. Gampel, "The Decline of Portuguese and Navarrese Jewries," in Assis and Kaplan, *Jews and Conversos*, 84.

97. Suarez Fernández, *Documentos acerca de la Expulsión*, 534–535.

98. Kamen, *Inquisition and Society*, 18.

99. Thus far, no attempt at quantification has been made; in actuality, any number given for any group of Jews or conversos at any time would be countered by other numbers. Gitlitz made a noble attempt to make sense out of the conflicting figures. For example, he estimated that there were between 7 million and 9 million inhabitants in Spain in 1491, and that 125,000–200,000 were Jews. As for the number of conversos, he ventured to use the figure of 225,000, supplemented by 25,000–50,000 in 1492. He calculated the number of exiles to be between 100,000 and 160,000, of whom 50,000 went to Portugal and 5,000–8,000 returned to Spain. For the details of which scholars give higher and lower figures, see Gitlitz, *Secrecy and Deceit*, 73–76.

100. See Beinart, *Records of the Trials*, 2:133–139.

101. Articles dealing with this movement include Haim Beinart, "A Prophesying Movement in Cordova in 1499–1502" (in Hebrew), *Zion* 44 (1980): 190–200; Beinart, "The Spanish Inquisition and a 'Converso Community' in Extremadura," *Medieval Studies* 43 (1981): 445–471; Beinart, "Herrera: Its Conversos and Jews" (in Hebrew), in *Proceedings of the Seventh World Congress of Jewish Studies*, vol. 2 (Jerusalem: World Union of Jewish Studies, 1981), 53–85; Beinart, "The Prophetess Inés and Her Movement in Pueblo de Alcocer and Talarrubias" (in Hebrew), *Tarbiz* 51 (1982): 633–658; Beinart, "Conversos of Chillón and the Prophecies of Mari Gómez and Inés, the Daughter of Juan Esteban" (in Hebrew), *Zion* 48 (1983): 241–272; Beinart, "The Prophetess Inés and Her Movement in Her Hometown, Herrera" (in Hebrew), in *Studies in Jewish Mysticism, Philosophy, and Ethical Literature*, ed. Yosef Dan and Yosef Hacker (Jerusalem: Magnes Press, 1986), 459–506; and Beinart, "Inés of Herrera del Duque: The Prophetess of Extremadura," in *Women in the Inquisition: Spain and the New World*, ed. Mary E. Giles (Baltimore: Johns Hopkins University Press, 1999), 42–52.

102. For a discussion of women and girls affected by this movement, see Levine Melammed, *Heretics or Daughters*, 45–72, 216–224.

103. The file for this trial can be found in the Archivo Histórico Nacional in Madrid; see leg. 165, n° 7. This particular case is also mentioned by Levine Melammed, *Heretics or Daughters*, 41–42; and by Francisco Cantera Burgos and Carlos Carrete Parrondo, "Las Juderías medievales en la provincia de Guadalajara," *Sefarad* 34, no. 2 (1974): 356–357. Guadalajara is in Castile, just northeast of Madrid.

104. For more details regarding this trial, see Levine Melammed, *Heretics or Daughters*, 43–44. The original trial is classified as leg. 158, n° 9 (1520–1523). Hita is in Castile, just north of Guadalajara.

105. Beatriz's charges are detailed in Levine Melammed, *Heretics or Daughters*, 42–43. Her trial was leg. 159, n° 15 (1520–21).

CHAPTER THREE   THE PORTUGUESE EXPERIENCE

1. See, for example, Jose Lúcio de Azevedo, *Historia dos Christãos Novos Portugueses* (Lisbon: Livraria Clássica Editora de A.M. Teixeira, 1921), 21; and Maria José Pimenta Ferro Tavares, *Os Judeos em Portugal seculo XV*, vol. 1 (Lisbon: Universidade Nova de Lisboa, 1984).

2. A brief survey of the Jewish situation in Portugal can be found in Elias Lipiner, *Two Portuguese Exiles in Castile: Dom David Negro and Dom Isaac Abravanel* (Jerusalem: Magnes Press, 1997), 9–24.

3. H. P. Salomon, *Portrait of a New Christian: Fernão Álvares Melo (1569–1632); Un "Portugués" entre los Castellanos: El primer proceso Inquisitorial contra Gonzalo Báez de Paiba, 1654–1657*, transcribed by David Willemse (Paris: Centro Cultural Portugués, 1982), 13. For greater detail about this as well as about other trials and tribulations of fifteenth-century Portuguese Jewry, see B. Netanyahu, *Don Isaac Abravanel* (Philadelphia: Jewish Publication Society, 1953), 6–12, 18–26.

4. See chapter 2 for references to fleeing to Portugal in 1391 and thereafter.

5. See Benjamin R. Gampel, "Ferdinand and Isabella and the Decline of Portuguese and Navarrese Jewries," in *Jews and Conversos at the Time of the Expulsion*, ed. Yom Tov Assis and Yosef Kaplan (in Hebrew) (Jerusalem: Zalman Shazar Center for Jewish History, 1999), 73, 83.

6. Maria José Pimenta Ferro Tavares, "Expulsion or Integration? The Portuguese Jewish Problem," in *Crisis and Creativity in the Sephardic World, 1391–1648*, ed. Benjamin R. Gampel (New York: Columbia University Press, 1997), 95–96; Gampel, "Ferdinand and Isabella," 74, 80; and Maria José Pimenta Ferro Tavares, *Judaísmo e Inquisição: Estudos* (Lisbon: Editorial Presença, 1987), 20–22.

7. Ferro Tavares, "Expulsion or Integration?" 96.

8. There is a chapter on anti-Jewish mentality in Portugal in Ferro Tavares, *Judaísmo e Inquisição*, 69–104.

9. Yosef Hayim Yerushalmi, "A Jewish Classic in the Portuguese Language," introduction to Samuel Usque, *Consolação às tribulações de Israel* (Lisbon: Fundaçãi Calouste Gulbenkian, 1989), 1:20.

10. According to Haim Beinart, there were more than five points of entry but only five points of departure from Spain. See *The Expulsion of the Jews from Spain*, trans. Jeffrey M. Green (Oxford: Littman Library of Civilization, 2002), 272.

11. Yerushalmi, "Jewish Classic," 21.

12. Ferro Tavares, "Expulsion or Integration?" 97.

13. São Tomé is an island located some 120 miles from the west-central coast of Africa; it was discovered by the Portuguese in 1470. Although it was not inhabited, the Portuguese hoped to take advantage of their tropical discovery and make it a lucrative locale for sugar crops. Slaves from the Congo were brought there along with criminals to provide labor. See Robert Garfield, "A Forgotten Fragment of the Diaspora: the Jews of São Tomé Island, 1492–1654," in *The Expulsion of the Jews: 1492 and After*, ed. Raymond B. Waddington and Arthur H. Williamson (New York: Garland Publishing, 1994), 73–74.

14. Samuel Usque, "Consolation for the Tribulations of Israel" in *The Expulsion 1492 Chronicles*, ed. David Raphael (North Hollywood, Calif.: Carmi House Press, 1992), 140–141.

15. This is the fifty-ninth conversion in the *Shevet Yehuda* (The Staff of Judah); see Raphael, *Expulsion 1492 Chronicles*, 100–101. São Tomé is discussed in Elias Lipiner, *Os baptizados em pé* (Lisbon: Vega, 1998), 20–34.

16. Garfield, "Forgotten Fragment," 75–78.

17. Ibid., 75.

18. Ibid., 75, 82.

19. According to Beinart, there were about 150,000 Jews in Portugal at this time: "As is well known, 120,000 exiles crossed the border from Spain into Portugal. The number of Jews in Portugal itself can be estimated at between 30,000 and 50,000." See Haim Beinart, "The Conversos in Spain and Portugal," in *Moreshet Sepharad = The Sephardi Legacy*, ed. Haim Beinart (Jerusalem: Magnes Press, 1992), 2:44 n. 5. However, contrasting figures abound. H. P. Salomon whittled the number of Spanish exiles down to 30,000 while noting that Abraham Zacuto gave an estimate of 120,000 (see Salomon, *Portrait of a New Christian*, 14 n.2); Andrés Bernaldez, an eyewitness, calculated 160,000 (see Raphael, *Expulsion 1492 Chronicles*, 73–74, 168). Salomon's preferred figure is based on "documental evidence" from Ferro Tavares, *Os Judeos em Portugal*. It is interesting to note, however, that in the article she published ten years later, she does not venture to give estimates of demographic figures. Jane Gerber chose the classic figure of 120,000, stating that of the 175,000 exiles, this was the number that opted to relocate to Portugal. See Gerber, *The Jews of Spain* (New York: Free Press, 1992), 139–140. An even larger figure appears in the "Writings of an Andalusian Rabbi" (Abraham Bokrat HaLevy), in Raphael, *Expulsion 1492 Chronicles*, 87: "And all [the Jews], about 200,000 on foot." An anonymous account recorded 120,000 "according to a compact which a prominent man, Don Vidal bar Benviste de la Cavalleria, had made with the king of Portugal" (Raphael, *Expulsion 1492 Chronicles*, 131).

20. The Muslims were also to be expelled; they left in April 1497. See Raphael, *Expulsion 1492 Chronicles*, 99–100.

21. For Hebrew sources and analysis, see I. Tishby, "Genizah Fragments of a Messianic-Mystical Text on the Expulsion from Spain and Portugal" (in Hebrew), *Zion* 48 (1983): 55–102.

22. The first occurred on March 19; the second applied to Lisbon. See Tishby, "Genizah Fragments," 100–101.

23. Yerushalmi, "Jewish Classic," 23.

24. Usque, "Consolation for the Tribulations of Israel," 142.

25. Raphael, *Expulsion 1492 Chronicles*, 154.

26. Jerónimo Osório, "Of the Life and Deeds of King Manuel," in Raphael, *Expulsion 1492 Chronicles*, 160.

27. Isaac Ibn Faradj, "The Family Origin of Isaac Ibn Faradj, the Pure Sephardi," in Raphael, *Expulsion 1492 Chronicles*, 123.

28. Ferro Tavares, "Expulsion or Integration?" 102.

29. Yerushalmi, "Jewish Classic," 27.

30. The Iberian Jews have the reputation of preferring conversion to martyrdom. For a discussion of this phenomenon emphasizing the cases of martyrdom in Portugal following the edict of 1497, see Avi Gross, "On the Ashkenazi Syndrome of Jewish Martyrdom in Portugal in 1497" (in Hebrew), *Tarbiz* 44 (1994): 83–114.

31. See, for example, literature on the mentality of the exiles and their tremendous sense of loss, often accompanied by a romanticization of their past. A classic article is Haim Hillel Ben-Sasson, "The Generation of Spanish Exiles [Reflects] on Itself" (in Hebrew), *Zion* 26 (1961): 23–64.

32. See Raymond P. Scheindlin, "Judah Abravanel to His Son," *Judaism* 41, no. 2 (1992): 190–199; Nahum Slousch, "Poesies de Don Jehuda Abrabanel," in *Revista de estudos hebraicos* (Lisbon, 1928), 1:192–223; Hayim Shirmann, *Mivhar ha-Shira ha-Ivrit Be-Italya* (*A Selection of Hebrew Poetry in Italy*; in Hebrew), (Berlin: Schocken Press, 1934): 216–222.

33. Scheindlin, "Judah Abravanel," 191. For a family history of sorts, see Alberto Dines, *O baú de Abravanel: Uma cronica de sete séculos até Silvio Santos* (São Paolo: Editora Schwarcz Ltda., 1990).

34. Netanyahu, *Don Isaac Abravanel*, 6. If the conversion had been voluntary, it would explain why he did not attempt to flee or observe secretly (ibid., 266–267 n. 12).

35. An interesting account is that of Rabbi Abraham Saba, who, after leaving Spain with his family in 1492, did not convert in Lisbon but, after having been imprisoned for about six months, was sent to North Africa on February 1, 1498. See Abraham Gross, *Iberian Jewry from Twilight to Dawn: The World of Rabbi Abraham Saba* (Leiden: Brill, 1995), 7–10.

36. Nevertheless, there were those who returned to Spain as converts or who converted at the border and then had their property reinstated, as mentioned in chapter 2. For documentation, see Luis Suarez Fernández, *Documentos acerca de la Expulsión de los Judios* (Valladolid: Ediciones Aldecoa, 1964), 64, 504–505, 520–522, 526–528; and Beinart, *Expulsion of the Jews*, 338–412.

37. A detailed analysis of the relationship between the Jews and the Crown appears in Yosef Hayim Yerushalmi, *The Lisbon Massacre of 1506 and the Royal Image in the Shebet Yehudah* (Cincinnati: Hebrew Union College Annual Supplements, 1976), 37–58.

38. See, for example, Moshe Orfali, "Images and Stereotypes of Jews in Portuguese Literature of the Sixteenth and Seventeenth Centuries" (in Hebrew), *Pe'amim* 69 (1996): 8–23; Frank Talmage, "To Sabbatize in Peace: Jews and New Christians in Sixteenth-Century Portuguese Polemics," *Harvard Theological Review* 74 (1983): 265–285; and Ferro Tavares, *Judaísmo e Inquisição*, 67–104. See also I. S. Révah's transcription of a work written in Lisbon in 1532 by João de Barros, *Ropica Pnefma*, "An Evangelical Dialogue on the Articles of Faith against the Talmud of the Jews," 2 vols. (Lisbon: Instituto Nacional de Investigação Científica, 1983).

39. See Salomon, *Portrait of a New Christian*, 17.

40. See Yerushalmi, *Lisbon Massacre*, 7.

41. Ibid., 8–9 n. 24.

42. The classic Hebrew account of this pogrom is found in Solomon Ibn Verga, *Shevet Yehudah*, ed. Yitzhak Baer (Jerusalem: Bialik Institute, 1947), 125–127. The English edition of the sixtieth conversion can be found in Raphael, *Expulsion 1492 Chronicles*, 101–102.

43. In *Lisbon Massacre*, Yerushalmi refers to one thousand victims (16). However, in "Jewish Classic," published thirteen years later, he cites double that number (28). Salomon is convinced that this would have been a less violent riot if the foreigners present had not participated. See his review of *Lisbon Massacre* in *American Sephardi* 9 (1978): 172.

44. Ellis Rivkin, *The Shaping of Jewish History: A Radical New Interpretation* (New York: Charles Scribner's Sons, 1971), 143–144.

45. See Yerushalmi, *Lisbon Massacre*, 1–91.

46. Alexandre Herculano, *History of the Origin and Establishment of the Inquisition in Portugal*, trans. John D. Branner (New York: KTAV Publishing House, 1972), 180–187.

47. This term has apparently been chosen to describe his unusual mission. See R. J. Zwi Werblowsky, "R. Joseph Caro, Solomon Molcho, Don Joseph Nasi," in Beinart, *Sephardi Legacy*, 2:187. Elias Lipiner, "Studies in the David Hareuveni and Shlomo Molko Affair," in *The Story of David Hareuveni Copied from the Oxford Manuscript*, by Aaron Zeev Aescoly (in Hebrew), rev. ed. (Jerusalem: Bialik Institute, 1993), xlv–xlviii, sheds new light on this figure.

48. A letter written by an inquisitor in 1528 in Badajoz, located on the western border of Spain, was sent to the king of Portugal complaining about a messianic Jew who might well have been Reubeni. See Carlos Carrete Parrondo and Yolanda Moreno Koch, "Movimiento mesiánico hispano-portugués: Badajoz 1525," *Sefarad* 52 (1992): 65–68.

49. See Werblowsky, "R. Joseph Caro," 188.

50. Yerushalmi, "Jewish Classic," 31. He adds, "It can be assumed that at least some of the New Christians who still managed to flee abroad did so because they saw the handwriting on the wall, but even this could not be a solution for the majority" (31).

51. Ibid., 31–32.

52. This method of employing one's own, in this case fellow members of "the Nation" or "the Portuguese Nation," was to be used quite effectively by the most eminent of Portuguese conversos, namely, Dona Gracia. This émigré successfully organized the equivalent of an underground railroad for navigating conversos smuggled out of Iberia to safer havens. The Nasi family used agents who were former Iberian conversos as their financial representatives. In other words, this policy of ethnic solidarity and mutual support was effective both in the homeland and in new locales. See, for example, Andrée Aelion Brooks, *The Woman Who Defied Kings: The Life and Times of Doña Gracia Nasi* (St. Paul, Minn.: Paragon House, 2002), 116–129.

53. Salomon, *Portrait of a New Christian*, 3. See also Henry Kamen, *The Spanish Inquisition* (New York: New American Library, 1965), 153. For a detailed discussion of historiographical issues, see Bruce Lorence, "The Inquisition and the New Christians

in the Iberian Peninsula: Main Historiographic Issues and Controversies," in *The Sepharadi and Oriental Jewish Heritage Studies*, ed. Issachar Ben-Ami (Jerusalem: Magnes Press, 1982), 13–72. Lorence calls Kamen "the Anglo-Marxist historian" (27).

54. See H. P. Salomon, "Samuel Usque et les problèmes de la *Consolação ds tribulações de Israel*," in *Deux études portugaises* (Braga: n.p., 1991), 33–34. Usque himself was a Portuguese New Christian who left his homeland in the 1530s. The Jewish knowledge reflected in the book is minimal and not surprising for someone brought up as a Catholic and who filled in bits and pieces of Jewish learning once he began to circulate among his brethren in the diaspora.

55. For details of the disputes and tensions between the king and the Church in Rome, see Herculano, *History of the Origin*, 262–314, 315.

56. See I. S. Révah, "Les Marranes Portugais et l'Inquisition au IVEᵉ siècle," in *The Sephardi Heritage*, vol. 1, ed. Richard D. Barnett (London: Vallentine, Mitchell, 1971), 505. One of the more recent histories of the Inquisition, originally written in Portuguese, is by Francisco Bethencourt, *La Inquisición en la época moderna: España, Portugal, Italia, Siglos XV–XIX* (Madrid: Ediciones Akal, 1997).

57. Yosef Hayim Yerushalmi, "Prolegomenon," in Herculano, *History of the Origin*, 18.

58. For an English translation, see Martin A. Cohen, *Samuel Usque's Consolation for the Tribulations of Israel* (Philadelphia: Jewish Publication Society, 1965).

59. Yerushalmi, "Jewish Classic," 112.

60. One study of Gracia's family using new documents is that of H. P. Salomon and Aron di Leone Leoni, "Mendes, Benveniste, de Luna, Micas, Nasci: The State of the Art (1532–1558)," *JQR* 88 (1998): 135–211. See also Brooks, *Woman Who Defied Kings*.

61. Yerushalmi, "Prolegomenon," 40, 43.

62. See António José Saraiva, *The Marrano Factory: The Portuguese Inquisition and its New Christians, 1536–1765* (Leiden: Brill, 2001); and I. S. Révah, "Les Marranes," *REJ* 118–119 (1959–1960): 29–77. The latter is a classic piece dealing with Marrano mentality and lifestyle.

63. Yerushalmi, "Prolegomenon," 38.

64. Ibid., 39.

65. See ibid., 44–45.

66. H. P. Salomon, review of *Un "Portugués" entre los Castellanos: El primer proceso Inquisitorial contra Gonzalo Báez de Paiba 1654–1657*, *American Sephardi* 7–8 (1975): 136.

67. Révah, "Les Marranes," 55.

68. Salomon, *Portrait of a New Christian*, 35.

69. See, for example, three articles that appeared in *Jews and Conversos*, ed. Yosef Kaplan (Jerusalem: Magnes Press, 1985): Elias Lipiner, "O cristão-novo: mito o realidade," 124–138; Amílcar Paulo, "O Ritual dos Criptojudeus Portugueses," 139–148; and Elvira Cunha de Azevedo Mea, "Orações Judaicas na Inquisição Portuguesa—Século XVI," 149–169. See also Amílcar Paulo, *Os judeus secretos em Portugal* (Porto: Editorial Labirinto, 1985); María José Ferro Tavares, "O criptojudaismo: a afirmação de alteridade dos cristãos novos portugueses," in *Xudeus e Conversos na Historia*, ed. Carlos Barros (Santiago de Compostela: Editorial de la Historia, 1994), 1:311–324; and Carsten Lorenz Wilke, "Conversion ou Retour? La Métamorphose du Noveau Chré-

tien en juif Portugais dans L'imaginaire sépharade du XVIIᵉ siècle," in *Mémoires juives e'Espagne et du Portugal*, ed. Esther Benbassa (Paris: Publisud, 1996), 53–67.

70. See Daniel M. Swetschinski, *Reluctant Cosmopolitans: The Portuguese Jews of Seventeenth-Century Amsterdam* (London: Littman Library of Jewish Civilization, 2000), 59–61, 70–75, 167–168; and Salomon, *Portrait of a New Christian*, 34–40.

71. This does not mean that there was total support of the king's policies. For an assessment of the debates about the conversos, see Reuven Faingold, "The 'New Christian Problem' in Portugal: 1601–1625" (in Hebrew), *Zion* 54 (1989): 379–400. See also Carmen Sanz Ayán, "Las finanzas de la monarquía y los Banqueros Judeo-conversos: Una aproximación a los sistemas ordinarios de financiación de la Corona en el reinado de Felipe IV," in Barros, *Xudeus e Conversos*, 2:185–200.

72. See Jonathan I. Israel, "Manuel López Pereira of Amsterdam, Antwerp, and Madrid: Jew, New Christian, and Advisor to the Conde-Duque de Olivares," *Studia Rosenthalia* 19 (1985): 109–126. I will discuss other similar figures in the context of the communities in which they settled, but I will note two more examples at this time, both of whom are known to us because they had encounters with the Inquisition upon their return. Cecil Roth, "The Strange Case of Hector Mendes Bravo," *Hebrew Union College Annual* 18 (1944): 221–245; and I. S. Révah, "Une famille de 'Nouveaux Chretiens': Les Bocarro Frances," *REJ* 116 (1957): 73–87.

73. Salomon contends that the Portuguese Inquisition was particularly cruel to the conversos around 1549 while the Spaniards did not begin to take steps to oppress the Portuguese conversos until there was economic distress in the 1650s. In his opinion, "the 'Portuguese' became the scapegoats for all the ills of Spain and the victims of numerous autos-da-fé held in various Spanish cities to pacify public opinion." Review of *Un "Portugués,"* 136. Again, the possibility that there were serious Judaizers among them is rejected by Salomon who ignores the fact that this series of trials began in 1630 and not in 1650.

74. See Edgar R. Samuel, "The Trade of the 'New Christians' of Portugal in the Seventeenth Century," in *The Sephardi Heritage*, vol. 2, ed. Richard D. Barnett and W. M. Schwab (Grendon, England: Gibraltar Books, 1989): 100–114; and Jonathan I. Israel, *European Jewry in the Age of Mercantilism, 1550–1750*, 2d ed. (Oxford: Oxford University Press, 1989).

75. See, for example, Salomon, *Portrait of a New Christian*; Pilar Huerga Criado, "Una Familia Judeoconversa: La Quiebra de la Solidaridad," *Sefarad* 49 (1989): 97–121; and Reuven Faingold, "Searching for Identity: The Trial of the Portuguese Converso Vicente Furtado, 1600–1615" (in Hebrew), *Pe'amim* 46–47 (1991): 235–259.

76. See, for example, Reuven Faingold, " 'Flight from the Valley of Death': Converso Physicians Leaving Portugal in the Early Seventeenth Century" (in Hebrew), *Pe'amim* 68 (1996): 105–138.

77. James C. Boyajian, "The New Christians Reconsidered: Evidence from Lisbon's Portuguese Bankers, 1497–1647," *Studia Rosenthalia* 13 (1979): 129–156.

78. Boyajian, "New Christians," 139.

79. Ibid., 142.

80. See Faingold, " 'New Christian Problem,' " 379–400. Regarding relations between Old Christian aristocracy and New Christians, see Claude Stuczynski, "*Capela dos Prazeres*: Bragança, Late Sixteenth Century—Inquisition and Memory" (in He-

brew), *Pe'amim* 69 (1996): 24–42. Interestingly enough, sometimes the Inquisition took a stance opposing the purity of blood statutes.

81. Boyajian, "New Christians," 143.

82. Ibid., 146. See also José Veiga Torres, "Da represão religiosa para a promoção social. A Inquisiçao como instância legitimadora da promoção social da burguesia mercantil," *Revista Critica de Ciências Sociais* 40 (1994): 109–135. For another study of Portuguese financiers in Spain, see Carmen Sanz Ayán, "Las finanzas de la monarquía y los banqueros judeoconversos: Una aprozimación a los sistemas ordinarios de financiación de la Corona en el reinado de Felipe IV," in Barros, *Xudeus e Conversos*, 2: 185–200.

83. Perhaps this holds true for these few well-connected families, but there were many more trials of accused Judaizers after 1580. As previously mentioned, the traditional periodization of the pursuit of Judaizers by the Spanish Inquisition began in 1481, ending the first period in either 1530 or 1550, followed by a period that ended in 1630 during which few Judaizers were on trial. The reactivization of trials of Judaizers followed the arrival of the Portuguese conversos. As a result, the second period of active trials of accused Judaizers lasted from 1630 to 1730. A look at the onomasticon of the defendants clearly confirms these developments, for the majority of those accused had Portuguese names. See, for example, Jean-Pierre Dedieu, "Les Quatre Temps d'Inquisition," in *L'Inquisition espagnole (XVe–XIXe siecle)*, ed. Bartolomé Benassar (Paris: Hachette, 1979), 15–42; Rafael Carrasco, "Preludio al 'siglo de los portugueses': La Inquisición de Cuenca y los judaizantes lusitanos en el siglo XVI," *Hispania* 47 (1987): 503–559; and Carrasco, "Solidarités et sociabilités judéo-converses en Castille au XVIe siècle," in *Etudes portugaises, publiées par les soins de Charles Amiel*, ed. I. S. Révah (Paris: Calouste Gulbenkian, 1975), 185–228.

84. See Boyajian, "New Christians," 155.

85. See Denise Helena Monteiro de Barros Carollo, "Family Dramas, Prison Dramas: Correspondence between Portuguese Businessmen in the Seventeenth Century," in *Troubled Souls: Conversos, Crypto-Jews, and Other Confused Jewish Intellectuals from the Fourteenth through the Eighteenth Century*, ed. Charles Meyers and Norman Simms (Hamilton, New Zealand: Outrigger Publishers, 2001), 91.

CHAPTER FOUR   AMSTERDAM

1. For details, see H. P. Salomon and Aron di Leone Leoni, "Mendes, Benveniste, de Luna, Micas, Nasci: The State of the Art (1532–1558)," *JQR* 88 (1998): 135–211. See also Andrée Aelion Brooks, *The Woman Who Defied Kings* (St. Paul, Minn.: Paragon House, 2002), 101–206, 497–513.

2. See Salomon and Leoni, "Mendes, Benveniste," 153.

3. Yosef Kaplan, "The Sephardim in North-Western Europe and the New World," in *Moreshat Sepharad = The Sephardi Legacy*, ed. Haim Beinart (Jerusalem: Magnes Press, 1992), 2:244.

4. Daniel M. Swetschinski, *Reluctant Cosmopolitans: The Portuguese Jews of Seventeenth-Century Amsterdam* (London: Littman Library of Jewish Civilization, 2000), 65. For additional information on Antwerp, see Hans Pohl, *Die Portugiesen in Antwerpen (1567–1648): Zur Geschichte einer Minderheit* (Wiesbaden: Steiner, 1977);

and I. S. Révah, "Pour l'histoire des Marranes à Anvers: Recensements de la 'Nation Portugaise' de 1571–1666," *REJ* 122 (1963): 123–147.

5. See Hermann Kellenbenz, "History of the Sephardim in Germany," in *The Sephardi Heritage*, vol. 2, ed. Richard D. Barnett and W. M. Schwab (Grendon, England: Gibraltar Books, 1989), 26–40.

6. Ibid., 28–29.

7. See Marion and Ramon F. Sarraga, "Some Episodes of Sefardic History as Reflected in Epitaphs of the Jewish Cemetery in Altona," in *Die Sefarden in Hamburg*, vol. 2, ed. Michael Studemund-Halévy (Hamburg: Helmut Buske Verlag, 1997), 662–663. Two communities, Hamburg and Altona, shared a cemetery; the latter city was controlled by Denmark until 1864 and served as the home of a small Sephardic community. See Rochelle Weinstein, "The Storied Stones of Altona: Biblical Imagery on Sefardic Tombstones at the Jewish Cemetery of Altona-Königstrasse, Hamburg," in Studemund-Halévy, *Sefarden in Hamburg*, 2:551–660.

8. See Swetschinski, *Reluctant Cosmopolitans*, 94–95; and Miriam Bodian, *Hebrews of the Portuguese Nation* (Bloomington: Indiana University Press, 1997), 158.

9. Sarraga, "Some Episodes," 662.

10. B. Z. Ornan Pinkus, "The Portuguese Community of Hamburg in the XVIIth Century" (in Hebrew), in *East and Magreb*, ed. A. Toaff (Ramat Gan: Bar-Ilan University Press, 1986), xxv.

11. See Sarraga, "Some Episodes," 662.

12. Bodian, *Hebrews of the Portuguese Nation*, ix.

13. For a detailed analysis of most of these stories, see Robert Cohen, "*Memoria para os siglos futuros*: Myth and Memory on the Beginnings of the Amsterdam Sephardi Community," *Jewish History* 2 (1987): 67–72. See also H. P. Salomon, "Myth or Anti-myth? The Oldest Account concerning the Origin of Portuguese Judaism at Amsterdam," *Lias* 16 (1989): 275–316.

14. Kaplan, "Sephardim in North-Western Europe," 248–249. Apparently there really was a trial in 1603 against this very rabbi, who was mentioned by de Barrios as having been arrested for conducting Yom Kippur services.

15. Wilhemina Chr. Pieterse, "The Sephardi Jews of Amsterdam," in Barnett and Schwab, *Sephardi Heritage*, 2:75. For the sake of comparison, see E. M. Koen, "The Earliest Sources Relating to the Portuguese Jews in the Municipal Archives of Amsterdam," *Studia Rosenthalia* 4, no. 1 (1970): 25–42.

16. See Bodian, *Hebrews of the Portuguese Nation*, 22.

17. See Arend H. Huussen Jr., "The Legal Position of Sephardi Jews in Holland, circa 1600," *Dutch Jewish History*, vol. 3, ed. Jozeph Michman (Jerusalem: Institute for Research on Dutch Jewry, 1993), 20.

18. Swetschinski, *Reluctant Cosmopolitans*, 12.

19. See, for example, Jonathan I. Israel, "The Changing Role of the Dutch Sephardim in International Trade, 1595–1715," in *Dutch Jewish History*, vol. 1, ed. Jozeph Michman and Tirtsah Levie (Jerusalem: Institute for Research on Dutch Jewry, 1984), 31–51; Israel, "The Dutch Republic and Its Jews during the Conflict over the Spanish Succession (1669–1715)," *Dutch Jewish History*, vol. 2, ed. Joseph Michman (Jerusalem: Institute for Research on Dutch Jewry, 1989), 117–136; and Israel, "Dutch Sephardi Jewry and the Rivalry of the European States," in *Society and Community*, ed. Abraham

Haim (Jerusalem: Misgav Yerushalayim, 1991), 173–196. Broader and more detailed studies are found in Israel, *Empires and Entrepôts: The Dutch, the Spanish Monarchy, and the Jews, 1585–1713* (London: Hambledon Press, 1990); and Israel, *European Jewry in the Age of Mercantilism, 1550–1750,* 2d ed. (Oxford: Oxford University Press, 1989).

20. An analysis of the cultural proclivities of this community appears in Daniel M. Swetschinski, "The Portuguese Jews of Seventeenth-Century Amsterdam: Cultural Continuity and Adaptation," in *Essays in Modern Jewish History: A Tribute to Ben Halpern,* ed. Frances Malino and Phyllis Cohen Albert (New York: Herzl Press, 1982), 56–80; and in Swetschinski, *Reluctant Cosmopolitans,* 278–314.

21. See Daniel M. Swetschinski, "Kinship and Commerce: The Foundations of Portuguese Jewish Life in Seventeenth-Century Holland," *Studia Rosenthalia* 15 (1981): 58–74.

22. Jonathan I. Israel, "The Economic Contribution of Dutch Sephardi Jewry to Holland's Golden Age, 1595–1713," *Tijdschrift voor Geschiedenis* 96 (1983): 505.

23. Richard H. Popkin, "The Historical Significance of Sephardic Judaism in 17th Century Amsterdam," *American Sephardi* 5 (1971): 21.

24. Ibid., 26.

25. The role of Venice is discussed in Miriam Bodian, "Amsterdam, Venice, and the Marrano Diaspora in the Seventeenth Century," Michman, *Dutch Jewish History,* 2: 46–65; Bodian, "The 'Portuguese' Dowry Societies in Venice and Amsterdam," *Italia* 6 (1987): 55–61; and Jonathan I. Israel, "The Jews of Venice and Their Links with Holland and with Dutch Jewry (1660–1710)," in *Gli Ebrei e Venezia secoli XIV–XVIII* (Milan: Edizioni Comunita, 1987), 95–116.

26. See H. P. Salomon, "Haham Saul Levi Morteira en de Portuguese Nieuw-Christenen," *Studia Rosenthalia* 10 (1976): 127–138 (in Dutch); 139–142 (in English); and Yosef Kaplan, "Rabbi Saul Morteira's Treatise 'Arguments against the Christian Religion' " (in Hebrew), in *Studies on the History of Dutch Jewry,* vol. 1, ed. Jozeph Michman (Jerusalem: Magnes Press, 1975), 9–31.

27. Bodian, *Hebrews of the Portuguese Nation,* 133.

28. Ibid., 146.

29. See, for example, Tirtsah Levie Bernfeld, "Caridade Escapa da Morte: Legacies to the Poor in Sephardi Wills from Seventeenth-Century Amsterdam," in Michman, *Dutch Jewish History,* 3:179–204; Robert Cohen, "Passage to a New World: The Sephardi Poor of Eighteenth Century Amsterdam," in *Neveh Ya'akov: Jubilee Volume Presented to Dr. Jaap Meijer on the Occasion of His Seventieth Birthday,* ed. Lea Dasberg and Jonathan N. Cohen (Assen, Netherlands: Van Gorcum, 1982), 31–42; and Swetschinski, *Reluctant Cosmopolitans,* 196–224.

30. Yosef Kaplan has written extensively on this topic. See, for example, "The Social Functions of the Herem in the Portuguese Jewish Community of Amsterdam in the Seventeenth Century," in Michman and Levie, *Dutch Jewish History,* 1:111–155; "Bans in the Sephardi Community of Amsterdam in the Late Seventeenth Century" (in Hebrew), in *Exile and Diaspora,* ed. Aharon Mirsky, Avraham Grossman, and Yosef Kaplan (Jerusalem: Ben Zvi Institute, 1991), 517–540; "The Place of Herem in the Sefardic Community of Hamburg during the Seventeenth Century," in *Die Sefarden in Hamburg,* vol. 1, ed. Michael Studemund-Halévy (Hamburg: Helmut Buske Verlag, 1994), 63–88; "From Apostasy to Return to Judaism: The Portuguese Jews in

Amsterdam," in *Binah: Studies in Jewish History, Thought, and Culture*, vol. 1, ed. Joseph Dan (New York: Praeger, 1989), 99–117; "The Portuguese Community of Amsterdam in the 17th Century: Tradition and Change," in Haim, *Society and Community*, 141–171 (he discusses "secularization" of the *herem* on 164); and "Wayward New Christians and Stubborn New Jews: The Shaping of a Jewish Identity," in *Robert Cohen Memorial Volume*, ed. Kenneth R. Stow and Lloyd Gartner (Haifa: Haifa University Press, 1994), 27–41.

31. See Kaplan, "Place of Herem," 75. Two chapters in Kaplan's new book, *From New Christians to New Jews* (in Hebrew) (Jerusalem: Zalman Shazar Center for Jewish History, 2003), are devoted to this topic; see 133–178.

32. See I. S. Révah, "La religion d'Uriel da Costa, Marrane de Porto," *Revue de L'Histoire des Religions* 161 (1962): 45–76; and Sanford Shepard, "The Background of Uriel da Costa's Heresy—Marranism, Scepticism, Karaism," *Judaism* 20 (1971): 341–350.

33. See I. S. Révah, "Spinoza et le hérétiques de la communauté judéo-portugaise d'Amsterdam," *Revue de L'Histoire des Religions* 154 (1958): 173–218; Révah, "Aux origines de la rupture spinozienne: Nouveaux documents sur l'incroyance dan la communauté judéo-portugaise d'Amsterdam a l'époque de l'excommunication de Spinoza," *REJ* 13 (1964): 359–431; Yosef Kaplan, "On the Relation of Spinoza's Contemporaries in the Portuguese Jewish Community of Amsterdam to Spanish Culture and the Marrano Experience," in *Spinoza's Political and Theological Thought*, ed. C. de Deugd (Amsterdam: North-Holland Publishing Co., 1984), 82–94; and Henry Méchoulan, *Être juif à Amsterdam au temps de Spinoza* (Paris: Albin Michel, 1991).

34. See I. S. Révah, *Spinoza et le Dr. Juan de Prado* (Paris: Mouton, 1959).

35. Swetschinski, *Reluctant Cosmopolitans*, 274.

36. Ibid., 276.

37. See, for instance, Yirmiyahu Yovel, *The Marrano of Reason*, vol. 1 of *Spinoza and Other Heretics* (Princeton, N.J.: Princeton University Press, 1989), 12–13.

38. Swetschinski, *Reluctant Cosmopolitans*, 277.

39. Yosef Hayim Yerushalmi, "Conversos Returning to Judaism in the 17th Century" (in Hebrew), in *Proceedings of the Fifth World Congress of Jewish Studies*, vol. 2 (Jerusalem: World Union of Jewish Studies, 1969), 201–209. See also Yosef Kaplan, "The Intellectual Ferment in the Spanish-Portuguese Community of Seventeenth Century Amsterdam," in Beinart, *Sephardi Legacy*, 2:288–314.

40. Carsten Lorenz Wilke, "Un judaïsme clandestin dans la France du XVIIe siècle: Un rite au rythme de l'imprimerie," in *Transmission et passages en monde juif*, ed. Esther Benbassa (Paris: Editiones du Cerf, 1997), 281.

41. Concerning memory and the Nation, see Daniel M. Swetschinski, "Un refus de mèmoire: Les Juifs portugais d'Amsterdam et leur passé marrane," in *Mémoires juives d'Espagne et du Portugal*, ed. Esther Benbassa (Paris: Publisud, 1996), 69–77; and Bodian, *Hebrews of the Portuguese Nation*, 76–95.

42. Yosef Hayim Yerushalmi, "The Re-education of Marranos in the Seventeenth Century," *The Third Annual Rabbi Louis Feinberg Memorial Lecture*, March 26, 1980 (Cincinnati, Ohio: University of Cincinnati, 1980), 1–16.

43. See Yosef Kaplan, "The Travels of Portuguese Jews from Amsterdam to the 'Lands of Idolatry,' " in *Jews and Conversos: Studies in Society and the Inquisition*, ed.

Yosef Kaplan (Jerusalem: Magnes Press, 1985), 197–224; and Kaplan, "Place of Herem," 68–69.

44. See Kaplan, "Portuguese Community of Amsterdam"; and Swetschinski, *Reluctant Cosmopolitans*, 213–221.

45. Bodian, *Hebrews of the Portuguese Nation*, 152.

46. Ibid., 155.

47. See ibid., 156.

48. Miriam Bodian, " 'Men of the Nation': The Shaping of *Converso* Identity in Early Modern Europe," *Past and Present* 143 (1994): 61.

49. Swetschinski, *Reluctant Cosmopolitans*, 316.

50. Ibid., 320.

51. Ibid., 321–322.

52. Ibid., 323.

53. Swetschinski describes what he calls "aristocratic tastes" and leisure time of the merchant class; see ibid., 278–314.

54. This term is not to be understood as synonymous with the "New Jew" in Yovel, *Marrano of Reason*, 49.

55. Swetschinski, *Reluctant Cosmopolitans*, 2 and n. 5.

56. This approach is also discussed in Swetschinski, *Reluctant Cosmopolitans*, 6.

57. Bodian, *Hebrews of the Portuguese Nation*, 135, 148–149.

58. Kaplan, "Portuguese Community of Amsterdam," 150–151.

59. Bodian claims that the Ashkenazim who were not in their immediate proximity were treated more kindly; see " 'Men of the Nation,' " 68. More detailed analyses of these interactions appear in Yosef Kaplan, "The Attitude of the Spanish and Portuguese Jews to the Ashkenazim in Seventeenth Century Amsterdam" (in Hebrew), in *Transition and Change in Modern Jewish History: Essays Presented in Honor of Shmuel Ettinger* (Jerusalem: Zalman Shazar Center, 1987), 389–412; and Joseph Michman, "Between Sephardim and Ashkenazim in Amsterdam" (in Hebrew), in *The Sephardi and Oriental Jewish Heritage*, ed. Issachar Ben Ami (Jerusalem: Magnes Press, 1982): 135–149.

CHAPTER FIVE   FRANCE

1. Two short documents refer to conversos from Spain who were sneaking through the Pyrenees from Catalan to France. See José Maria Millás Vallicrosa, "Emigración masiva de conversos por la frontera Catalona-Francesa en el año 1608," *Sefarad* 19 (1959): 140–144.

2. Quoted by Gérard Nahon, "The Sephardim of France," in *The Sephardi Heritage*, vol. 2, ed. Richard D. Barnett and W. M. Schwab (Grendon, England: Gibraltar Books, 1989), 47.

3. Ibid., 48. Zvi Loker discusses the fact that the authorities in essence were projecting ambivalence via their policy. See "From Converso Congregation to Holy Community: The Shaping of the Jewish Community of Bordeaux during the 18th Century" (in Hebrew), *Zion* 42 (1976): 51.

4. "Les Nouveaux Chrétiens ou Marchands Portugais maintiennent leur observance juive et édifient des institutions communautaires semi-clandestines dans des

conditions bien meilleures que dans la Péninsule ibérique: C'est une raison de leur traversée—relativement paisible—du XVIIe siècle." Gérard Nahon, "Les Rapports des Communautés Judeo-Portugaises de France avec celle d'Amsterdam au XVIIe et XVIIIe siècles," *Studia Rosenthalia* 10 (1976): 161.

5. Frances Malino, *The Sephardic Jews of Bordeaux* (University, Alabama: University of Alabama Press, 1978), 5.

6. Loker, "From Converso Congregation," 50–51.

7. Carsten Lorens Wilke, "Un judaïsme clandestin dans la France du XVIIe siècle: Un rite au rythem de l'imprimerie," in *Transmission et passages en monde juif*, ed. Esther Benbassa (Paris: Editiones du Cerf, 1997), 282.

8. See Gérard Nahon, "Bayonne dans la Diaspora sefarade d'Occident (XVIIe— XVIIIe siecle), in *Proceedings of the Seventh World Congress of Jewish Studies*, vol. 4 (Jerusalem: World Union of Jewish Studies, 1981), 47.

9. Michael Alpert, *Crypto-Judaism and the Spanish Inquisition* (Hampshire, England: Palgrave, 2001), 95.

10. Nahon, "Sephardim of France," 52.

11. Gérard Nahon, "From New Christians to the Portuguese Jewish Nation in France," in *Moreshet Sepharad = Sephardi Legacy*, ed. Haim Beinart (Jerusalem: Magnes Press, 1992), 2:341.

12. Nahon, "Sephardim of France," 47–53.

13. I. S. Révah, "Le Premiere établissement des Marranes portugais à Rouen (1603–1607)," in *Annuaire de l'Institut de Philologie et d'histoire Orientales et Slaves* 13 (1953) [=*Mélanges Isidore Lévy*], 539–540.

14. See Malino, *Sephardic Jews*, 1–26, 117–125.

15. See Zosa Szajkowski, "The Marranos and Sephardim of France," in *The Abraham Weiss Jubilee Volume* (New York: Abraham Weiss Jubilee Committee, 1964), 107.

16. Ibid., 109. Szajkowski lists over eighty conversions to Catholicism between 1667 and 1782, the majority of which were voluntary and took place in Bordeaux. This is a large number for a small community. See 122–127 for a detailed list.

17. Ibid., 113, 116–119.

18. Szajkowski points out that the percentage of elderly members of the Nation in France was unusually high. See "Marranos and Sephardim," 114.

19. Gérard Nahon, "The Impact of the Expulsion from Spain on the Jewish Community of Pre-Revolutionary France, 1550–1791," *Judaism* 41 (1992): 172–173.

20. An early article on this community was written by Cecil Roth, "Les Marranes à Rouen: Un chapitre ignoré de l'histoire des Juifs de France," *REJ* 88 (1929): 113–155. This was followed by I. S. Révah, "Le Premiere établissement," 539–552; and Haim Beinart, "The Spanish Inquisition at Work outside the Peninsula" (in Hebrew), in *Proceedings of the Fifth World Congress of Jewish Studies*, vol. 2 (Jerusalem: World Union of Jewish Studies, 1972), 55–73. An attempt to reconstruct life in Rouen appeared in Alpert, *Crypto-Judaism and the Spanish Inquisition*, 64–85.

21. Nahon, "Sephardim of France," 68. Nahon published two articles by the same name that deal with this topic and related material: "Les Rapports des Communautés Judeo-Portugaises de France avec celle d'Amsterdam au XVIIe et XVIIIe siècles," in *Proceedings of the Sixth World Congress of Jewish Studies*, vol. 2 (Jerusalem: World Union of Jewish Studies, 1973), 77–84, and a lengthier version, already mentioned, in *Studia Rosenthalia* 10 (1976): 37–78, 151–188 (163–188 contain documenta-

tion). See also Nahon, *Métropoles et périphéries sefarades d'Occident* (Paris: Les Édiciones du Cerf, 1993), 95–183.

22. Nahon, "Les Rapports," *Studia Rosenthalia*, 161. The community of Bayonne had to cope with a substantial number of poor in their midst. See Nahon, "Bayonne dans la Diaspora," 52–53.

23. Nahon, "Sephardim of France," 49.

24. See Nahon, "Les Rapports," *Proceedings*, 78; Nahon, "Les Rapports," *Studia Rosenthalia*, 51.

25. For details, see Nahon, "Les Rapports," *Studia Rosenthalia*, 162.

26. Ibid., 70–72.

27. Nahon, "Les Rapports," *Proceedings*, 84 (my translation).

28. Nahon discusses this in "Les Rapports," *Studia Rosenthalia*, 77, although there was a parity of sorts between Bayonne and Bordeaux.

29. See Nahon, "Sephardim of France," 52–53.

30. Ibid., 77.

31. Wilke provides a detailed discussion of this phenomenon including the role played by Menasseh ben Israel in his article, "Un judaïsme clandestin," 291–299.

32. Nahon, "Sephardim of France," 53.

33. Timothy Oelman, ed. and trans., *Marrano Poets of the Seventeenth Century*, (London: Associated University Presses, 1982), 27.

34. Concerning the man and his community, see Rafael Carrasco, "Preludio al 'Siglo de los Portugueses': La Inquisición de Cuenca y los judaizantes lusitanos en el siglo XVI," *Hispania* 47 (1987): 503–559; Charles Amiel, "El criptojudaísmo castellano en La Mancha a fines del siglo XVI," in *Judíos. Sefarditas. Converso. La expulsión de 1492 y sus consecuencias*, ed. Ángel Alcalá (Valladolid: Ámbito Ediciones, 1995), 503–512; and Renée Levine Melammed, *Heretics or Daughters of Israel? The Crypto-Jewish Women of Castile* (New York: Oxford University Press, 1999), 150–165, 236–240.

35. See I. S. Révah, "Un pamphlet contre l'Inquisition d'Antonio Enríquez Gómez: La second partie de la 'Politíca Angélica," *REJ* 121 (1962): 112. This account became popularized, attributing various remarks to Gómez upon witnessing his effigy. See introduction to Teresa de Santos, *Antonio Enríquez: El siglo pitagórico y Vida de don Gregorio Guadaña* (Madrid: Ediciones Cátedra, 1991), 12–13, 18.

36. This was a messianic movement that took place from 1665 to 1666 and stemmed from Turkey but affected Jewish communities worldwide. When the messianic pretender apostasized, the majority of his disillusioned followers returned to their normal lives. Nevertheless, a small number of Jews (who did not convert with him) continued to believe in Sabbatai Zevi despite the fact that he had become a Muslim.

37. For example, Refael d'Aguilar of Amsterdam received queries from Antwerp and from Bayonne in the mid-sixteenth century. See Yosef Kaplan, "The Place of Rabbi Moshe Refael D'Aguilar in the Context of His Connections with Refugees from Spain and Portugal in the 17th Century" (in Hebrew), in *Proceedings of the Sixth World Congress of Jewish Studies*, vol. 2 (Jerusalem: World Union of Jewish Studies, 1975); 95–106.

38. The rabbis did not have an official status and were more or less at the mercy of their congregations. Rabbis serving in Bayonne usually came from Amsterdam, although one came from Italy. See Nahon, "Sephardim of France," 55.

39. See Wilke, "Un judaïsme clandestin," 309.

40. No mention was made of the Sephardi tradition of *hadas*, which was a celebration held for both male and female infants on the eighth night after they were born. For more details, see Renée Levine Melammed, "Noticias sobre los ritos de los nacimientos y de la pureza de las judeo-conversas castellanas del siglo XVI," *El Olivo* 13, nos. 29-30 (1989): 235-243.

41. Nahon, "Sephardim of France," 53.

42. Ibid., 162. Nahon has also pointed out that the undesired poor arrivals could now be encouraged to go to France.

43. See Nahon, "Les Rapports," *Studia Rosenthalia*, 163.

44. Nahon, "Sephardim of France," 51.

45. Ibid., 51-52.

46. See Loker, "From Converso Congregation."

47. For a discussion of attitudes toward death, see Gérard Nahon, "Pour un approche des attitudes devant la mort au XVIIIe siècle: Sermonnaires et testateurs juifs portugais à Bayonne," *Métropoles et périphéries*, 261-369.

48. See, for example, Gérard Nahon, "The Spanish Register of Circumcisions by Samuel Gomes Atias (Bidache 1725-1773)," *Bulletin hispanique* 86 (1974): 142-182.

49. See Nahon, "Sephardim of France," 54.

50. Malino, *Sephardic Jews*, 7.

51. Ibid., 12.

52. Ibid., 20.

53. Ibid., 24-25.

54. Nahon, "Sephardim of France," 57.

55. The story of the French community changed as the result of the ideological changes in late eighteenth-century France; these changes seriously affected the Jews of France and forced them to reconsider their identity as Jews and as Frenchmen.

56. Richard Menkis, "Patriarchs and Patricians: The Gradis Family of Eighteenth-Century Bordeaux," in *From East and West: Jews in a Changing Europe, 1750-1870*, ed. Frances Malino and David Sorkin (Oxford: Blackwell, 1990), 32. He also refers to the name of their firm as a "surrogate noble title" (33).

57. Ibid., 25.

58. Ibid., 26.

59. Ibid., 44.

60. Alpert, *Crypto-Judaism and the Spanish Inquisition*, 193; see also 170-171, 190.

61. See Claude B. Stucyznski, "Cristãos-Novos e Judaísmo no Início da Época Moderna: Identidade Religiosa e 'Razão de Estado,'" *Lusitania Sacra*, 2d ser., vol. 12 (2000): 355-366, and his discussion of a double but not necessarily simultaneous identity "of being Jews and of being Sephardi-Portuguese."

CHAPTER SIX   ENGLAND

1. See Gérard Nahon, "The Sephardim of France," in *The Sephardi Heritage*, vol. 2, ed. Richard D. Barnett and Walter M. Schwab (Grendon, England: Gibraltar Books, 1989), 57. It is quite probable that the French tolerated them because of economic utility.

2. See Benjamin Kaplan, "Fictions of Privacy: House Chapels and the Spatial Ac-

commodation of Religious Dissent in Early Modern Europe," *American Historical Review* 107, no. 4 (2002): 1031–1064, for a discussion of foreign embassies and rights to pray in their chapels.

3. Daniel M. Swetschinski, *Reluctant Cosmopolitans: The Portuguese Jews of Seventeenth-Century Amsterdam* (London: Littman Library of Jewish Civilization, 2000), 65.

4. Yosef Kaplan, "The Jewish Profile of the Spanish-Portuguese Community of London," *Judaism* 41 (1992): 230–231. See also Y. Kaplan, *From New Christians to New Jews* (Jerusalem: Zalman Shazar Center, 2003).

5. For details, see Lucien Wolf, "The First English Jew: Notes on Antonio Fernandez Carvajal, with some Biographical Documents," *TJHSE* 2 (1894–1895): 14–48. For an early history of this phase of the community, see Wolf, "Crypto-Jews under the Commonwealth," *TJHSE* 1 (1893–1894): 55–88.

6. A. S. Diamond, "The Community of the Resettlement, 1656–1684: A Social Survey," *TJHSE* 24 (1974): 135.

7. This well-known figure who was born as Manoel Dias Soeiro has been the subject of many studies. See, for instance, *Menasseh ben Israel and His World*, ed. Yosef Kaplan, Henry Méchoulan and Richard H. Popkin (Leiden: Brill, 1989); and Ismar Schorsch, "From Messianism to Realpolitik: Menasseh Ben Israel and the Readmission of the Jews to England," *PAAJR* 45 (1978): 187–208.

8. For details, see R. D. Barnett, "Sephardim of England," in Barnett and Schwab, *The Sephardi Heritage*, 2:6–7; Y. Kaplan, "Jewish Profile," 232–233; Y. Kaplan, "Sephardim in North-Western Europe and the New World," in *Moreshet Sepharad = The Sephardi Legacy*, ed. Haim Beinart (Jerusalem: Magnes Press, 1992), 2:261–262; and Wilfred S. Samuel, "The First London Synagogue of the Resettlement," *TJHSE* 10 (1924): 1–147.

9. See A. S. Diamond, "The Cemetery of the Resettlement," *TJHSE* 19 (1960): 183; and Edgar Samuel, "1680–1780: The Golden Age of the Portuguese Jewish Community of London," in *Society and Community*, ed. Abraham Haim (Jerusalem: Misgav Yerushalayim, 1991), 201.

10. Barnett, "Sephardim of England," 9.

11. Ibid., 6.

12. Swetschinski, *Reluctant Cosmopolitans*, 51.

13. See Matt Goldish, "Jews, Christians, and Conversos: Rabbi Solomon Aailion's Struggles in the Portuguese Community of London," *Journal of Jewish Studies* 45 (1994): 234–235. See also David S. Katz, "The Jews of England and 1688," in *From Persecution to Toleration: The Glorious Revolution and Religion in England*, ed. Ole Peter Grell, Jonathan I. Israel, and Nicholas Tyacke (Oxford: Clarendon Press, 1991), 217–249.

14. Y. Kaplan, "Jewish Profile," 229–240, quotation on 233. See also Diamond, "Community of the Resettlement," 134–150.

15. Y. Kaplan, "Sephardim in North-Western Europe," 264, and Lucien Wolf, "Jewry of the Restoration," *TJHSE* 5 (1902–1905): 5–33.

16. See Wolf, "Crypto-Jews under the Commonwealth," 65.

17. See Y. Kaplan, "Jewish Profile," 230–231.

18. Goldish, "Jews, Christians, and Conversos," 228.

19. See also Evelyne Oliel-Grausz, "A Study in Intercommunal Relations in the

Sephardi Diaspora: London and Amsterdam in the Eighteenth Century," in *Dutch Jews as Perceived by Themselves and by Others*, ed. Chaya Brasz and Yosef Kaplan (Leiden: Brill, 2001), 42.

20. For a discussion of the statutes, see Miriam Bodian, "The Escamot of the Spanish-Portuguese Jewish Community of London," *Michael* 9 (1985): 9–26.

21. Goldish, "Jews, Christians and Conversos," 243–257.

22. Y. Kaplan discusses this phenomenon in "Jewish Profile," 233–234; for insight into the friction during Sasportas's stay, see Y. Tishby, "New Information on the 'Converso' Community in London according to the Letters of Sasportas from 1664/1665" (in Hebrew), in *Exile and Diaspora*, ed. Aharon Mirsky, Avraham Grossman, and Yosef Kaplan (Jerusalem: Ben Zvi Institute, 1988): 470–496. Sasportas fled when an epidemic broke out in the summer of 1665.

23. Regarding this difficulty, see Y. Kaplan, "Jewish Profile," 233–234.

24. Richard Barnett, "Mr. Pepys' Contacts with the Spanish and Portuguese Jews of London," in Mirsky et al., *Exile and Diaspora* (English volume; Jerusalem: Ben Zvi Institute, 1991), 226–228.

25. Ibid., 228–229.

26. The letter was translated and published by Matt Goldish in "Jews, Christians, and Conversos," 238–242. His spelling of the family name is Aailion; there was controversy around the rabbi himself as discussed in this article; Barnett called him a "dubious figure" in "Sephardim of England," 13.

27. Barnett, "Mr. Pepys' Contacts," 230.

28. Oliel-Grausz, "Study in Intercommunal Relations," 48.

29. Y. Kaplan, "Jewish Profile," 234.

30. Goldish, "Jews, Christians, and Conversos," 248–249.

31. Ibid., 248.

32. R. D. Barnett, "The Correspondence of the Mahamad of the Spanish and Portuguese Congregation of London during the Seventeenth and Eighteenth Centuries," *TJHSE* 20 (1964): 4–5.

33. Y. Kaplan, "Jewish Profile," 239.

34. Barnett, "Correspondence of the Mahamad," 23–25.

35. Ibid., 25–33.

36. The Inquisition was still active in Spain at the beginning of the eighteenth century, arresting locals as well as Portuguese who were probably on their way to France. The War of the Spanish Succession (1700–1713) seems to have hampered activities only temporarily. A look at the Judaizing of these conversos can be found in Michael Alpert, *Crypto-Judaism and the Spanish Inquisition* (Hampshire, England: Palgrave, 2001), 176–199.

37. E. Samuel, "1680–1780," 203.

38. Barnett, "Correspondence of the Mahamad," 33.

39. Nahon, "Sephardim of France," 59.

40. Swetschinski, *Reluctant Cosmopolitans*, 69.

41. See Oliel-Grausz, "Study in Intercommunal Relations," 50–56.

42. Barnett, "Correspondence of the Mahamad," 33.

43. E. Samuel, "1680–1780," 205.

44. Todd M. Endelman has downplayed any intellectual achievements among the members of this community in *The Jews of Georgian England, 1714–1830* (Philadel-

phia: Jewish Publication Society, 1979); David B. Ruderman attempts to correct this impression with the examples discussed in his book, *Jewish Enlightenment in an English Key: Anglo-Jewry's Construction of Modern Jewish Thought* (Princeton, N.J.: Princeton University Press, 2000). See also, for example, Richard Popkin, "David Levi, Anglo-Jewish Theologian," *JQR* 87 (1996): 79–101; and Matt Goldish, "Newtonian, Converso, and Deist: The Lives of Jacob (Henrique) de Castro Sarmento," *Science in Context* 10 (1997): 651–675.

45. Barnett, "Sephardim of England," 10–11.

46. Todd M. Endelman, *Radical Assimilation in English Jewish History, 1656–1945* (Bloomington: Indiana University Press, 1990), 11–13.

47. Ibid., 17.

48. See Y. Kaplan, "Jewish Profile," 238, and n. 24 in chapter 5 of this book.

49. Endelman, *Radical Assimilation,* 20.

50. Ibid., 30.

51. Todd M. Endelman, " 'A Hebrew to the End': The Emergence of Disraeli's Jewishness," in *The Self-Fashioning of Disraeli, 1818–1851,* ed. C. Richmond and P. Smith (Cambridge: Cambridge University Press, 1998), 111.

52. Endelman, *Radical Assimilation,* 21–22.

53. See Ruderman, *Jewish Enlightenment,* 8.

54. Ibid., 7. He even entitled a chapter in the book "Translation and Transformation: The Englishing of Jewish Culture."

55. Michael Galchinsky, "Engendering Liberal Jews: Jewish Women in Victorian England," in *Jewish Women in Historical Perspective,* 2d ed., ed. Judith R. Baskin (Detroit: Wayne State University Press, 1998), 219.

56. See Renée Levine Melammed, "The Ultimate Challenge: Safeguarding the Crypto-Judaic Heritage," *PAAJR* 53 (1986): 91–109.

57. Galchinsky, "Engendering Liberal Jews," 213, discusses the novel in which the Jewess did not choose a Christian suitor but rather a Jew.

58. Ibid., 219.

59. Endelman, *Radical Assimilation,* 33.

60. See Barnett, "Sephardim of England," 20.

61. See Ruderman, *Jewish Enlightenment,* 57.

CHAPTER SEVEN   ITALY

1. I will attempt here to reconstruct converso life on the basis of some unusual Inquisition trials along with other assorted material.

2. Nadia Zeldes has attempted to reconstruct the history of this community by means of analyzing inventories and other material; see, for example, "Tracing a Profile of the New Christians of Sicily" (in Hebrew), *Zion* 65 (2000): 307–342; and for more details, Zeldes, *Converted Jews in Sicily before and after the Expulsion (1460–1550)* (in Hebrew), Ph.D. diss., Tel Aviv University, 1997. It should also be noted that the Jews were expelled from Naples in 1519 and 1541.

3. See Robert Bonfil, "The History of the Spanish and Portuguese Jews in Italy," in *Moreshet Sepharad = The Sephardi Legacy,* ed. Haim Beinart (Jerusalem: Magnes Press, 1992), 2:217.

4. Ibid., 221.

5. See, for example, Ariel Toaff, "Ebrei spagnoli e marrani nell'Italia del cinque-cento: Caratteristiche di una mentalitá," in *Xudeus e Conversos na Historia*, ed. Carlos Barros (Santiago de Compostela: Editorial de la Historia, 1994), 1:195–204.

6. Anna Foa, "Converts and *Conversos* in Sixteenth-Century Italy: Marranos in Rome," in *The Jews of Italy: Memory and Identity*, ed. Bernard D. Cooperman and Barbara Garvin (Bethesda, Md.: University Press of Maryland, 2000), 111. Foa points out that during this period absolutions were granted by the pope, but the Spanish rulers pressured Rome to cancel them.

7. See ibid., 112–115, regarding the unusual saga of Aranda. See also Cecil Roth, "Joseph Saralvo, A Marrano Martyr at Rome," in *Festschrift zu Simon Dubnows siebzig-stem Geburtstag*, ed. Ismar Elbogen, Josef Meisl, and Mark Wischnitzer (Berlin: Jü-discher Verlag, 1930), 180–186.

8. See chapter 3, n. 57.

9. These two figures are discussed in chapter 3.

10. Bonfil, "History of the Spanish and Portguese Jews," 227.

11. Ibid., 230. Individuals of this type will be discussed in the section regarding Venice.

12. Bonfil adds, "By contrast, those states in which political, social or religious pressure was exercised against the Conversos, particularly from the side of Spain, were considered less attractive, and some failed completely to attract a Converso set-tlement, even if their rulers so wished" ("History of the Spanish and Portuguese Jews," 223). Savoy was an example of the latter, namely, a failed attempt by a duke.

13. I have found little concerning Florence except for an Italian book on the Jews of the Renaissance written in the early twentieth century by M. D. Cassuto, *Gli Ebrei a Firenze nell'età del Rinascimento* (Florence, 1905), and some references in Lucia Frat-tarelli Fischer, "Urban Forms of Jewish Settlement in Tuscan Cities (Florence, Pisa, Leghorn) during the 17th Century," in *Papers in Jewish Demography, 1989*, ed. Uziel O. Schmelz and Sergio Della Pergola (Jerusalem: Institute of Contemporary Jewry, 1993), 48–60.

14. See Benjamin Ravid, "Venice, Rome, and the Reversion of New Christians to Judaism," in *L'identità dissumulata, Guidaizzanti iberici nell'Europa Cristiana dell'età moderna*," ed. Pier Cesare Ioly Zorattini (Florence: Leo S. Olschki Editore, 2000), 153–154.

15. See Abraham David, "Concerning the Martyr's Death of the Proselyte Joseph Saralvo" (in Hebrew), *Kiryat Sefer* 59 (1984): 243.

16. See Renata Segre, "Sephardic Refugees in Ferrara: Two Notable Families," in *Crisis and Creativity in the Sephardic World, 1391–1648*, ed. Benjamin R. Gampel (New York: Columbia University Press, 1997), 167.

17. This Portuguese publication was translated by Martin A. Cohen into English as *Samuel Usque's Consolation for the Tribulations of Israel* (Philadelphia: Jewish Publi-cation Society, 1965).

18. See Cecil Roth, " 'Salusque Lusitano,' " *JQR* 34 (1943): 65–85. See also Roth, "The Marrano Press at Ferrara 1552–1555," *Modern Language Review* 38 (1943): 307–317.

19. Roth, " 'Salusque Lusitano,' " 70.

20. See Andrée Aelion Brooks, *The Woman Who Defied Kings: The Life and Times of Doña Gracia Nasi* (St. Paul, Minn.: Paragon House, 2002), 222, 241, 262.

21. Ibid., 74.

22. Brooks states that he was a cousin of Dona Gracia's and had been named as her replacement as the bank's head if anything were to happen to her. See *Woman Who Defied Kings*, 167, 396, 407.

23. Ibid., 369, 383–384. Gomez's trial is discussed on 379–382; Enríquez's on 382–383; da Costa's on 376–379.

24. Roth, " 'Salusque Lusitano,' " 71–73. Greed and jealousy cannot be ruled out as possible motives for bringing these men to trial.

25. Ibid., 75.

26. See Brooks, *Woman Who Defied Kings*, 140.

27. The fate of the conversos of Ancona will be described next.

28. Brooks, *Woman Who Defied Kings*, 339.

29. See Segre, "Sephardic Refugees," 169 n. 26.

30. Ibid., 164–165, 183–184.

31. Ibid., 180.

32. Regarding her visit and business enterprises in the Ragusan Republic, see Moises Orfali, "Doña Gracia Mendes and the Ragusan Republic: The Successful Use of Economic Institutions in 16th Century Commerce," in *The Mediterranean and the Jews*, ed. Elliott Horowitz and Moises Orfali (Ramat Gan: Bar Ilan University Press, 2002): 175–201.

33. See, for example, Libby Garshowitz, "Gracia Mendes: Power, Influence, and Intrigue," in *Power of the Weak: Studies on Medieval Women*, ed. Jennifer Carpenter and Sally-Beth MacLean (Champaign: University of Illinois Press, 1995), 94–125.

34. Segre, "Sephardic Refugees," 166.

35. See Roth, "Joseph Saralvo," 180–186; and David, "Concerning the Martyr's Death," 244, regarding an elegy to Saralvo.

36. For details regarding Portuguese in Ancona as of 1532, see Aron di Leone Leoni, "Per una storia della Nazione Portoghese ad Ancona e a Pesaro," in Zorattini, *L'identità dissimulata*, 28–78.

37. Shlomo Simonsohn, "Marranos in Ancona under Papal Protection," *Michael* 9 (1985): 238. For a detailed analysis of the negotiations, precedents, and repercussions of this charter, see Bernard D. Cooperman, "Portuguese *Conversos* in Ancona: Jewish Political Activity in Early Modern Italy," in *In Iberia and Beyond: Hispanic Jews between Cultures*, ed. Bernard D. Cooperman (Newark, Del.: University of Delaware Press, 1998), 297–352.

38. The original text appears in Simonsohn, "Marranos in Ancona," 259, and is referred to on p. 238.

39. For details, see ibid., 239–241.

40. Ibid., 242.

41. See Bonfil, "History of the Spanish and Portuguese Jews," 224.

42. See David Kaufmann, "Les Martyrs D'Ancone," *REJ* 11 (1885): 149–153, for a list of the martyrs and for reference to the elegies written in their memory.

43. Details concerning Portuguese who arrived in Pesaro even prior to this attempted settlement can be found in Leoni, "Per una storia," 72–78.

44. Bonfil, "History of the Spanish and Portuguese Jews," 224–225. See also Marc Saperstein, "Martyrs, Merchants, and Rabbis: Jewish Communal Conflict as Reflected in the Responsa on the Boycott of Ancona," *Jewish Social Studies* 43 (1981):

215–228. For a detailed report, see Brooks, *Woman Who Defied Kings*, 336–345, 349–364.

45. Roth, "Joseph Saralvo," 182.

46. Bonfil, "History of the Spanish and Portuguese Jews," 228, 232.

47. Pier Cesare Ioly Zorattini describes the confrontation with normative Judaism on Italian soil as slow and progressive and that resulted at times in the adoption of a definite Catholic identity and also created numerous intermediary options, such as adopting a selective and critical Judaism. See *"Derekh Teshuvah*: La Via del Ritorno," in Zorattini, *L'Identità' dissimulata*, 195–248; and the review by Claude B. Stuczynski, "Cristãos-Novos e Judaísmo no Início da Época Moderna: Identidade Religiosa e 'Razão de Estado,' " *Lusitania Sacra*, 2d ser., vol. 12 (2000): 355–366.

48. Cecil Roth, *Venice* (Philadelphia: Jewish Publication Society, 1930), 46.

49. For details, see Benjamin Ravid, "The First Charter of the Jewish Merchants of Venice, 1589," *AJS Review* 1 (1976): 187–222; and Ravid, "The Legal Status of the Jewish Merchants of Venice, 1541–1638," *Journal of Economic History* 35 (1975): 274–279. For details, see 192–209.

50. Pier Cesare Ioly Zorattini, "Jews, Crypto-Jews, and the Inquisition," in *The Jews of Early Modern Venice*, ed. Robert C. Davis and Benjamin Ravid (Baltimore: Johns Hopkins University Press, 2001), 106.

51. See Cecil Roth, "The Strange Case of Hector Mendes Bravo," *Hebrew Union College Annual* 18 (1944): 221–245.

52. See Bonfil, "History of the Spanish and Portuguese Jews," 232; see also Miriam Bodian, "The 'Portuguese' Dowry Societies in Venice and Amsterdam: A Case Study within the Marrano Diaspora," *Italia* 6 (1987): 30–61; and Elliott Horowitz, "The Dowering of Brides in the Ghetto of Venice: Between Tradition and Change, Ideas and Reality" (in Hebrew), *Tarbiz* 56 (1987): 347–371.

53. See Moises Orfali, "The Portuguese Dowry Society in Livorno and the Marrano Diaspora," *Studia Rosenthalia* 35, no. 2 (2001): 147–148, esp. n. 23.

54. Brian Pullan, *The Jews of Europe and the Inquisition of Venice, 1550–1670* (Oxford: Blackwell, 1983), 60.

55. See Pullan, *Jews of Europe*, 9–10.

56. Zorattini, "Jews, Crypto-Jews," 98–100.

57. Ibid., 107–108.

58. Pullan, *Jews of Europe*, 58.

59. Zorattini, "Jews, Crypto-Jews," 104.

60. Pullan, *Jews of Europe*, 60–61.

61. Zorattini, "Jews, Crypto-Jews," 113.

62. Pullan, *Jews of Europe*, 201.

63. See Brooks, *Woman Who Defied Kings*, 225, 366, 379, 387.

64. Pullan, *Jews of Europe*, 214.

65. For information on these restrictions, see Benjamin Ravid, "From Yellow to Red: On the Distinguishing Head-Covering of the Jews of Venice," *Jewish History* 6 (1992): 179–210.

66. Pullan, *Jews of Europe*, 217.

67. Zorattini, "Jews, Crypto-Jews," 102.

68. Pullan, *Jews of Europe*, 224.

69. Ibid., 225–227.

70. See ibid., 223–224, for examples of seeking Jews for help when one's fortune was down.

71. Ibid., 217–218.

72. Pier Cesar Ioly Zorattini, "Anrriquez Nunez alias Abraham alias Righetto: A Marrano Caught between the S. Uffizio of Venice and the Inquisition of Lisbon," in *The Mediterranean and the Jews*, ed. Ariel Toaff and Simon Schwarzfuchs (Ramat Gan: Bar Ilan University Press, 1989), 307.

73. Brian Pullan, " 'A Ship with Two Rudders': 'Righetto Marrano' and the Inquisition in Venice," *Historical Journal* 20 (1977): 37–38.

74. See Zorattini, "Anrriquez Nunez," 291–292.

75. Ibid., 302.

76. Pullan, *Jews of Europe*, 218.

77. Zorattini, "Anrriquez Nunez," 303.

78. Pullan, *Jews of Europe*, 218–219.

79. Pullan, " 'Ship with Two Rudders,' " 44.

80. Pullan, *Jews of Europe*, 219–220.

81. Lepanto is located in southwestern Greece.

82. Zorattini, "Anrriquez Nunez," 305–307.

83. The information on this figure has been culled from Pullan, *Jews of Europe*, 230–241; and Pullan, "The Inquisition and the Jews of Venice: The Case of Gaspare Ribeiro, 1580–1581," *Bulletin of the John Rylands Library* 62 (1979): 207–231.

84. On women's roles in religion and particularly in converso society, see Renée Levine Melammed, *Heretics or Daughters of Israel? The Crypto-Jewish Women of Castile* (New York: Oxford University Press, 1999); and Levine Melammed, "The Ultimate Challenge: Safeguarding the Crypto-Judaic Heritage," *PAAJR* 53 (1986): 91–109.

85. Pullan, *Jews of Europe*, 225.

86. For an interesting account, see Pier Cesare Ioly Zorattini, "Estevão Noghera, A Portuguese Spy among the Marranos in Venice during the Sixteenth Century," in *Society and Community*, ed. Abraham Haim (Jerusalem: Misgav Yerushalayim, 1991), 81–90.

87. Pullan, *Jews of Europe*, 230.

88. See Cecil Roth, *The History of the Jews of Italy* (Philadelphia: Jewish Publication Society, 1946), 225.

89. Bonfil, "History of the Spanish and Portuguese Jews," 230–231.

90. See Ravid, "Venice, Rome," 173–174.

91. The paths of New Christians and "New Jews" in Tuscany was traced in Lucia Frattarelli Fischer, "Cristiani Nuovi e Nuovi Ebrei in Toscana fra Cinque e Seicento: Legittimazioni e percorse indiviudali," in Zorattini, *L'identità dissimulata*, 99–149.

92. For an analysis of their role in international commerce, see Jean Pierre Filippini, "Le Role des Négociants et des Banquiers juifs de Livourne dans le Grand Commerce International en Méditerranée au XVIII siècle," in Toaff and Schwarzfuchs, *Mediterranean and the Jews*, 123–149.

93. Roth, *History of the Jews of Italy*, 399.

94. For a very detailed study of this charter, see Bernard Cooperman, "Trade and Settlements: The Establishment and Early Development of the Jewish Communities in Leghorn and Pisa (1591–1626)," Ph.D. diss., Harvard University, 1976.

95. A third option was to return to Iberia. For cases of this sort, see Haim Bei-

nart, "Jewish-Converso Connections from Italy to Spain" (in Hebrew), in *Jews in Italy*, ed. Haim Beinart (Jerusalem: Magnes Press, 1988), 275–288.

96. Renata Segre, "Sephardic Settlements in Sixteenth-Century Italy: A Historical and Geographical Survey," *Mediterranean Historical Review* 6 (1991): 115.

97. See Benjamin Ravid, "A Tale of Three Cities and Their *Raison d'Etat*: Ancona, Venice, Livorno, and the Competition for Jewish Merchants in the Sixteenth Century," *Mediterranean Historical Review* 6 (1991): 156.

98. See Moises Orfali, "Danielillo of Leghorn: Image versus Historic Reality" (in Hebrew), in Haim, *Society and Community*, 147 n. 12.

99. The ban in Leghorn seemed to be aimed mostly at those who were not observing the dietary laws. Community decisions and regulations were discussed in Moises Orfali, "Reforming and Conforming: A History of the Jews of Livorno, 1693–1707," *Mediterranean Historical Review* 7 (1992): 208–218.

100. See Frattarelli Fischer, "Urban Forms of Jewish Settlement," 55.

101. Ibid., 56.

102. See Flora Aghib Levi d'Ancona, "The Sephardi Community of Leghorn (Livorno)," in *The Sephardi Heritage*, vol. 2, ed. Richard D. Barnett and W. M. Schwab (Grendon, England: Gibraltar Books, 1989), 181.

103. For more information about the history of this community, see Cecil Roth, "Notes sur les marranes de Livourne, *REJ* 90 (1931): 1–27; Renzo Toaff, *La Nazione ebrea a Livorno e a Pisa (1591–1700)* (Florence: Leo S. Olschki Editore, 1990); and Lionel Lévy, *La Communaté juive de Livourne* (Paris: Éditions L'Harmattan, 1996). For the later period, see J. P. Filippini, "Juifs émigrés et immigrés dans le port de Livourne pendant le période Napolónienne," *East and Magreb* 4 (1983): 31–91.

104. Levi d'Ancona, "Sephardi Community of Leghorn," 182.

105. Orfali, "Portuguese Dowry Society," 144.

106. Ibid., 150–151.

107. Levi d'Ancona, "Sephardi Community of Leghorn," 194.

108. See Bernard Cooperman, "Eliahu Montalto's 'Suitable and Incontrovertible Propositions': A Seventeenth-Century Anti-Christian Polemic," in *Jewish Thought in the Seventeenth Century*, ed. Isadore Twersky and Bernard Septimus (Cambridge: Harvard University Press, 1987), 470–471, 479.

109. Orfali, "Daniellilo of Leghorn," 148.

110. Ibid., 148–149.

111. There is a distinction between the exiles of 1492 and those who experienced life as conversos, although much of the literature of the Spanish exiles appealed to and was appropriate for the conversos. One example is *Shevet Yehudah* by Solomon Ibn Verga, which was published in Adrianople in 1554; this author had probably experienced a forced conversion in Portugal, yet he inspired Sephardi and converso readers alike.

112. The title of this novel is *La historia de los amores de Clareo y Florisea y de los trabajos de la sin ventura Isea*; the volume also has seventeen poems that expand upon the fiction and shed light upon the author's own life. Constance Hubbard Rose, *Alonso Núñez de Reinoso: The Lament of a Sixteenth-Century Exile* (Rutherford, N.J.: Fairleigh Dickinson University Press, 1971), 85, 136, 145, 152.

113. Ibid., 69.

114. Ibid., 55 n. 75, with a reference to Bataillon.

115. Ibid., 89.

116. Ibid., 161.

117. Ibid., 164.

CHAPTER EIGHT   MODERN MANIFESTATIONS

1. Yitzhak Baer, *A History of the Jews in Christian Spain*, 2d ed. (Philadelphia: Jewish Publication Society, 1992), 2:102.

2. Ibid., 2:102–103.

3. Ibid., 121.

4. Kenneth Moore, *Those of the Street: The Catholic-Jews of Mallorca* (Notre Dame, Ind.: University of Notre Dame Press, 1976), 108.

5. Ibid., 109.

6. Ibid., 210. It is hard to verify this claim, for it would mean, among other things, that the purity of blood statutes played no role here.

7. Baruch Braunstein, *The Chuetas of Majorca: Conversos and the Inquisition of Majorca*, 2d ed. (New York: KTAV Publishing House, 1972), 46–55.

8. Ibid., 56.

9. See Angela S. Selke, *The Conversos of Majorca: Life and Death in a Crypto-Jewish Community in XVII Century Spain* (Jerusalem: Magnes Press, 1986), 101.

10. Ibid., 91.

11. Moore, *Those of the Street*, 120–121.

12. Braunstein, *Chuetas of Majorca*, 105.

13. Moore, *Those of the Street*, 137.

14. See Braunstein, *Chuetas of Majorca*, 105–114.

15. For details, see ibid., 57–93. There were those who successfully escaped to Valencia, Nice, Leghorn, and Alexandria; see Selke, *Conversos of Majorca*, 110, 112.

16. Selke, *Conversos of Majorca*, 182.

17. Ibid., 88.

18. Moore, *Those of the Street*, 136.

19. Braunstein, *Chuetas of Majorca*, 94.

20. Ibid.

21. See Selke, *Conversos of Majorca*, 211; and Braunstein, *Chuetas of Majorca*, 122.

22. Selke, *Conversos of Majorca*, 105.

23. Moore, *Those of the Street*, 139.

24. See Braunstein, *Chuetas of Majorca*, 122.

25. Selke, *Conversos of Majorca*, 12–14. She translated the title of this popular book as *Faith Triumphant in Four Autos*.

26. For additional examples of his writing style, see Selke, *Conversos of Majorca*, 207–210.

27. Moore, *Those of the Street*, 155.

28. The book was called *Comments on the Religious and Social Situation on the Island of Mallorca*. For details, see Braunstein, *Chuetas of Majorca*, 129–130; and Moore, *Those of the Street*, 157–158.

29. Moore, *Those of the Street*, 158.

30. Braunstein, *Chuetas of Majorca*, xxxi.

31. Ibid., xxxii, 130, 131.

32. For a detailed analysis of the role of tourism on the island and its repercussions in Chueta life, see Moore, *Those of the Street*, 164–171. He claims that the "consequences of industrial tourism were nothing less than a total reordering of Mallorcan society" (170).

33. Ibid., 165.

34. See Selke, *Conversos of Majorca*, 211 n. 25.

35. Moore, *Those of the Street*, 177.

36. This expression appears in Moore, *Those of the Street*, 179; "cultural patterns" appears on 190. Moore points to a concern with the Jews as a people and the role of the Vatican and its Jewish policy (182–184). Ironically, twenty-four Majorcans went to Israel in 1966, but all save one returned. Their motives seem to have been opportunistic, as none of them was of Jewish background (193–197).

37. Ibid., 11. For another anthropological perspective that often converges with that of Moore, see Eva and Juan F. Laub, *El mito triunfante: Estudio antropológico de los Chuetas mallorquines* (Palma de Mayorca: Miquel Font, 1987).

38. See Samuel Schwarz, *Inscrições hebraicas em Portugal* (reprint from *Arcqueologia e historia*) (Lisbon: Tipografia do Comercio, 1923), 23–28.

39. See Ignacio Steinhardt, "A Lone Community of Conversos in North Portugal" (in Hebrew), *Ha-Aretz*, September 20, 1964, 15.

40. Lucien Wolf, *Report on the "Marranos" or Crypto-Jews of Portugal*, presented to the Alliance Israélite Universelle and the Council of the Anglo-Jewish Association (London, March 1926), 10.

41. Cardozo de Bethencourt, "The Jews in Portugal from 1773 to 1902," *JQR* 15 (1903): 251–274, 529–530.

42. Claude B. Stuczynski refers to a piece in *The Jewish Chronicle* in 1920 that seems to be plagiarized from Schwarz and to two books that appeared in Portuguese in 1925; one was written by a priest and the other was extremely anti-Semitic. See his introduction to *The New Christians in Portugal in the Twentieth Century*, by Samuel Schwarz (in Hebrew) (Jerusalem: Dinur Center, 2004).

43. Nahum Shlouscz, *The Anusim in Portugal* (in Hebrew) (Dvir: Tel Aviv, 1932), 99.

44. Samuel Schwarz, *Os Cristãos-novos em Portugal no Século XX* (Lisbon: Empresa Portuguesa de Livros, 1926). This book is due to appear soon in Hebrew translation along with a collection of prayers that were recorded by Schwarz. Stuczynzki has written an in-depth introduction and translation which he graciously allowed me to read in draft form; as a result, references to this Hebrew work will be without pagination. Here he points out that there was antagonism to the publication of Schwarz's book and some church figures as high up as in the Vatican tried to prevent its publication; there was also a fear of Old Christian reactions.

45. Samuel Schwarz, "The Crypto-Jews of Portugal," *Menorah Journal* 12 (1926): 149.

46. Ibid., 140.

47. In his introduction to Schwarz, Stuczynski notes the irony in the fact that up to this day, many of the Judaizers use this book to access their own prayers!

48. See Elvira de Azevedo Mea and Ignacio Steinhardt, "The Contributions of Captain Barros Basto, 'Apostle of the Marranos,' " *Shofar* 18 (1999): 68. This article is

based on the final chapter of their important book, *Ben-Rosh: Biografia do Capitão Barros Basto, o apóstolo dos Marranos* (Porto: Edições Afrontamento, 1997).

49. There is a discussion of this in Stuczynski's introduction.

50. Schwarz, "Crypto-Jews of Portugal," 143.

51. David Augusto Canelo, *The Last Crypto-Jews of Portugal*, 2d ed. (n.p.: IJS, 1990), 67.

52. The predominance of women in crypto-Judaism was noted in earlier periods. See, for example, Renée Levine Melammed, "The Ultimate Challenge: Safeguarding the Crypto-Judaic Heritage," *PAAJR* 53 (1986): 91–109; and Levine Melammed, "Crypto-Jewish Women Facing the Spanish Inquisition: Transmitting Religious Practices, Beliefs, and Attitudes," in *Christians, Muslims, and Jews in Medieval and Early Modern Spain: Interaction and Social Change*, ed. Mark D. Meyerson and Edward D. English (Notre Dame, Ind.: University of Notre Dame Press, 2000), 197–219.

53. The recitation of prayers while preparing these wicks is reminiscent of the prayers in Yiddish called *tehinnot* that are recited when preparing wicks for memorial candles. See Chava Weissler, *Voices of the Matriarchs* (Boston: Beacon Press, 1998), 126–146.

54. See Yosef Hayim Yerushalmi, "Les Derniers Marranes," in *Marranes*, ed. Fredric Brenner (Paris: Éditiones de la Différence, 1992), 31, 42.

55. Sarica Molho is a Tel Aviv sociologist who spent many months living with the crypto-Jews of Belmonte between 1994 and 1997 and is preparing a Hebrew book on the topic. She provided this information during a private conversation on November 6, 2001.

56. See Anita Novinsky and Amilcar Paulo, "The Last Marranos," *Commentary* 43 (May 1967): 79. For information on Judaizing customs, see Renée Levine Melammed, "Some Death and Mourning Customs of Castilian Conversas," in *Exile and Diaspora*, ed. Aharon Mirsky, Avraham Grossman and Yosef Kaplan (Jerusalem: Ben Zvi Institute, 1991), 157–167; and Encarnación María Padilla, "Relacíon judeoconversa durante la segunda mitad del siglo XV en Aragón: Enfermedades y muertes," *Sefarad* 43, no. 2 (1983): 251–344.

57. Stuczynski, in the aforementioned introduction, relates how a rabbi from Salonika was infuriated when he encountered this phenomenon.

58. Novinsky and Paulo, "Last Marranos," 77–78.

59. Canelo, *Last Crypto-Jews*, 88–90, 167.

60. Information about specific observances in greater detail can be found in Schwarz, "Crypto-Jews of Portugal," 146–149, 283–292; Steinhardt, "Lone Community of Conversos," 3, 15; Novinsky and Paulo, "Last Marranos," 76–81; Yerushalmi, "Les Derniers Marranes," 41–42; Canelo, *Last Crypto-Jews*, 59–148; and Wolf, *Report on the "Marranos,"* 11.

61. Wolf, *Report on the "Marranos,"* 11.

62. See Stuczynski, introduction to Schwarz.

63. See Avraham Milgram, "The Attempt to Return the Conversos of Portugal to Judaism from 1925 to 1931" (in Hebrew), *Gesher* 125, no. 38 (1992): 90–99.

64. See Wolf, *Report on the "Marranos,"* 3, 19; and *Marranos in Portugal*, Survey by the Portuguese Marranos Committee, London, 1926–1938 (London: Vestry Offices, Bevis Marks, 1938), 1–4.

65. Wolf, *Report on the "Marranos,"* 4.

66. *Marranos in Portugal*, 3–4.

67. Basto was compared at times to Moses as well as to Herzl because they all grew up outside the Jewish community. After examining his identity formation, some have concluded that rejections by his fiancée and by noblemen in the army were significant factors in his development. See Mea and Steinhardt, "Contributions of Captain Barros Basto," 71–72. It should be pointed out that H. P. Salomon questions the New Christian background of Barros Basto and attributes this phenomenon to a desire not to be part of the Catholic majority. See "The Captain, the Abade, and 20th Century Marranism in Portugal," *Archivos do Centro Cultural Portugues* 10 (1976): 631–642.

68. See Milgram, "Attempt to Return," 93.

69. Goodman was the secretary of the Portuguese Marranos Committee. See *Marranos in Portugal*, 9

70. Claude B. Stuczynski, review of *Ben-Rosh: Biografia do Capitão Barros Basto, o apóstolo dos Marranos*, by Elvira de Azevedo Mea and Inácio Steinhardt, *Hispania Judaica* 2 (1999): 93.

71. Ibid.

72. Mea and Steinhardt, "Contributions of Captain Barros Basto," 68.

73. Schwarz, "Crypto-Jews of Portugal," 145–146.

74. Stuczynski, introduction to Schwarz.

75. See Milgram, "Attempt to Return," 97.

76. See Stuczynski, introduction to Schwarz.

77. Canelo, *Last Crypto-Jews*, 160.

78. See *Marranos in Portugal*, 1–2. The truth is that the synagogue rarely had a quorum. See Elaine Rosenthal and Robert Rosenthal, "The Portuguese Dreyfus," *Midstream* 33, no. 2 (1987): 46.

79. See Joshua Stampfer, prologue to Canelo, *Last Crypto-Jews*, xiii.

80. Milgram, "Attempt to Return," 97.

81. Stuczynski, review of *Ben-Rosh*, 90.

82. For details, see *Marranos in Portugal*, 15.

83. Stuczynski, review of *Ben-Rosh*, 90.

84. See Rosenthal, "Portuguese Dreyfus," 44–48; and the book by Mea and Steinhardt, *Ben-Rosh*, which refutes this contention.

85. Stuczynski, review of *Ben-Rosh*, 90.

86. See Canelo, *Last Crypto-Jews*, 162–165.

87. See Issar Steinhardt, "The Conversos of Belmonte" (in Hebrew), *Apiryon* 40 (1995): 26. Sarika Molho contends that the terms "family" and "nation" are interchangeable in Belmonte. See "Masks for Yom Kippur, Masks for Passover: A Sociological Look at the Conversos of Belmonte Today" (in Hebrew), in *Proceedings of the Twelfth World Congress of Jewish Studies*, vol. 5 (Jerusalem: World Union of Jewish Studies, 2001), 263.

88. Steinhardt, "Lone Community of Conversos," 3.

89. By this time, there seems to have been nothing left in the other villages. Yerushalmi, "Les Derniers Marranes," 39.

90. Novinsky and Paulo, "Last Marranos," 81.

91. Interview on November 6, 2001.

92. See Stuczynski, introduction to Schwarz.

93. Molho, interview.

94. See Yerushalmi, "Les Derniers Marranes," 42–43.

95. According to Molho, today most of them go or send representatives to Madrid to make bulk purchases, as they now have deep freezers, which enable long-term storage of meats and other foods.

96. Yerushalmi, "Les Derniers Marranes," 43.

97. Mea and Steinhardt, "Contributions of Captain Barros Basto," 76.

98. Canelo, *Last Crypto-Jews*, 166.

99. Yerushalmi discusses the sentiments of some of the leaders of the community, such as Dona Emilia, who was one of the central informants in Brenner's movie; see "Les Derniers Marranes," 43–44.

100. Information provided by Molho, interview.

101. Canelo, *Last Crypto-Jews*, 151.

102. Yerushalmi, "Les Derniers Marranes," 38–39.

103. All of the data concerning the conversions and attitudes of these individuals is based on information provided by Molho, either in a lecture delivered to my class in the spring of 1999, or in private conversations; see also "Masks for Yom Kippur," 264, for figures.

104. Molho, "Masks for Yom Kippur," 264.

105. In 1990 Canelo wrote that this religion would only "continue for as long as the more traditionalist members will live because the mixed marriages of their sons and daughters, which are increasingly frequent, will cause a gradual extinction of the 'Marranic' worship of Belmonte" (*Last Crypto-Jews*, 169). While intermarriage was cited as responsible for the eventual disappearance of the Chueta identity, Molho cites examples of nonconverso men who took on the crypto-Jewish customs ("Masks for Yom Kippur," 264).

106. Molho, "Masks for Yom Kippur," 264.

107. Ibid., 262.

108. Ibid., 265.

109. Ibid.

110. Ibid., 266.

111. This debate has taken place primarily in the fields of folklore and ethnology, but it goes beyond them as well. One can see signs of the debate in academic professional journals and newspapers and on various sites on the Internet.

112. There are famous trials and individuals from this era; for example, the most famous Judaizer was Luis Carvajal, the nephew of the governor of New Spain. See Martin Cohen, *The Martyr* (Philadelphia: Jewish Publication Society, 1973); and Seymour Liebman, *The Enlightened* (Coral Gables, Fla.: University of Miami Press, 1967).

113. Stanley Hordes, "The Inquisition and the Crypto-Jewish Community in Colonial New Spain and New Mexico," in *Cultural Encounters: The Impact of the Inquisition in Spain and the New World*, ed. Mary Elizabeth Perry and Anne J. Cruz (Berkeley: University of California Press, 1993), 213–214.

114. Hordes, "Inquisition and the Crypto-Jewish Community," 214.

115. Frances Hernández, "The Secret Jews of the Southwest," in *Sephardim in the Americas: Studies in Culture and History*, ed. Martin A. Cohen and Abraham J. Peck (Tuscaloosa: University of Alabama Press, 1993), 414.

116. Interestingly, three-quarters of those condemned to exile never left the shores of Mexico.

117. This revolt also brought about the destruction of most of the local documentation. See Hordes, "Inquisition and the Crypto-Jewish Community," 214.

118. Hernández, "Secret Jews," 416.

119. Details about the sequence of discovery by the media can be found in Barbara Ferry and Debbie Nathan, "Mistaken Identity? The Case of New Mexico's 'Hidden Jews,' " Atlantic Monthly (December 2000): 85. See also Kathleen Teltsch, "Scholars and Descendants Uncover Hidden Legacy of Jews in Southwest," New York Times, November 11, 1990, 30.

120. Hordes's dissertation, entitled "The Crypto-Jewish Community of New Spain, 1620–1649," was written under the supervision of Richard Greenleaf at Tulane University and submitted in 1980. The emphasis in this work is on the economic activities of the conversos of Mexico and the circumstances leading to the sudden inquisitorial activity that occurred there.

121. See Seth D. Kunin, "Juggling Identities among the Crypto-Jews of the American Southwest," Religion 31 (2001): 43, 57.

122. This is worded in an abstract yet scientific-sounding way, as it uses the terms "research," "information," and "development."

123. This Web site is located at the Library of Congress in Washington, D.C.

124. Conferences in Belmonte were also organized, but the Judaizers there were unimpressed with the Jews and Israelis who have passed through. They were also extremely angry with Brenner for giving them unwanted publicity by screening his movie without their permission after promising not to do so.

125. See, for example, Jewish magazines such as the B'nai Brith Monthly (December 1989 and October 1991); Echoes of Sefarad (October 1991); Atlantic Monthly (December 2000); and Ha-Aretz (April 6, 2001). This is by no means a comprehensive list, but rather a sampling. On the academic level, Hordes and his colleague Tomás Atencio proposed a project in which they hoped to trace the origins of the New Mexican crypto-Jewish families. Their stated goal was to analyze Mexican archives and to ascertain the identity of those who migrated to New Mexico, utilizing Inquisition documents when possible. Documentation would be based on registrations of birth, baptism, marriage, census records, Church archives, and Spanish army induction lists. These scholars hoped to create a database of all confirmed and suspected crypto-Jews, as well as Spanish settlers, soldiers, and missionaries in New Mexico from 1598 to 1821. Unfortunately, this research has not been published. See Stanley Hordes and Tomás Atencio, A Prospectus: New Mexico's Sephardic Legacy (Albuquerque: University of New Mexico, 1987) for the proposal.

126. Kunin, "Juggling Identities," 47, 51.

127. See Janet Leibman Jacobs, Hidden Heritage: The Legacy of the Crypto-Jews (Berkeley: University of California Press, 2002), 12.

128. Schulamith C. Halevy, "Manifestations of Crypto-Judaism in the American Southwest," Jewish Folklore and Ethnology Review 18 (1996): 69.

129. See ibid., 69, as compared to Stanley Hordes, "Report: 'The Sephardic Legacy in the Southwest: The Crypto-Jews of New Mexico,' Historical Research Project Sponsored by the Latin American Institute," Jewish Folklore and Ethnology Review 15 (1993): 137.

130. See Kunin, "Juggling Identities," 52–57, and especially his discussion of *bricolage*, the act of building with materials from different cultures and times.

131. See Kunin, "Juggling Identities," 56.

132. Hernández, "Secret Jews," 423–436.

133. Numerous other examples of Jewish rites that might not be so Jewish appear in Richard Santos, "Chicanos of Jewish Descent in Texas," *Western States Jewish Historical Quarterly* 15 (1983): 329–332.

134. See D. S. Nidel and P. J. Citrin, "Modern Descendants of Conversos in New Mexico," *Western States Jewish Historical Quarterly* 16 (1984): 261.

135. On the other hand, the further one lived from Mexico City, the further one was from the Inquisition and its tentacles. In addition, as we have seen, the Mexican Inquisition actively pursued Judaizers during two rather concentrated time periods. In between these two periods as well as pursuant to them, there was almost no direct threat to the crypto-Jews in these areas, so perhaps the threat of the Inquisition is overemphasized here.

136. Richard G. Santos, "Silent Heritage: The Sephardim and the Colonization of the Spanish North American Frontier," *Shofar* 18, no. 1 (1999): 116.

137. Ibid., 117.

138. Santos, "Chicanos of Jewish Descent," 327.

139. Santos, "Silent Heritage," 117. His conclusion is rather problematic: "There are indeed some descendants of anusim or Converso families which sincerely embraced Christianity. Still others are descendants of true crypto-Judaic families, living in a marginal religious and cultural milieu and commonly referred to as 'Catholics by culture' or 'Sunday Catholics.' Basically anti-clerical and anti-organized religion, many Catholic Hispanics in this group tend to reject the Christian concept of the Trinity and the infallibility of the Pope. Moreover, regardless of their religiosity, many descendants of the Spanish/Portuguese colonial Sephardim are totally unaware of their rich historical and cultural heritage" (122).

140. See Tomás Atencio, "Crypto-Jewish Remnants in Manito Society and Culture," *Jewish Folklore and Ethnology Review* 18 (1996): 59–97. *Manito* is the shortened diminutive of brother (*hermano*); these are the Indo-Hispanics dating to the colonial period who include *mestizos*, of mixed Spanish and Indian heritage.

141. Schulamith Halevy, "Jewish Practices among Contemporary Anusim," *Shofar* 18, no. 1 (1999): 82.

142. Janet Jacobs, "Conversa Heritage, Crypto-Jewish Practice, and Women's Rituals," *Shofar* 18, no. 1 (1999): 103–104.

143. Jacobs, *Hidden Heritage*, 154.

144. Neither Atencio nor Jacobs has a strong grasp of the historical issues at hand, and both relied upon an eclectic collection of literature and sources for information. See Janet Liebman Jacobs, "Women, Ritual, and Secrecy: The Creation of Crypto-Jewish Culture," *Journal for the Scientific Study of Religion* 35 (1996): 97–98; and Jacobs, *Hidden Heritage*, 1–19.

145. In electronic mail communications on February 14, 2004, I discussed these confessions with César J. Ayala Casás of the Sociology department of UCLA. He explained to me that this "takes the form of refusing to receive the Catholic ritual of *extrema unción* and it is that refusal which then acquires meaning to the children and relatives. . . . Children then take this and run with it, the refusal of the Catholic ritual

takes the form of the moment of truth, the moment of definition, for the children, so they then relate that moment as the moment of revelation."

146. This is not always easily discerned. For example, why should "Semitic bread," essentially made without lard, be a carryover of *matzoh*, made without leavening?

147. Jacobs, "Women, Ritual, and Secrecy," 99.

148. Jacobs, "Conversa Heritage," 107–108.

149. Ibid., 106. Jacobs also sees the ritual bath as a release from oppressions, and speculates about these women's exile, alienation and cultural survival. See also Jacobs, *Hidden Heritage*, 42–66.

150. Schulamith Halevy, introduction to *Shofar* 18, no. 1 (1999): 2.

151. This statement was distributed through the H-Judaic electronic mail list on December 6, 1997.

152. See Judith Neulander, "Crypto-Jews of the Southwest: An Imagined Community," *Jewish Folklore and Ethnology Review* 16 (1994): 64.

153. Judith Neulander, "The New Mexican Crypto-Jewish Canon: Choosing to Be 'Chosen' in Millennial Transition," *Jewish Folklore and Ethnology Review* 18 (1996): 19.

154. Kunin, "Juggling Identities," 43.

155. Jacobs, *Hidden Heritage*, 40.

156. Seth Ward, "Converso Descendants in the American Southwest: A Report on Research, Resources, and the Changing Search for Identity," in *Jewish Studies at the Turn of the Twentieth Century*, ed. Judit Targarona Barrós and Angel Sáenz-Badillos (Leiden: Brill, 1999), 2:685.

CONCLUSION

The opening epigraph is a footnote discussing Isaac Abravanel's perceptions of conversion and ethnicity. See *From Spanish Court to Italian Ghetto: Isaac Cardoso: A Study in Seventeenth-Century Marranism and Jewish Apologetics* (New York: Columbia University Press, 1971), 20 n. 30.

1. See chapter 3, nn. 32–34, regarding the fate of his namesake and grandson, the son of Yehuda Abravanel.

2. Thomas F. Glick refers to "the existence of rather extensive familial and patronage relationships. Such associations would be necessary to provide a sufficiently high degree of enclosure to perpetuate group identity after the first generation of converts." See "On Converso and Marrano Ethnicity," in *Crisis and Creativity in the Sephardic World, 1391–1648*, ed. Benjamin R. Gampel (New York: Columbia University Press, 1997), 68.

Bibliography

BOOKS

Aescoly, Aaron Zeev. *The Story of David Hareuveni Copied from the Oxford Manuscript* (in Hebrew). Rev. ed. Jerusalem: Bialik Institute, 1993.

Albert, Bath Sheva. *The Case of Baruch: The Earliest Report of the Trial of a Jew by the Inquisition, 1320* (in Hebrew). Ramat Gan: Bar Ilan University, 1974.

Alcalá, Ángel, ed. *The Spanish Inquisition and the Inquisitorial Mind.* New York: Columbia University Press, 1987.

———, ed. *Judíos. Sefarditas. Conversos. La expulsión de 1492 y sus consecuencias.* Valladolid: Ámbito Ediciones, 1995.

Alpert, Michael. *Crypto-Judaism and the Spanish Inquisition.* Hampshire, England: Palgrave, 2001.

Ashtor, Eliyahu. *The Jews of Moslem Spain.* 3 vols. Philadelphia: Jewish Publication Society, 1973.

Assis, Yom Tov, and Yosef Kaplan, eds. *Jews and Conversos at the Time of the Expulsion* (in Hebrew). Jerusalem: Zalman Shazar Center for Jewish History, 1999.

Azevedo, Jose (Joaõ) Lúcio de. *Historia dos Christãos Novos Portugueses.* Lisbon: Livraria Clássica Editora de A.M. Teixeira, 1921.

Baer, Yitzhak. *A History of the Jews in Christian Spain.* 2d ed. 2 vols. Philadelphia: Jewish Publication Society, 1992.

Barnett, Richard D., ed. *The Sephardi Heritage.* Vol. 1. London: Vallentine, Mitchell, 1971.

Barnett, Richard D., and W. M. Schwab, eds. *The Sephardi Heritage.* Vol. 2. Grendon, England: Gibraltar Books, 1989.

Barros, Carlos, ed. *Xudeus e Conversos na Historia.* 2 vols. Santiago de Compostela: Editorial de la Historia, 1994.

Beinart, Haim. *Conversos on Trial: The Inquisition in Ciudad Real.* Jerusalem: Magnes Press, 1981.

———. *Records of the Trials of the Spanish Inquisition in Ciudad Real.* 4 vols. Jerusalem: Israel National Academy of Sciences and Humanities, 1974–1985.

———. *The Expulsion of the Jews from Spain.* Trans. Jeffrey M. Green. Oxford: Littman Library of Jewish Civilization, 2002.

———, ed. *Moreshet Sepharad = The Sephardi Legacy.* 2 vols. Jerusalem: Magnes Press, 1992.

Benbassa, Esther, ed. *Mémoires juives d'Espagne et du Portugal.* Paris: Publisud, 1996.

———, ed. *Transmission et passages en monde juif.* Paris: Editiones du Cerf, 1997.

Bethencourt, Francisco. *La Inquisición en la época moderna: España, Portugal, Italia, Siglos XV–XIX.* Madrid: Ediciones Akal, 1997.

Bodian, Miriam. *Hebrews of the Portuguese Nation.* Bloomington, Ind.: Indiana University Press, 1997.

Braunstein, Baruch. *The Chuetas of Majorca: Conversos and the Inquisition of Majorca.* 2d ed. New York: KTAV Publishing House, 1972.

Brenner, Fredric, ed. *Marranes.* Paris: Éditions de la Différence, 1992.

Brooks, Andrée Aelion. *The Woman Who Defied Kings: The Life and Times of Doña Gracia Nasi.* St. Paul, Minn.: Paragon House, 2002.

Burns, Robert I. *Jews in the Notarial Culture: Latinate Wills in Mediterranean Spain, 1250–1350.* Berkeley: University of California Press, 1996.

Canelo, David Augusto. *The Last Crypto-Jews of Portugal.* 2d ed. N.p.: IJS, 1990.

Carrete Parrondo, Carlos. *El judaísmo español y la Inquisición.* Madrid: Editorial MAPFRE, 1992.

Cohen, Jeremy. *The Friars and the Jews: The Evolution of Medieval Anti-Judaism.* Ithaca, N.Y.: Cornell University Press, 1982.

Cohen, Martin A. *Samuel Usque's Consolation for the Tribulations of Israel.* Philadelphia: Jewish Publication Society, 1965.

Cooperman, Bernard D. *Trade and Settlements: The Establishment and Early Development of the Jewish Communities in Leghorn and Pisa (1591–1626).* Ph.D. diss., Harvard University, 1976.

———, ed. *In Iberia and Beyond: Hispanic Jews between Cultures.* Newark, Del.: University of Delaware Press, 1998.

Cooperman, Bernard D., and Barbara Garvin, eds. *The Jews of Italy: Memory and Identity.* Bethesda, Md.: University Press of Maryland, 2000.

Coronas Tejada, Luis. *Conversos and Inquisition in Jaén.* Jerusalem: Magnes Press, 1988.

Endelman, Todd M. *The Jews of Georgian England, 1714–1830.* Philadelphia: Jewish Publication Society, 1979.

———. *Radical Assimilation in English Jewish History, 1656–1945.* Bloomington, Ind.: Indiana University Press, 1990.

Ferro Tavares, Maria José Pimenta. *Os Judeos em Portugal seculo XV.* Vol. 1. Lisbon: Universidade Nova de Lisboa, 1984.

———. *Judaísmo e Inquisição: Estudos.* Lisbon: Editorial Presença, 1987.

Gampel, Benjamin R. *The Last Jews on Iberian Soil.* Berkeley: University of California Press, 1989.

————, ed. *Crisis and Creativity in the Sephardic World, 1391–1648*. New York: Columbia University Press, 1997.

Gerber, Jane. *The Jews of Spain*. New York: Free Press, 1992.

Gitlitz, David M. *Secrecy and Deceit: The Religion of the Crypto-Jews*. Philadelphia: Jewish Publication Society, 1996.

Gross, Abraham. *Iberian Jewry from Twilight to Dawn: The World of Rabbi Abraham Saba*. Leiden: Brill, 1995.

Haim, Abraham, ed. *Society and Community* (in Hebrew and English). Jerusalem: Misgav Yerushalayim, 1991.

Haliczer, Stephen. *Inquisition and Society in the Kingdom of Valencia, 1478–1834*. Berkeley: University of California Press, 1990.

Henningsen, Gustav, John Tedeschi, and Charles Amiel, eds. *The Inquisition in Early Modern Europe: Studies on Sources and Methods*. DeKalb, Ill.: Northern Illinois University Press, 1986.

Herculano, Alexandre. *History of the Origin and Establishment of the Inquisition in Portugal*. Trans. John D. Branner. New York: KTAV Publishing House, 1972.

Hordes, Stanley. *The Crypto-Jewish Community of New Spain, 1620–1649*. Ph.D. diss., Tulane University, 1981.

Hordes, Stanley, and Tomás Atencio. *A Prospectus: New Mexico's Sephardic Legacy*. New Mexico: University of New Mexico, 1987.

Horowitz, Elliott, and Moises Orfali, eds. *The Mediterranean and the Jews: Society, Culture, and Economy in Early Modern Times*. Ramat Gan: Bar-Ilan University Press, 2002.

Ibn Verga, Solomon. *Shevet Yehudah*. Ed. Yitzhak Baer. Jerusalem: Bialik Institute, 1947.

Israel, Jonathan I. *European Jewry in the Age of Mercantilism, 1550–1750*. 2d ed. Oxford: Oxford University Press, 1989.

————. *Empires and Entrepôts: The Dutch, the Spanish Monarchy, and the Jews, 1585–1713*. London: Hambledon Press, 1990.

Jacobs, Janet Liebman. *Hidden Heritage: The Legacy of the Crypto-Jews*. Berkeley: University of California Press, 2002.

Jewish Folklore and Ethnology Review 15 (1993).

Jewish Folklore and Ethnology Review 16 (1994).

Jewish Folklore and Ethnology Review 18 (1996).

Kamen, Henry. *The Spanish Inquisition*. New York: New American Library, 1965.

————. *Inquisition and Society in Spain*. London: Weidenfeld & Nicolson, 1985.

Kaplan, Yosef, ed. *Jews and Conversos: Studies in Society and the Inquisition*. Jerusalem: Magnes Press, 1985.

Kaplan, Yosef, Henry Méchoulan, and Richard H. Popkin, eds. *Menasseh ben Israel and His World*. Leiden: Brill, 1989.

Kaplan, Yosef, and Chaya Brasz, eds. *Dutch Jews as Perceived by Themselves and by Others*. Leiden: Brill, 2001.

Laub, Eva, and Juan F. Laub. *El mito triunfante: Estudio antropológico de los Chuetas mallorquines*. Palma de Mayorca: Miquel Font, 1987.

Lazar, Moshe, and Stephen Haliczer, eds. *The Jews of Spain and the Expulsion of 1492*. Lancaster, Calif.: Labyrinthos, 1997.

Levine Melammed, Renée. *Heretics or Daughters of Israel? The Crypto-Jewish Women of Castile.* New York: Oxford University Press, 1999.

Lipiner, Elias. *Two Portuguese Exiles in Castile: Dom David Negro and Dom Isaac Abravanel.* Jerusalem: Magnes Press, 1997.

———. *Os baptizados em pé.* Lisbon: Vega, 1998.

Malino, Frances. *The Sephardic Jews of Bordeaux.* University, Ala.: University of Alabama Press, 1978.

Marranos in Portugal. Survey by the Portuguese Marranos Committee, London, 1926–1938. London: Vestry Offices, Bevis Marks, 1938.

Méchoulan, Henry. *Être juif à Amsterdam au temps de Spinoza.* Paris: Albin Michel, 1991.

Meyuhas Ginio, Alisa. *La forteresse de la foi.* Paris: Ediciones du Cerf, 1998.

Meyers, Charles, and Norman Simms, eds. *Troubled Souls: Conversos, Crypto-Jews, and Other Confused Jewish Intellectuals from the Fourteenth through the Eighteenth Century.* Hamilton, New Zealand: Outrigger Publishers, 2001.

Mirsky, Aharon, Avraham Grossman, and Yosef Kaplan, eds. *Exile and Diaspora* (in Hebrew). Vol. 1. Jerusalem: Ben Zvi Institute, 1988.

———, eds. *Exile and Diaspora.* Vol. 2. Jerusalem: Ben Zvi Institute, 1991.

Monter, William. *Frontiers of Heresy.* Cambridge: Cambridge University Press, 1990.

Moore, Kenneth. *Those of the Street: The Catholic-Jews of Mallorca.* Notre Dame, Ind.: University of Notre Dame Press, 1976.

Nahon, Gérard. *Métropoles et périphéries sefarades d'Occident.* Paris: Les Édiciones du Cerf, 1993.

Netanyahu, B. *Don Isaac Abravanel: Statesman and Philosopher.* Philadelphia: Jewish Publication Society, 1953.

———. *The Marranos of Spain from the Late 14th to the Early 16th Century according to Contemporary Hebrew Sources.* 3d ed. Ithaca, N.Y.: Cornell University Press, 1999.

———. *The Origins of the Inquisition in Fifteenth-Century Spain.* New York: Random House, 1994.

Oelman, Timothy, trans. and ed. *Marrano Poets of the Seventeenth Century.* London: Associated University Presses, 1982.

Paulo, Amílcar. *Os judeus secretos em Portugal.* Porto: Editorial Labirinto, 1985.

Peters, Edward. *Inquisition.* Berkeley: University of California Press, 1988.

Pullan, Brian. *The Jews of Europe and the Inquisition of Venice, 1550–1670.* Oxford: Blackwell, 1983.

Raphael, David, ed. *The Expulsion 1492 Chronicles.* North Hollywood, Calif.: Carmi House Press, 1992.

Révah, I. S. *Spinoza et le Dr. Juan de Prado.* Paris: Mouton, 1959.

———. *Ropica Pnefma.* 2 vols. Lisbon: Instituto Nacional de Investigação Científica, 1983.

Rivkin, Ellis. *The Shaping of Jewish History: A Radical New Interpretation.* New York: Charles Scribner's Sons, 1971.

Rose, Constance. *Alonso Núñez de Reinoso: The Lament of a Sixteenth-Century Exile.* Rutherford, N.J.: Fairleigh Dickinson University Press, 1971.

Roth, Cecil. *The History of the Jews of Italy.* Philadelphia: Jewish Publication Society, 1946.

Roth, Norman. *Conversos, Inquisition, and the Expulsion of the Jews from Spain.* Madison, Wis.: University of Wisconsin Press, 1995.

Ruderman, David B. *Jewish Enlightenment in an English Key: Anglo-Jewry's Construction of Modern Jewish Thought.* Princeton, N.J.: Princeton University Press, 2000.

Salomon, H. P. *Portrait of a New Christian: Fernão Álvares Melo (1569–1632); Un "Portugués" entre los Castellanos: El primer proceso Inquisitorial contra Gonzalo Báez de Paiba, 1654–1657.* Vol. 1. Transcribed by David Willemse. Paris: Centro Cultural Portugués, 1982.

————. *Deux études portugaises.* Braga: n.p., 1991.

Saraiva, António José. *The Marrano Factory: The Portuguese Inquisition and Its New Christians, 1536–1765.* Leiden: Brill, 2001.

Schwarz, Samuel. *Inscrições hebraicas em Portugal* (reprint from *Arcqueologia e Historia*). Lisbon: Tipografia do Comercio, 1923.

Selke, Angela S. *The Conversos of Majorca: Life and Death in a Crypto-Jewish Community in XVII Century Spain.* Jerusalem: Magnes Press, 1986.

Shlouscz, Nahum. *The Anusim in Portugal* (in Hebrew). Dvir: Tel Aviv, 1932.

Shofar 18, no. 1 (Fall 1999).

Sicroff, Albert A. *Les controverses des statuts de pureté de sang en Espagne du XVe au XVIIe siècle.* Paris: Didier, 1960.

Studemund-Halévy, Michael. *Die Sefarden in Hamburg.* 2 vols. Hamburg: Helmut Buske Verlag, 1994–1997.

Suarez Fernández, Luis. *Documentos acerca de la Expulsión de los Judios.* Valladolid: Ediciones Aldecoa, 1964.

Swetschinski, Daniel M. *Reluctant Cosmopolitans: The Portuguese Jews of Seventeenth-Century Amsterdam.* London: Littman Library of Jewish Civilization, 2000.

Toaff, Ariel, and Simon Schwarzfuchs, eds. *The Mediterranean and the Jews.* Ramat Gan: Bar Ilan University Press, 1989.

Waddington, Raymond B., and Arthur H. Williamson, eds. *The Expulsion of the Jews 1492 and After.* New York: Garland Publishing, 1994.

Yerushalmi, Yosef Hayim. *From Spanish Court to Italian Ghetto: Isaac Cardoso: A Study in Seventeenth-Century Marranism and Jewish Apologetics.* New York: Columbia University Press, 1971.

————. *The Lisbon Massacre of 1506 and the Royal Image in the Shebet Yehudah.* Cincinnati: Hebrew Union College Annual Supplements, 1976.

Yovel, Yirmiyahu. *The Marrano of Reason.* Vol. 1 of *Spinoza and Other Heretics.* Princeton: Princeton University Press, 1989.

Zorattini, Pier Cesare Ioly, ed. *L'identità dissimulata: Guidaizzanti iberici nell'Europa Cristiana dell'età moderna.* Florence: Leo S. Olschki Editore, 2000.

ARTICLES AND ESSAYS

Abbreviations for Journals

AJS Review: Association of Jewish Studies Review
JQR: Jewish Quarterly Review
PAAJR: Proceedings of the American Academy for Jewish Research

REJ: Revue des Études Juives
TJHSE: Transactions of the Jewish Historical Society of England

Amiel, Charles. "El criptojudaísmo castellano en La Mancha a fines del siglo XVI."
In Judíos. Sefarditas. Converso. La explusión de 1492 y sus consecuencias, ed. Ángel
Alcalá, 503–512. Valladolid: Ámbito Ediciones, 1995.

Assaf, Simha. "The Conversos of Spain and Portugal in Rabbinic Literature" (in
Hebrew). Zion 5 (1933): 19–60.

Barnett, R. D. "The Correspondence of the Mahamad of the Spanish and Portuguese
Congregation of London during the Seventeenth and Eighteenth Centuries."
TJHSE 20 (1964): 1–50.

Beinart, Haim. "Three Generations, Members of One Family Tried by the
Inquisition" (in Hebrew). Tarbiz 30 (1960): 46–61.

———. "The Spanish Inquisition at Work outside the Peninsula" (in Hebrew). In
Proceedings of the Fifth World Congress of Jewish Studies. Vol. 2, 55–73. Jerusalem:
World Union of Jewish Studies, 1972.

———. "A Prophesying Movement in Cordova in 1499–1502" (in Hebrew). Zion 44
(1980): 190–200.

———. "The Spanish Inquisition and a 'Converso Community' in Extremadura."
Medieval Studies 43 (1981): 445–471.

———. "Herrera: Its Conversos and Jews" (in Hebrew). In Proceedings of the Seventh
World Congress of Jewish Studies. Vol. 2, 53–85. Jerusalem: World Union of
Jewish Studies, 1981.

———. "The Prophetess Inés and Her Movement in Pueblo de Alcocer and
Talarrubias" (in Hebrew). Tarbiz 51 (1982): 633–658.

———. "Conversos of Chillón and the Prophecies of Mari Gómez and Inés, the
Daughter of Juan Esteban" (in Hebrew). Zion 48 (1983): 241–272.

———. "The Prophetess Inés and Her Movement in Her Hometown, Herrera" (in
Hebrew). In Studies in Jewish Mysticism, Philosophy, and Ethical Literature, ed.
Yosef Dan and Yosef Hacker, 459–506. Jerusalem: Magnes Press, 1986.

———. "Jewish-Converso Connections from Italy to Spain" (in Hebrew). In Jews in
Italy, ed. Haim Beinart, 275–288. Jerusalem: Magnes Press, 1988.

———. "Inés of Herrera del Duque: The Prophetess of Extremadura." In Women in
the Inquisition: Spain and the New World, ed. Mary E. Giles, 42–52. Baltimore:
Johns Hopkins University Press, 1999.

Ben-Sasson, Haim Hillel. "The Generation of Spanish Exiles [Reflects] on Itself" (in
Hebrew). Zion 26 (1961): 23–64.

Bethencourt, Cardozo de. "The Jews in Portugal from 1773 to 1902." JQR 15 (1903):
251–274, 529–530.

Bodian, Miriam. "The Escamot of the Spanish-Portuguese Jewish Community of
London." Michael 9 (1985): 9–26.

———. "The 'Portuguese' Dowry Societies in Venice and Amsterdam: A Case Study
within the Marrano Diaspora." Italia 6 (1987): 30–61.

———. "Amsterdam, Venice, and the Marrano Diaspora in the Seventeenth
Century." In Dutch Jewish History. Vol. 2, ed. Jozeph Michman, 46–65.
Jerusalem: Institute for Research on Dutch Jewry, 1989.

──────. " 'Men of the Nation': The Shaping of *Converso* Identity in Early Modern Europe." *Past and Present* 143 (1994): 48–76.

Boyajian, James C. "The New Christians Reconsidered: Evidence from Lisbon's Portuguese Bankers, 1497–1647." *Studia Rosenthalia* 13 (1979): 129–156.

Cabezudo Astrain, José. "Los conversos aragoneses según los procesos de la Inquisición." *Sefarad* 18 (1958): 272–282.

Cantera, Francisco. "Fernando de Pulgar y los Conversos." *Sefarad* 4 (1944): 295–348.

Cantera Burgos, Francisco, and Carlos Carrete Parrondo. "Las Juderías medievales en la provincia de Guadalajara." *Sefarad* 33 (1973): 3–44; 34, no. 1 (1974): 43–78; and 34, no. 2 (1974): 313–386.

Cantera Montenegro, Enrique. "Judios de Torrelaguna: Retorno de algunos expulsados entre 1493 y 1495." *Sefarad* 39 (1979): 333–346.

Carrasco, Rafael. "Solidarités et sociabilités judéo-converses en Castille au XVIᵉ siècle." In *Etudes portugaises, publiées par les soins de Charles Amiel*, 185–228. Paris: Calouste Gulbenkian, 1975.

──────. "Preludio al 'Siglo de los Portugueses': La Inquisición de Cuenca y los judaizantes lusitanos en el siglo XVI." *Hispania* 47 (1987): 503–559.

Carrete Parrondo, Carlos, and Yolanda Moreno Koch. "Movimiento mesiánico hispano-portugués: Badajoz 1525." *Sefarad* 52 (1992): 65–68.

Cohen, Gershon. Review of *The Marranos of Spain. Jewish Social Studies* 29 (1967): 178–184.

Cohen, Robert. "Passage to a New World: The Sephardi Poor of Eighteenth Century Amsterdam." In *Neveh Ya'akov: Jubilee Volume Presented to Dr. Jaap Meijer on the Occasion of His Seventieth Birthday*, ed. Lea Dasberg and Jonathan N. Cohen, 31–42. Assen, Netherlands: Van Gorcum, 1982.

──────. "*Memoria para os siglos futuros*: Myth and Memory on the Beginnings of the Amsterdam Sephardi Community." *Jewish History* 2 (1987): 67–72.

Cooperman, Bernard. "Eliahu Montalto's 'Suitable and Incontrovertible Propositions': A Seventeenth-Century Anti-Christian Polemic." In *Jewish Thought in the Seventeenth Century*, ed. Isadore Twersky and Bernard Septimus, 469–497. Cambridge: Harvard University Press, 1987.

Coronas Tejada, Luis. "El motín antijudío de 1473 en Jaén." In *Proceedings of the Seventh World Congress of Jewish Studies*, 141–177. Jerusalem: World Union of Jewish Studies, 1981.

David, Abraham. "Concerning the Martyr's Death of the Proselyte Joseph Saralvo" (in Hebrew). *Kiryat Sefer* 59 (1984): 243–245.

Dedieu, Jean-Pierre. "Les Quatre Temps d'Inquisition." In *L'Inquisition espagnole (XVᵉ–XIXᵉ siecle)*, ed. Bartolomé Benassar, 15–42. Paris: Hachette, 1979.

Diago Hernando, Máximo. "Los judeoconversos en Soria después de 1492." *Sefarad* 51 (1991): 259–297.

──────. "El ascenco sociopolítico de los judeoconversos en la Castilla del siglo XVI: El Ejemplo de la Familia Beltrán en Soria." *Sefarad* 56 (1996): 221–250.

Diamond, A. S. "The Cemetery of the Resettlement." *TJHSE* 19 (1960): 163–190.

──────. "The Community of the Resettlement, 1656–1684: A Social Survey." *TJHSE* 24 (1974): 134–150.

Edwards, John. "Was the Spanish Inquisition Truthful?" *JQR* 87, nos. 3–4 (1997): 351–366.

Endelman, Todd M. " 'A Hebrew to the End': The Emergence of Disraeli's Jewishness." In *The Self-Fashioning of Disraeli, 1818–1851*, ed. C. Richmond and P. Smith, 106–130. Cambridge: Cambridge University Press, 1998.

Faingold, Reuven. "The 'New Christian Problem' in Portugal: 1601–1625" (in Hebrew). *Zion* 54 (1989): 379–400.

———. " 'Flight from the Valley of Death': Converso Physicians Leaving Portugal in the Early Seventeenth Century" (in Hebrew). *Pe'amim* 68 (1996): 105–138.

Ferry, Barbara, and Debbie Nathan. "Mistaken Identity? The Case of New Mexico's 'Hidden Jews.' " *Atlantic Monthly* (December 2000): 85–96.

Frattarelli Fischer, Lucia. "Urban Forms of Jewish Settlement in Tuscan Cities (Florence, Pisa, Leghorn) during the 17th Century." In *Papers in Jewish Demography, 1989*, ed. Uziel O. Schmelz and Sergio Della Pergola, 48–60. Jerusalem: Institute of Contemporary Jewry, 1993.

Freund, Scarlett, and Teofilo F. Ruiz. "Jews, *Conversos,* and the Inquisition in Spain, 1391–1492: The Ambiguities of History." In *Jewish-Christian Encounters over the Centuries,* ed. Marvin Perry and Frederick M. Schweitzer, 169–195. New York: Peter Lang, 1994.

Galchinsky, Michael. "Engendering Liberal Jews: Jewish Women in Victorian England." In *Jewish Women in Historical Perspective.* 2d ed., ed. Judith R. Baskin, 208–226. Detroit: Wayne State University Press, 1998.

Garshowitz, Libby. "Gracia Mendes: Power, Influence, and Intrigue." In *Power of the Weak: Studies on Medieval Women,* ed. Jennifer Carpenter and Sally-Beth MacLean, 94–125. Champaign: University of Illinois Press, 1995.

Gitlitz, David. "Divided Families in *Converso* Spain." *Shofar* 11 (1993): 5–14.

Glatzer, Michael. "Pablo de Santa Maria on the Events of 1391." In *Antisemitism through the Ages,* ed. Shmuel Almog, 127–137. Oxford: Pergamon Press, 1988.

———. "Between Yehoshua Halorki and Shelomo Halevi—Towards an Examination of the Causes of Conversion among Jews in Spain in the Fourteenth Century" (in Hebrew). *Pe'amim* 54 (1993): 103–115.

Goldish, Matt. "Jews, Christians, and Conversos: Rabbi Solomon Aailion's Struggles in the Portuguese Community of London." *Journal of Jewish Studies* 45 (1994): 227–257.

Gross, Avi. "On the Ashkenazi Syndrome of Jewish Martyrdom in Portugal in 1497" (in Hebrew). *Tarbiz* 44 (1994): 83–114.

Gutwirth, Eleazer. "Jewish-Converso Relations in XVth Century Segovia." In *Proceedings of the Eighth World Congress of Jewish Studies.* Vol. 2, 49–53. Jerusalem: World Union of Jewish Studies, 1982.

Hacker, Joseph. "New Chronicles on the Expulsion of the Jews from Spain, Its Causes and Results" (in Hebrew). *Zion* 44 (1979) = *Yitzhak F. Baer Memorial Volume,* 219–223.

Hernández, Frances. "The Secret Jews of the Southwest." In *Sephardim in the Americas: Studies in Culture and History,* ed. Martin A. Cohen and Abraham J. Peck, 422–454. Tuscaloosa: University of Alabama Press, 1993.

Hordes, Stanley. "The Inquisition and the Crypto-Jewish Community in Colonial New Spain and New Mexico." In *Cultural Encounters: The Impact of the*

Inquisition in Spain and the New World, ed. Mary Elizabeth Perry and Anne J. Cruz, 207–217. Berkeley: University of California Press, 1993.

Horowitz, Elliott. "The Dowering of Brides in the Ghetto of Venice: Between Tradition and Change, Ideas and Reality" (in Hebrew). *Tarbiz* 56 (1987): 347–371.

Huerga Criado, Pilar. "Una familia judeoconversa: La quiebra de la solidaridad." *Sefarad* 49 (1989): 97–121.

Huussen Jr., Arend H. "The Legal Position of Sephardi Jews in Holland, *circa* 1600." *Dutch Jewish History.* Vol. 3, ed. Jozeph Michman, 19–41. Jerusalem: Institute for Research on Dutch Jewry, 1993.

Israel, Jonathan I. "The Economic Contribution of Dutch Sephardi Jewry to Holland's Golden Age, 1595–1713." *Tijdschrift voor Geschiedenis* 96 (1983): 505–535.

———. "The Changing Role of the Dutch Sephardim in International Trade, 1595–1715." *Dutch Jewish History.* Vol. 1, ed. Joseph Michman and Tirtsah Levie, 31–51. Jerusalem: Institute for Research on Dutch Jewry, 1984.

———. "Manuel López Pereira of Amsterdam, Antwerp, and Madrid: Jew, New Christian, and Advisor to the Conde-Duque de Olivares." *Studia Rosenthalia* 19 (1985): 109–126.

———. "The Jews of Venice and Their Links with Holland and with Dutch Jewry (1660–1710)." In *Gli Ebrei e Venezia secoli XIV–XVIII,* ed. Gaetano Cozzi, 95–116. Milan: Edizioni Comunita, 1987.

———. "The Dutch Republic and Its Jews during the Conflict over the Spanish Succession (1669–1715)." In *Dutch Jewish History.* Vol. 2, ed. Jozeph Michman, 117–136. Jerusalem: Institute for Research on Dutch Jewry, 1989.

Jacobs, Janet Liebman. "Women, Ritual, and Secrecy: The Creation of Crypto-Jewish Culture." *Journal for the Scientific Study of Religion* 35 (1996): 97–108.

Kaplan, Yosef. "The Place of Rabbi Moshe Refael D'Aguilar in the Context of His Connections with Refugees from Spain and Portugal in the 17th Century" (in Hebrew). In *Proceedings of the Sixth World Congress of Jewish Studies.* Vol. 2, 95–106. Jerusalem: World Union of Jewish Studies, 1975.

———. "Rabbi Saul Morteira's Treatise 'Arguments against the Christian Religion' " (in Hebrew). In *Studies on the History of Dutch Jewry.* Vol. 1, ed. Joseph Michman, 9–23. Jerusalem: Magnes Press, 1975.

———. "On the Relation of Spinoza's Contemporaries in the Portuguese Jewish Community of Amsterdam to Spanish Culture and the Marrano Experience." In *Spinoza's Political and Theological Thought,* ed. C. de Deugd, 82–94. Amsterdam: North-Holland Publishing Co., 1984.

———. "The Social Functions of the Herem in the Portuguese Jewish Community of Amsterdam in the Seventeenth Century." In *Dutch Jewish History.* Vol. 1, ed. Jozeph Michman and Tirtsah Levie, 111–155. Jerusalem: Institute for Research on Dutch Jewry, 1984.

———. "The Attitude of the Spanish and Portuguese Jews to the Ashkenazim in Seventeenth Century Amsterdam" (in Hebrew). In *Transition and Change in Modern Jewish History: Essays Presented in Honor of Shmuel Ettinger,* 389–412. Jerusalem: Zalman Shazar Center, 1987.

———. "From Apostasy to Return to Judaism: The Portuguese Jews in Amsterdam."

In *Binah: Studies in Jewish History, Thought, and Culture.* Vol. 1, ed. Joseph Dan, 99–117. New York: Praeger, 1989.

―――. "The Jewish Profile of the Spanish-Portuguese Community of London." *Judaism* 41 (1992): 229–240.

―――. "Wayward New Christians and Stubborn New Jews: The Shaping of a Jewish Identity." In *Robert Cohen Memorial Volume,* ed. Kenneth R. Stow and Lloyd P. Gartner, 27–41. Haifa: Haifa University Press, 1994.

Kaufmann, David. "Les Martyrs D'Ancone." *REJ* 11 (1885): 149–153.

Koen, E. M. "The Earliest Sources Relating to the Portuguese Jews in the Municipal Archives of Amsterdam." *Studia Rosenthalia* 4, no. 1 (1970): 25–42.

Kunin, Seth D. "Juggling Identities among the Crypto-Jews of the American Southwest." *Religion* 31 (2001): 41–61.

Levie Bernfeld, Tirtsah. "Caridade Escapa da Morte: Legacies to the Poor in Sephardi Wills from Seventeenth-Century Amsterdam." In *Dutch Jewish History.* Vol. 3, ed. Jozeph Michman, 179–204. Jerusalem: Institute for Research on Dutch Jewry, 1993.

Levine Melammed, Renée. "The Ultimate Challenge: Safeguarding the Crypto-Judaic Heritage." *PAAJR* 53 (1986): 91–109.

―――. "Noticias sobre los ritos de los nacimientos y de la pureza de las judeo-conversas castellanas del siglo XVI." *El Olivo,* 13, nos. 29–30 (1989): 235–243.

―――. "Sephardi Women in the Medieval and Early Modern Periods." In *Jewish Women in Historical Perspective.* 2d ed., ed. Judith R. Baskin, 115–134. Detroit: Wayne State University Press, 1998.

―――. "Crypto-Jewish Women Facing the Spanish Inquisition: Transmitting Religious Practices, Beliefs, and Attitudes." In *Christians, Muslims, and Jews in Medieval and Early Modern Spain: Interaction and Social Change,* ed. Mark D. Meyerson and Edward D. English, 197–219. Notre Dame, Ind.: University of Notre Dame, 2000.

Loker, Zvi. "From Converso Congregation to Holy Community: The Shaping of the Jewish Community of Bordeaux during the 18th Century" (in Hebrew). *Zion* 42 (1976): 49–94.

Lorence, Bruce. "The Inquisition and the New Christians in the Iberian Peninsula: Main Historiographic Issues and Controversies." In *The Sepharadi and Oriental Jewish Heritage Studies,* ed. Issachar Ben-Ami, 13–72. Jerusalem: Magnes Press, 1982.

Lourie, Elena. "A Society Organized for War: Medieval Spain." *Past and Present* 35 (1966): 54–76.

MacKay, Angus. "Popular Movements and Pogroms in Fifteenth-Century Castile." *Past and Present* 55 (1972): 33–67.

―――. "The Hispanic-*Converso* Predicament." *Transactions of the Royal Historical Society* 35 (1985): 159–179.

Marín Padilla, Encarnación. "Relación judeoconversa durante la segunda mitad del siglo XV en Aragón: Matrimonio." *Sefarad* 42, no. 2 (1982): 243–298.

―――. "Relación judeoconversa durante la segunda mitad del siglo XV en Aragón: Nacimiento, hadas, circuncisiones." *Sefarad* 41, no. 2 (1981): 273–300; and 42, no. 3 (1982): 59–77.

————. "Relación judeoconversa durante la segunda mitad del siglo XV en Aragón: Enfermedades y muertes." *Sefarad* 43, no. 2 (1983): 251–344.

Menkis, Richard. "Patriarchs and Patricians: The Gradis Family of Eighteenth-Century Bordeaux." In *From East and West: Jews in a Changing Europe, 1750–1870*, ed. Frances Malino and David Sorkin, 11–45. Oxford: Blackwell, 1990.

Meyuhas Ginio, Alisa. "The Fortress of Faith—At the End of the West: Alonso de Espina and His *Fortalitium Fidei*." In *Contra Iudaeos*, ed. Ora Limor and Guy G. Stroumsa, 215–237. Tübingen: J. C. B. Mohr, 1996.

Michman, Jozeph. "Between Sephardim and Ashkenazim in Amsterdam" (in Hebrew). In *The Sephardi and Oriental Jewish Heritage*, ed. Issachar Ben Ami, 135–149. Jerusalem: Magnes Press, 1982.

Milgram, Avraham. "The Attempt to Return the Conversos of Portugal to Judaism from 1925 to 1931" (in Hebrew). *Gesher* 125, no. 38 (1992): 90–99.

Millás Vallicrosa, José Maria. "Emigración masiva de conversos por la frontera Catalona-Francesa en el año 1608." *Sefarad* 19 (1959): 140–144.

Molho, Sarica. "Masks for Yom Kippur, Masks for Passover: A Sociological Look at the Conversos of Belmonte Today" (in Hebrew). In *Proceedings of the Twelfth World Congress of Jewish Studies*. Vol. 5, 261–268. Jerusalem: World Union of Jewish Studies, 2001.

Moreno Koch, Yolanda. "La comunidad judaizante de Castillo de Garcimuñoz." *Sefarad* 37, nos. 1–2 (1977): 351–371.

————. "De la diáspora hacia Sefarad: La primera carta de regreso de un judio convertido?" *Michael* 11 (1989): 257–265.

————. "Las Deudas de los Judíos de Segovia después de la Expulsión." In *Hispano-Jewish Civilization after 1492*, ed. Michel Abitbol, Yom-Tov Assis, and Galit Hassan-Rokem, 3–13. Jerusalem: Misgav Yerushalayim, 1997.

Nahon, Gérard. "Les Rapports des Communautés Judeo-Portugaises de France avec celle d'Amsterdam au XVIIe et XVIIIe Siècles." *Studia Rosenthalia* 10 (1976): 37–78, 151–188.

————. "Bayonne dans la Diaspora Sefarade d'Occident (XVIIe–XVIIIe Siècle)." In *Proceedings of the Seventh World Congress of Jewish Studies*. Vol. 4, 47–55. Jerusalem: World Union of Jewish Studies, 1981.

————. "The Impact of the Expulsion from Spain on the Jewish Community of Pre-Revolutionary France, 1550–1791." *Judaism* 41 (1992): 169–179.

Netanyahu, B. "Alonso de Espina—Was He a New Christian?" *PAAJR* 43 (1976): 107–165.

Nidel, D. S., and P. J. Citrin. "Modern Descendants of Conversos in New Mexico." *Western States Jewish Historical Quarterly* 16 (1984): 249–263.

Novinsky, Anita, and Amilcar Paulo. "The Last Marranos." *Commentary* 43 (May 1967): 76–81.

Orfali, Moises (Moshe). "Reforming and Conforming: A History of the Jews of Livorno, 1693–1707." *Mediterranean Historical Review* 7 (1992): 208–218.

————. "Images and Stereotypes of Jews in Portuguese Literature of the Sixteenth and Seventeenth Centuries" (in Hebrew). *Pe'amim* 69 (1996): 8–23.

————. "The Portuguese Dowry Society in Livorno and the Marrano Diaspora," *Studia Rosenthalia* 35, no. 2 (2001): 143–156.

———. "Doña Gracia Mendes and the Ragusan Republic: The Successful Use of Economic Institutions in 16th Century Commerce." In *The Mediterranean and the Jews*, ed. Elliott Horowitz and Moises Orfali, 175–201. Ramat Gan: Bar-Ilan University Press, 2002.

Ornan Pinkus, B. Z. "The Portuguese Community of Hamburg in the XVIIth Century" (in Hebrew). In *East and Magreb*, ed. A. Toaff, 7–51. Ramat Gan: Bar-Ilan University Press, 1986.

Perry, Mary Elizabeth. "Beatas and the Inquisition in Early Modern Seville." In *Inquisition and Society in Early Modern Europe*, ed. Stephen Haliczer, 147–167. London: Croom Helm, 1987.

Popkin, Richard H. "The Historical Significance of Sephardic Judaism in 17th Century Amsterdam." *American Sephardi* 5 (1971): 18–27.

Pullan, Brian. " 'A Ship with Two Rudders': 'Righetto Marrano' and the Inquisition in Venice." *Historical Journal* 20 (1977): 37–38.

———. "The Inquisition and the Jews of Venice: The Case of Gaspare Ribeiro, 1580–1581." *Bulletin of the John Rylands Library* 62 (1979): 207–231.

Ravid, Benjamin. "The Legal Status of the Jewish Merchants of Venice, 1541–1638." *Journal of Economic History* 35 (1975): 274–279.

———. "The First Charter of the Jewish Merchants of Venice, 1589." *AJS Review* 1 (1976): 187–222.

———. "A Tale of Three Cities and Their *Raison d'Etat*: Ancona, Venice, Livorno, and the Competition for Jewish Merchants in the Sixteenth Century." *Mediterranean Historical Review* 6 (1991): 138–162.

———. "From Yellow to Red: On the Distinguishing Head-Covering of the Jews of Venice." *Jewish History* 6 (1992): 179–210.

Révah, I. S. "Le Premiere Établissement des Marranes portugais à Rouen (1603–1607)." *Annuaire de l'Institut de Philologie et d'histoire Orientales et Slaves* 13 (1953) [=*Mélanges Isidore Lévy*]: 539–552.

———. "Une famille de 'Nouveaux Chretiens': Les Bocarro Frances." *REJ* 116 (1957): 73–87.

———. "Spinoza et le hérétiques de la communauté judéo-portugaise d'Amsterdam." *Revue de L'Histoire des Religions* 154 (1958): 173–218.

———. "Les Marranes." *REJ* 118–119 (1959–1960): 29–77.

———. "La religion d'Uriel da Costa, Marrane de Porto." *Revue de L'Histoire des Religions* 161 (1962): 45–76.

———. "Pour l'histoire des Marranes à Anvers: Recensements de la 'Nation Portugaise' de 1571–1666." *REJ* 122 (1963): 123–147.

———. "Aux origines de la rupture spinozienne: Nouveaux documents sur l'incroyance dan la communauté judéo-portugaise d'Amsterdam a l'époque de l'excommunication de Spinoza." *REJ* 13 (1964): 359–431.

———. "La Controverse sur les statuts de pureté de sang—Un document inédit." *Bulletin Hispanique* 73 (1971): 263–306.

Rosenthal, Elaine, and Robert Rosenthal. "The Portuguese Dreyfus." *Midstream* 33, no. 2 (1987): 44–48.

Roth, Cecil. "Les marranes à Rouen: Un chapitre ignoré de l'histoire des Juifs de France." *REJ* 88 (1929): 113–155.

———. "Joseph Saralvo, A Marrano Martyr at Rome." In *Festschrift zu Simon*

Dubnows siebzigstem Geburtstag, ed. Ismar Elbogen, Josef Meisl, and Mark Wischnitzer, 180–186. Berlin: Jüdischer Verlag, 1930.

———. "Notes sur les marranes de Livourne." *REJ* 90 (1931): 1–27.

———. "Immanuel Aboab's Proselytization of the Marranos." *JQR* 23 (1932): 131–134.

———. "The Marrano Press at Ferrara, 1552–1555." *Modern Language Review* 38 (1943): 307–317.

———. " 'Salusque Lusitano.' " *JQR* 34 (1943): 65–85.

———. "The Strange Case of Hector Mendes Bravo." *Hebrew Union College Annual* 18 (1944): 221–245.

Salomon, H. P. Review of *Un "Portugués" entre los Castellanos: El Primer Proceso Inquisitorial contra Gonzalo Báez de Paiba 1654–1657*, by David Willemse. *American Sephardi* 7–8 (1975): 135–137.

———. "The Captain, the Abade, and 20th Century Marranism in Portugal." *Archivos do Centro Cultural Portugues* 10 (1976): 631–642.

———. "Haham Saul Levi Morteira en de Portuguese Nieuw-Christenen." *Studia Rosenthalia* 10 (1976): 127–138 (in Dutch); 139–142 (in English).

———. Review of *The Lisbon Massacre of 1506*, by Yosef Hayim Yerushalmi. *The American Sephardi* 9 (1978): 170–172.

———. "Myth or Anti-myth? The Oldest Account concerning the Origin of Portuguese Judaism at Amsterdam." *Lias* 16 (1989): 275–316.

Salomon, H. P., and Aron di Leone Leoni. "Mendes, Benveniste, de Luna, Micas, Nasci: The State of the Art (1532–1558)." *JQR* 88 (1998): 135–211.

Samuel, Wilfred S. "The First London Synagogue of the Resettlement." *TJHSE* 10 (1924): 1–147.

Santos, Richard. "Chicanos of Jewish Descent in Texas." *Western States Jewish Historical Quarterly* 15 (1983): 327–333.

Saperstein, Marc. "Martyrs, Merchants, and Rabbis: Jewish Communal Conflict as Reflected in the Responsa on the Boycott of Ancona." *Jewish Social Studies* 43 (1981): 215–228.

Scheindlin, Raymond P. "Judah Abravanel to His Son." *Judaism* 41, no. 2 (1992): 190–199.

Schorsch, Ismar. "From Messianism to Realpolitik: Menasseh Ben Israel and the Readmission of the Jews to England." *PAAJR* 45 (1978): 187–208.

Schwarz, Samuel. "The Crypto-Jews of Portugal." *Menorah Journal* 12 (1926): 138–149, 283–297, 325.

Segre, Renata. "Sephardic Settlements in Sixteenth-Century Italy: A Historical and Geographical Survey." *Mediterranean Historical Review* 6 (1991): 114–115.

Shell, Marc. "Marranos (Pigs), or From Coexistence to Toleration." *Critical Inquiry* 17, no. 2 (1991): 306–335.

Shepard, Sanford. "The Background of Uriel da Costa's Heresy—Marranism, Scepticism, Karaism." *Judaism* 20 (1971): 341–350.

Simonsohn, Shlomo. "Marranos in Ancona under Papal Protection." *Michael* 9 (1985): 234–243.

Steinhardt, Ignacio (Issar). "A Lone Community of Conversos in North Portugal" (in Hebrew). *Ha-Aretz*, September 20, 1964, 3, 15.

———. "The Conversos of Belmonte" (in Hebrew). *Apiryon* 40 (1995): 21–30.

Stuczynski, Claude B. "*Capela dos Prazeres:* Bragança, Late Sixteenth Century—
Inquisition and Memory" (in Hebrew). *Pe'amim* 69 (1996): 24–42.
———. Review of *Ben-Rosh: Biografia do Capitão Barros Basto o Apóstolo dos
Marranos,* by Elvira de Azevedo Mea and Inácio Steinhardt. *Hispania Judaica* 2
(1999): 89–95.
———. "Cristãos-Novos e Judaísmo no Início da Época Moderna: Identidade
Religiosa e 'Razão de Estado,' " *Lusitania Sacra,* 2d ser., vol. 12 (2000): 355–366.
———. Introduction to *The New Christians in Portugal in the Twentieth Century,* by
Samuel Schwarz (in Hebrew). Jerusalem: Dinur Center, 2004.
Swetschinski, Daniel M. "Kinship and Commerce: The Foundations of Portuguese
Jewish Life in Seventeenth-Century Holland." *Studia Rosenthalia* 15 (1981): 58–
74.
———. "The Portuguese Jews of Seventeenth-Century Amsterdam: Cultural
Continuity and Adaptation." In *Essays in Modern Jewish History: A Tribute to Ben
Halpern,* ed. Frances Malino and Phyllis Cohen Albert, 56–80. New York: Herzl
Press, 1982.
Szajkowski, Zosa. "The Marranos and Sephardim of France." In *The Abraham Weiss
Jubilee Volume,* 109–129. New York: Abraham Weiss Jubilee Committee, 1964.
Talmage, Frank. "To Sabbatize in Peace: Jews and New Christians in Sixteenth-
Century Portuguese Polemics." *Harvard Theological Review* 74 (1983): 265–285.
Teltsch, Kathleen. "Scholars and Descendants Uncover Hidden Legacy of Jews in
Southwest." *New York Times,* November 11, 1990, 30.
Tishby, I. "Genizah Fragments of a Messianic-Mystical Text on the Expulsion from
Spain and Portugal" (in Hebrew). *Zion* 48 (1983): 55–102.
Ward, Seth. "Converso Descendants in the American Southwest: A Report on
Research, Resources, and the Changing Search for Identity." In *Jewish Studies at
the Turn of the Twentieth Century.* Vol. 2, ed. Judit Targarona Barrós and Angel
Sáenz-Badillos, 677–686. Leiden: Brill, 1999.
Wolf, Lucien. "Crypto-Jews under the Commonwealth." *TJHSE* 1 (1893–1894): 55–
88.
———. "The First English Jew: Notes on Antonio Fernandez Carvajal, with some
Biographical Documents." *TJHSE* 2 (1894–1895): 14–48.
———. "The Jewry of the Restoration." *TJHSE* 5 (1902–1905): 5–33.
———. *Report on the "Marranos" or Crypto-Jews of Portugal.* Presented to the Alliance
Israélite Universelle and the Council of the Anglo-Jewish Association. London,
March, 1926.
Wolff, Philippe. "The 1391 Pogrom in Spain: Social Crisis or Not." *Past and Present*
50 (1971): 4–18.
Yerushalmi, Yosef Hayim. "Conversos Returning to Judaism in the 17th Century" (in
Hebrew). In *Proceedings of the Fifth World Congress of Jewish Studies.* Vol. 2, 201–
209. Jerusalem: World Union of Jewish Studies, 1969.
———. "The Re-education of Marranos in the Seventeenth Century." *Third Annual
Rabbi Louis Feinberg Memorial Lecture,* March 26, 1980, 1–16. Cincinnati, Ohio:
University of Cincinnati, 1980.
———. "A Jewish Classic in the Portuguese Language." Introduction to *Consolação
às tribulações de Israel,* by Samuel Usque, 18–123. Lisbon: Fundaçãi Calouste
Gulbenkian, 1989.

Yovel, Yirmiyahu. "The New Otherness: Marrano Dualities in the First Generation."
The 1999 Swig Lecture. University of San Francisco, September 13, 1999, 1–14.

Zeldes, Nadia. "Tracing a Profile of the New Christians of Sicily" (in Hebrew). *Zion*
65 (2000): 307–342.

Zorattini, Pier Cesare Ioly. "Jews, Crypto-Jews, and the Inquisition." In *The Jews of
Early Modern Venice*, ed. Robert C. Davis and Benjamin Ravid, 97–116.
Baltimore: Johns Hopkins University Press, 2001.

Index